THE MEXICAN PEOPLE: THEIR STRUGGLE FOR FREEDOM

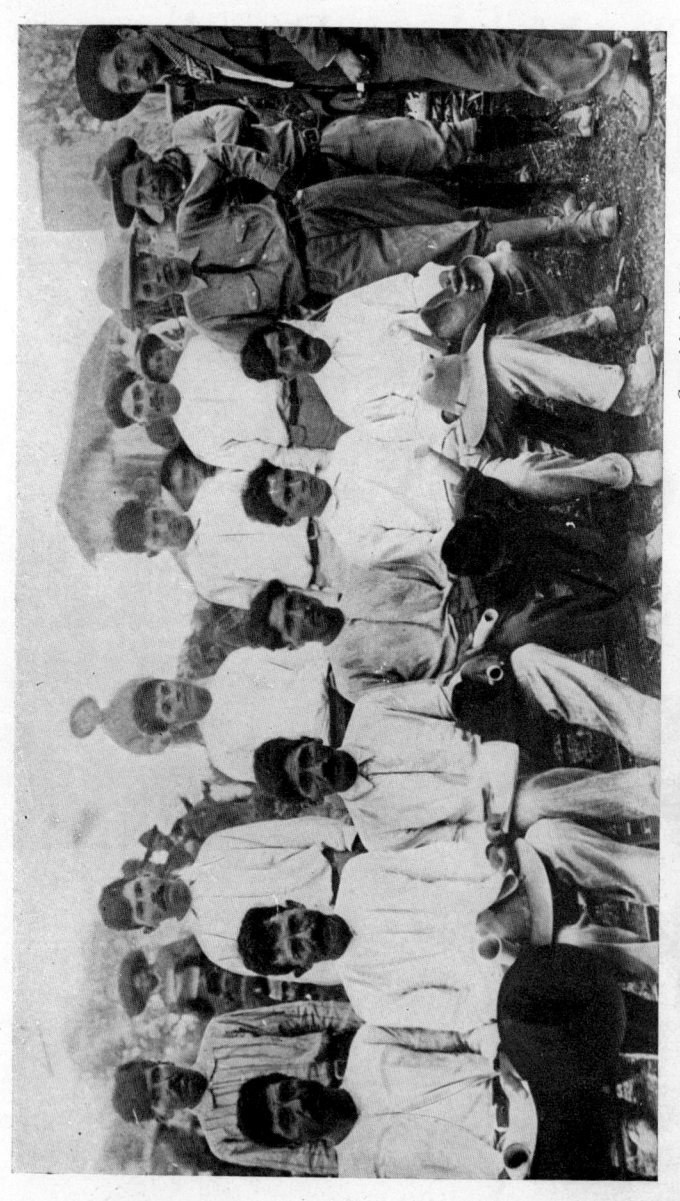

WHAT THE MEXICAN PEOPLE ARE FIGHTING FOR

The revolution in Mexico is distinctly a fight for the land which was taken from the small land-holders early in the Diaz reign. This picture shows some of the natives who bought the land, following the seizure by the Constitutionalists, of the 73,000-acre estate of Felix Diaz, in Matamoros

The Mexican People:
Their Struggle for Freedom

BY

L. GUTIERREZ DE LARA

Author of
"Story of a Political Refugee" and "Les Bribones"

AND

EDGCUMB PINCHON

Illustrated from Photographs

GARDEN CITY   NEW YORK
DOUBLEDAY, PAGE & CO.
1917

Copyright, 1914, by

DOUBLEDAY, PAGE & COMPANY

All rights reserved, including that of translation into foreign languages, including the Scandinavian

PREFACE

THIS book is deliberately given the title of "The Mexican People: Their Struggle for Freedom." We know that to the average mind Mexico and freedom seem almost antithetical terms; that is why we wrote this book. The Mexican people have democratic traditions as grand, pure, and sane as those of any race in the world. Like all peoples, they have suffered bitter oppression at the hands of their own master class, but unlike the majority of peoples their weakness has made of them the peculiar prey of the foreign exploiter as well. For a hundred years they have maintained the bloodiest, most heroically abandoned fight for their liberties, not only against their own master class but against that master class leagued with Spain, with the United States, with France, and with England. We have long wished to tell of this struggle. It constitutes one of the most exalted dramas of the social process. If by this book, wrought out amidst many difficulties, we shall awaken the spirit of brotherhood and understanding in the hearts of some, for the battling proletariat of Mexico, our work will not have been without reward.

L. GUTIÉRREZ DE LARA.
EDGCUMB PINCHON.

CONTENTS

		PAGE
Preface		v

CHAPTER

		PAGE
I.	The Real Mexico	3
II.	The Genesis of the Mexican Master Class	7
III.	The Origin of the Mexican Agrarian Revolts	15
IV.	Political and Ecclesiastical Constitution of Mexico in the Colonial Period	19
V.	The Revolution of Independence	26
VI.	The First Empire	61
VII.	The Republic	74
VIII.	The Presidency of Bustamante	87
IX.	The Texas War	100
X.	Clerical Prætorianism and the Supreme Conservative Power	121
XI.	The War with the United States	139
XII.	Clerical Intrigues for the Establishment of a Monarchy in Mexico	167
XIII.	The Ayutla Revolution	179
XIV.	The Constitution of 1857	201
XV.	The Upholding of the Constitution	220
XVI.	The French Intervention of 1861-1865	233
XVII.	The Withdrawal of the French Troops and the End of the Empire	257

CONTENTS

CHAPTER		PAGE
XVIII.	Reëstablishment of the Republic and the Constitution of 1857	265
XIX.	Agrarian and Political Democracy	271
XX.	The Diaz Cuartelazo	289
XXI.	Porfirio Diaz, President of Mexico	297
XXII.	The Dictatorship	312
XXIII.	The Railroads	335
XXIV.	The Revolution of 1910-1914	341
XXV.	The Downfall of Madero	351
Epilogue.	A Dispatch from the Front	359

ILLUSTRATIONS

What the Mexican People Are Fighting For	*Frontispiece*
	FACING PAGE
President Diaz and His Cabinet	20
The Cost of the Battle of Ojinaga	21
Map for the Period of Independence	28
The Constitutionalists' Agrarian Plan	42
José Maria Morelos	43
Vincente Guerrero — President of Mexico in 1827	68
General Carranza Addressing a Crowd of Constitutionalists	69
Native Maya Girls	84
Ore Sorting	85
Native Silver Smelter	85
Mexican Types	116
Chapultepec Castle	117
Mexico Penitentiary	117
Second epoch of the history of Mexico, showing places where war with the United States, Ayutla Revolution, and French Intervention took place	142
The Famous Floating Gardens Near Mexico City	148
Federals	149
Constitutionalists	149
A Little Rebel Patriot	164

ILLUSTRATIONS

	FACING PAGE
General Luis Terrazas Claims United States Protection	164
A Troop of Rurales	165
A Battery of Mexican Federal Artillery	165
The National Palace	196
Constitutionalists and Their Families	196
Chapultepec Castle	197
Mexico City After the Bombardment of February, 1913	197
General Carranza on Campaign	212
Yaqui Soldiers	212
General Zapata, Called "The Atilla of the South"	213
Zapata and His Men	213
Mexican Planter and Peon	246
Cultivation of Hennequin, Yucatan	246
The Toilers	247
Constitutionalists	258
Yaqui Rebels in Camp	259
A Rebel Barricade in Juarez	259
President Huerta and His Advisers	292
Enrique C. Creel	293
José Y. Limantour	293
Ramón Corral	293
Rebel Scouts	308
The People and War News	308
General Pascual Orozco	309
General Pancho Villa	309

Third epoch of the history of Mexico, showing places where

ILLUSTRATIONS

FACING PAGE

farmers were disposessed of their lands	322
Victoriano Huerta	340
Venustiano Carranza	340
Francisco Madero	341
Porfirio Diaz	341
The Climax in the 1912–1914 Revolt	356
Non-Combatants in the Bombardment of Mexico City	356
Non-Combatants from Ojinaga	357
Federal Lines of Defence at Ojinaga	357

THE MEXICAN PEOPLE: THEIR STRUGGLE FOR FREEDOM

The Mexican People: Their Struggle for Freedom

CHAPTER I

THE REAL MEXICO

IT IS commonly supposed that the Mexican race is made up of degraded half-castes, the joint product of the most backward nation in Europe (the Spanish) and the primitive savages of the southern portion of North America. None of the popular superstitions in regard to Mexico could be more falsely cruel. The Aztecs, Toltecs, Zapotecs, Mistecs, Mayas, and allied races which made up the entire population of Mexico at the time of the Conquest still constitute 60 per cent. of the population, and in spite of the fact that they have been compelled to adopt Spanish names and the Spanish language, this 60 per cent. of the nation — the working class of Mexico — still retain their ancient blood in all its purity.

Again, these peoples are not Indians.* Modern archæological and philological research bear emphatic witness to the fact that they are ethnologically as remote from the wild nomads of North America as are the so-called white races themselves. At the time of the Conquest they were in full enjoyment of a civilization greatly superior in many respects to that of Teutonic Europe, and certainly superior in every respect to that of the

---

*The real Indians (akin to the North American Indians) form a small proportion of the population of Mexico. They reside for the most part in the hills and mountains and are entirely outside of the main currents of Mexican politics.

Spanish nation which subjugated and enslaved them. Much has been written, particularly by Spanish historians, of the barbarous religious practices of these native races. It is true that the degraded native priesthood, who founded their wisdom-religion in Mexico more than three thousand years ago, practised human sacrifice as did the British druids. Even so, this deliberate blood sacrifice of the Aztecs was intrinsically no more inhuman than the martyr holocausts of Smithfield, the Massacre of St. Bartholomew, or the complicated cruelties of the Spanish Inquisition.

The magnificent architecture, splendid engineering works, exquisite craftsmanship, and sane social arrangements of these native races of Mexico (or Anahuac, as it was called in pre-Conquest days) mark them out as a people of ancient lineage and advanced culture. Compared with the Conquistadores they were enlightened, peaceable, and humane, and if the practices of their priesthood (a small and degenerate section of the master class) bring a shudder to the modern mind, it must be remembered that the barbarity they betray is not an Aztec peculiarity, but the common barbarity of priestcraft in all ages and climes: it is an essential component of class rule wherever it be found, and as such it is a class characteristic — not a race characteristic. The Spanish Conquest was, in fact, the triumph of a nation brutal and ignorant, but warlike, over a highly intelligent, artistic people so long accustomed to peace as to know but little of arms. And thus the history of Mexico from the Spanish Conquest of the sixteenth century to the Revolution of Independence in 1810 is the history of the domination of a small foreign element, backed, however, by a large foreign army, over a subjugated but intrinsically superior nation.

At the time of the Revolution of Independence in 1810, when the history of Mexico as an independent political entity begins, there were thus two main classes in Mexican society divided by the deepest racial and economic distinctions: the pure Spanish aristocracy — the official and large land-owning class, constituting not more than 10 per cent. of the population, and the dispossessed and enslaved native class — the peons,* constituting about 80 per cent. of the population. Between these two lay a third class, of mixed Spanish and native blood — the trading and professional class constituting the remaining 10 per cent. of the population.

This distinction of blood between the three economic divisions of Mexican society has remained, with some modifications, to the present day. Consequently, with the exception of the glorious period of the native supremacy beginning with the Ayutla Revolution of 1856, and ending with the accession of Diaz to power in 1876, the government of the country has been entirely in the hands of the Spanish and mixed Spanish element; and the chain of disasters which constitutes this hundred years of Mexican history is the direct outcome of the atrocities committed by this element — the master class of the country — upon the native element — the working class of the country.

To-day, of course, the Mexican people may be fairly regarded as a homogeneous race, but they cannot be regarded as a half-caste race in the general acceptance of the term, for 60 per cent. of the population still retain the ancient blood in all its purity. As for the mixed class the term half-caste is only applicable to them in the sense that they are the result of an alliance between a European blood and a superior Western blood — itself partially European in origin. The superiority of this mixed class — essentially the Mexican intellectual class — over the pure, Spanish class, shows that the native blood is dominant, and that eventually it will overcome the evil legacy of Spanish blood in the Mexican nation. The Revolution of Independence in 1810, therefore, was the revolt of the native races against the power of Spain for national independence and possession of the land. Its issues, consequently, were both racial and economic.

---

*While the strict meaning of the word "peon" in Mexico is "farmhand," to-day its actual meaning is serf — the man held in bondage by indebtedness or other legal trickery

Finally and summarily the history of Mexico is the history of a class struggle in which the opposing classes, master class and working class, are of distinct bloods, traditions, and psychologies, with the balance of racial development entirely in favour of the latter. Thus all that we know of the evil that is Mexican is the product of a small, parasitic and originally alien section of the nation; and all that we know of the good that is Mexican (and the world in general knows little enough) — the arts, the crafts, the poetry, the gentleness and good faith, the heroic struggle for democracy — is the product of the working class native races.

Bearing these simple basic facts in mind the maze of Mexican history may be threaded with ease. It is a record of profound significance and dramatic interest, the record of a struggle for racial expression and economic freedom on the part of an oppressed people, unusually gifted, of abandoned valour, of wonderful human kindness and gentleness — a struggle carried on against the most bloodthirsty and depraved master class the world has ever witnessed.

Since it is the Spanish and mixed Spanish master class which has controlled Mexico throughout the larger part of her modern history, it will be necessary for us to consider the origin of that master class, its psychology, and the economic, topographical and ethnological conditions with which it had to cope in the conquest and colonization of the country. We shall thus, as the first step in our study, find the key to that bewildering Saturnalia of crime which constitutes Spain's gift to the land of the Aztecs.

CHAPTER II

THE GENESIS OF THE MEXICAN MASTER CLASS

IN ORDER thus to investigate our subject from the roots we shall endeavour to trace the two distinct economic and psychological evolutions which have resulted in the present civilization of Mexico, on the one hand, and of the United States on the other. In this way we shall be able to take advantage of a number of illuminating comparisons between the two processes which will throw into relief the particular idiosyncrasies of the former.

PSYCHOLOGICAL

In the sixth century of the Christian era, Mohammed began preaching his doctrine to the Arabians; and a few years later Mohammedanism entered upon its bloody conquest of the Christian world. These two religions, Christianity and Mohammedanism, in their gigantic struggles for dominion in Europe and in northern Africa, converted the shores of the Mediterranean into one vast amphitheatre of slaughter. For over a thousand years the sun rose and sank on the carnage of the hosts of Islam and Christ, and millions of human lives perished by the sword before equilibrium between these two huge forces was obtained. This thousand years of combat profoundly modified — as might be expected — the psychology of the nations involved. In the case of Spain, which far more than any other nation in Europe bore the brunt of the fight, it evolved in the national character a distinctive idiosyncrasy which has remained the key to the Spanish and Spanish-American psychology to this day.

In their setting forth to the conquest of the world the hordes of Islam first overran Asia Minor and the Valley of the Nile. They swept northward and westward along the southern shores of the Mediterranean until by fire and sword they had carried the word of the prophet into all those regions now known as Barca, Tripoli, Tunis, and Morocco. Here, at the Straits of Gibraltar, but a narrow ribbon of water withheld them from the glorious subjugation of Spain, and through Spain, all Europe. Djeb Al Tarik, the Moorish general, at the head of his hosts walked into the strait, crying above the murmur of the waters: "Bear witness, God of Mohammed, that the conquest of this land is but a small thing, but not my faithfulness to you." He advanced into Spain at the head of an army, continually reinforced by the uncounted legions of Asia, and planted the Crescent in the very citadel of the Cross. In the meantime the Mohammedan conquests had stretched over Arabia, Palestine, Asiatic Turkey, and the lower Roman Empire. When at last Constantinople fell, the last stronghold of ancient Rome had become the appanage of the all-conquering Mussulman. Northward and westward the invading hordes swept on until they dominated the whole territory known to-day as the Balkans.

All Europe was alarmed by that tremendous conflict. Already, as we have seen, Spain and the lower Roman Empire lay in the clutch of Islam. The Spaniards, contesting every inch of the ground, were slowly driven backward into the mountains of Asturias, where Palayo and a handful of his followers hid themselves in the caves of Covadonga, still fighting for Christ and their country; while at sea the battleships of Spain maintained an equally dismal and stubborn resistance.

It is well for us to examine the important modifications wrought in the economic and psychological development of the peoples of Europe by this thousand years of war, for it will supply us with the keynote of our historical investigations.

Standing at the gate of Europe, Spain, desperately fighting for her own preservation, was the bulwark which prevented the Moors from invading the northern, central, and western states. Her daily sacrifice of blood was the safeguard of her sister Christian nations. For in the whole eight hundred years during which the Islamic invasion was principally concentrated on her conquest, Spain was never actually vanquished. The mountains of Asturias constituted a line of defence beyond which the Moors were unable to penetrate, and Europe remained inviolate. This tremendous struggle for religion and country left an indelible impression on the psychology of the Spanish people. The passion for Catholicism and country became the very substance of their souls. It is easy to understand, then, that when, at the surrender of Boabdil in Granada, the Spanish people under Isabella and Ferdinand inflicted the last blow on the Moorish power in Spain, nothing short of the Inquisition could satisfy their spirit of burning fanaticism. The discovery of the New World at the same time opened to them a sphere for the expression of that lust of blood and conquest developed in them during their long, cruel struggle with the Moors.

On the other hand, England, France, and Germany, sheltered behind Spain, had been spared all direct contact with the Mussulman. Indeed, the Holy War was of distinct service to these countries, in that it provided a beneficent sewer through which from time to time they were enabled to drain off from the body social the scum of their brigand kings, parasitic noblemen, adventurers, and vagrants, both titled and untitled. Thus, the conflict which impoverished and perverted Spain performed a genuine social service for the rest of Europe, and permitted these more favoured nations to develop their arts, industries, and commerce in comparative peace.

Wars there were, of course. But, whereas the intense religious nature of the Holy War served only to pervert the Christianity of Spain to bloody fanaticism, these lesser wars of the northern nations were either sheer economic conflicts or struggles between Catholics and reformed Catholics, which resulted in the purification, rather than in the perversion of the Christian faith among them; and in the long intervals of peace and prosperity their material progress gave rise in turn to a proportional development of political science, philosophy, and the liberal arts. Thus, while Spain was exhausting her best blood in the incessant strife with Mohammed, the rest of Europe conserved their best blood for the enrichment of society, casting only their social offal to the dogs of war. Truly Spain had become "her brother's keeper" at the cost of her own misery and retrogression.

In these comparisons Italy occupies a place apart. In a position less exposed than that of Spain, and more exposed than that of the central and northern states, to the attacks of the Mussulman, she shared with the former the miserable consequences of the protracted struggle, but not nearly in the same degree.

Thus we have in Europe two well-defined psychologies, Spanish and non-Spanish, which were to influence profoundly the history of the New Worlds, South and North. The first was to impart to the great Continent of Latin-America its own characteristic lust of blood, despotism, and intolerance; and the second, which, owing to the small part played by the Latin peoples in the colonization of the United States and Canada, was essentially a Saxon psychology, was to impart to the great Continent of North America its own characteristic love of peace, justice, and industry.

By the light of the foregoing comparisons we have been able to investigate the genesis of the Mexican master class. Later we shall examine that tremendous tragedy which constitutes Mexico's history — the unceasing struggle of the native working class against this foreign master class, for human liberty and

THE MEXICAN MASTER CLASS

democratic institutions. The most backward and least favoured of the nations, her brilliant Aztec intellect tinged with the Iberian fire, has not suffered her to rest content in degradation and stultification; but has impelled her to make almost inhuman efforts to reach the rank of the most advanced nations of the world. It is this great struggle for human liberty and national development which is the one continuous and consistent force beneath all her upheavals so often characterized by the unreflective as sporadic explosions without aim or meaning.

ECONOMIC AND ETHNOLOGICAL

While England in the north was engaged in the conquest and colonization of the territory afterward known as the "Thirteen Colonies," and the eastern part of Canada, Spain was occupied in the south in the conquest of Mexico and South America. The history of the conquest of Mexico and of its subsequent development is a type of all Latin-American history, just as the history of the Thirteen Colonies is the type of all Saxon-American history. In drawing our comparisons, therefore, between the colonial evolution of the Spaniard and the Saxon we shall confine our considerations to Mexico on the one hand, and the Thirteen Colonies on the other.

First, let us glance at the respective physical conditions with which the Saxons and the Spaniards had to cope in their settlement of the New World. In the area now known as the Thirteen Colonies the Saxon colonists found themselves in possession of an immense area of fertile land, level, easily worked, and ready to respond to the roughest cultivation with bounteous crops. The snowy mantle of winter protects these lands from the frost and leaves them at the spring thaw, warm, moist, and in ideal condition for the rapid and vigorous sprouting of seed. Immense rivers — the Mississippi, Missouri, Ohio, St. Lawrence, and others — cross the land in divers directions, sufficiently deep and slow moving to permit the ready use of their waters for navigation. In addition to these great assets of fertile land, and efficient communication and transportation, the settlers were enriched by the discovery of great deposits of coal — the food of machinery. Here, then, were combined all the conditions most favourable to the development of a rich and varied agriculture and industry.

In Mexico, on the contrary, the land is not level, but interlaced and fretted throughout its length and breadth with mountain ranges, which constitute a serious hindrance to communication and transportation, and are perfectly useless for agriculture. The valleys between these mountain ranges are uneven and arid. There is no snow in winter, and consequently no snow-water in the spring; in summer the rains are scarce, and even in the rainy season the tempestuous torrents which rave down the *arroyos* are too deeply channelled for use in irrigation. As for navigation, there is not a mile of navigable river in all Mexico. Under such conditions as these, the land, in colonial times, could scarcely provide for its inhabitants, much less produce — as was the case in the Thirteen Colonies — that accumulation of capital necessary for further development.

Again, another powerful differentiating factor in the evolution of the two civilizations is to be found in the immense difference existing between the aboriginal races which they respectively displaced and absorbed — between the haughty nomadic hunters of the north, barbarous tribal communists, among whom slavery and subjection were unknown; and the gentle, intellectual Aztecs, Toltecs, and Mayas of the south, not Indians at all, but highly civilized peoples of Aryan origin — feudal agriculturists, among whom a mild form of serfdom had existed for centuries.

In spite of the utmost effort on the part of the Saxon invaders to enslave the Indian, he remained free. A nomad, a hunter, living in brotherly equality with his fellows, he either succumbed to the bullets of the white man in desperate defence of his hunting grounds, or retreated to remoter fastnesses. Slavery, sub-

THE MEXICAN MASTER CLASS

jection, restraint, were all utterly against his nature. The Saxon colonist, unable to possess himself of slaves, was compelled to perform his own labour; and, therefore, confined himself to the appropriation of just as much land as he could conveniently cultivate unaided. Of what use was more to him? His fellow-colonists, his equals on the physical, social, and economic fields, were by no means fit subjects for servitude. Hence arose, by economic necessity, a relative agrarian democracy, in which a very large proportion of the colonists became owners of as much land as they could personally cultivate. It was not till a later period that the introduction of the negro destroyed to some extent this democratic equilibrium.*

In Mexico, on the other hand, the invading Spaniards found not barbarism, but a feudal civilization, private ownership of land in place of communal ownership, and serfdom in place of nomadic liberty. With fire and sword they laid waste a civilization in many respects superior to their own; and the fighting element among the natives, once subjugated or exterminated, the serfs fell perforce into the most abject servitude to their new masters. Thus the Spanish colonists in Mexico, far from being limited, like the Saxon colonists in the north, to as much land as they could personally cultivate, were enabled to appropriate immense tracts, limited in extent only by the number of natives whom they could force to perform serf-labour for them. Through the private ownership of these immense estates and the corresponding servitude of the toilers of the soil, there arose in Mexico an economic system closely resembling the feudal system then predominant in Europe. But, while in Europe and all the European colonies capitalism has superseded feudalism, in Mexico, feudalism still remains to a large extent the economic foundation of the country. Now, as then, Mexico is a country of great land-owners and landless peons.

---

*We take into account only the ordinary private land owners, and not the exceptional feudal land holdings established by a few privileged individuals and chartered corporations.

To this contrast of the respective natural conditions met by the Saxon and the Spaniard in their colonial enterprises must be added the psychological differences of the two races themselves. In freedom from the pressure of the Asiatic hordes the Saxon nations had achieved a well-developed civilization characterized by a purified form of faith, and a high degree of religious tolerance. Spain, on the other hand, brought to Mexico an arrested civilization, and a fanatic Romanism embittered and perverted by the fierce conflict with Islam. The Holy Inquisition set its bloody fangs in the heart of the people; persecution, fire, and torment quenched all liberty of conscience, and the soul of Mexico lay degraded and shackled as even her body. The ignorant priests went so far in their hatred of all enlightenment that emanated from any source other than the Vatican, that they burned to ashes the invaluable library in the Imperial Palace of the Aztecs, destroying at a blow the records of a culture beyond their comprehension.

Thus, summing up our comparison between the two colonial evolutions, we have: in the north, Nature rich and abundant in her gifts; in the south, Nature arid and niggardly; in the north, a vast field for labour and a plentiful reward for the labourer; in the south, labour without reward to the many, idleness and luxury for the few; in the north, an agrarian democracy in which a very large proportion of the males shared, to some extent at least, in the administration of society; in the south, a despotic feudalism, under which the administration of society remained in the hands of the few, utterly without responsibility to the many; in the north, the peaceable habits of the Saxon and a spirit of coöperation; in the south, the lust of blood and selfish individualism which characterized the perverted Spanish psychology; and, finally, in the north, religious tolerance and general intellectual enlightenment; in the south, religious bigotry and intellectual darkness. On these two foundations have arisen what we know to-day as the United States, and modern Mexico.

CHAPTER III

THE ORIGIN OF THE MEXICAN AGRARIAN REVOLTS

WE HAVE examined the deep roots of Mexico's history. Let us now investigate the immediate causes of her modern social movements. To those unaccustomed to view the historical process as an unbroken, evolving continuity, it may seem a strange assertion that the agrarian revolt which gloriously founded the democracy of America, and the agrarian revolt which is now agitating Mexico, are the true and lineal descendants of the great agrarian revolt which arose in England in the fourteenth century. But such is the fact. In England — the home of all the great mediæval and modern revolutionary movements — broke out in 1381 A. D. the first powerful uprising of the peasantry against the feudal system. John Ball, a bold priest of those times, marched up and down the country arousing the people to their first vision of democracy with his famous quip:

> "When Adam delved and Eve span
> Who was then the gentleman?"

His harangues to the peasantry sound curiously like the harangues of another bold priest four centuries later, the heroic Hidalgo, who first aroused the democratic spirit of Mexico.

"My friends," said Ball, "things will never go well in England till there shall be no longer lords or masters, till we be our own masters, as much as they are now. What right have they to keep us in bondage? How ill they use us! Are we not all descendants of Adam and Eve? Our masters are clothed in velvet and ermine, while we must be content with the poorest rags! They have wines and spices and fine bread, and handsome houses, while we have only rye and water for food and drink, and we must brave the wind and rain in the fields. Let us go to the King, who is young, and tell him of our servitude, and let us tell him that we must have it otherwise, or we shall find a remedy for ourselves."

The rebellion was suppressed with terrible slaughter by the feudal aristocracy of the time, but it was the first spark of the fire destined ultimately to envelop the world. A century and a half later the peasants of Germany arose likewise in revolt against their feudal oppressors, and the dawn of a great era of widespread revolution seemed close at hand. Two powerful agencies, however, combined to divert, retard, and stifle the power of this tremendous awakening: the Reformation under Luther, and the colonization of America.

In regard to the former we quote the following passage from "Riforma e Rivoluzione Sociale" by the great Italian sociologist, Labriola:

> The German peasants, reduced to the condition of beasts through centuries of untold oppression, made their masters suffer all that savagery which the feudal régime had developed in them, without pity for sex, state or condition. As they had been made by their masters, so did they act. Luther, who was the mouthpiece of the master class, before they gathered their great armies to crush the insurrection, used the prestige of his name to reduce the peasants to obedience, hurling at them his pamphlet "Wider die mörderischen und räuberischen Rotten der Bauer," which is considered the code of the future oppression. Luther, fuming with rage before the revolt of the peasants, called down upon them the wrath of God and the revenge of men. "This ass needs to be whipped," he said, "and the people to be shaken with violence." And he did not hesitate to compel the princes to sink their petty differences and combine to show a resolute front to the revolt, and to suppress it without mercy or consideration. The princes obeyed him. They combined and crushed the rebellion. Then followed the most dreadful reprisals that the imagination can conceive, dwarfing, indeed, the terrible ravages of the Roman emperors upon the Christians."

The second great cause of the suppression of this widespread agrarian revolt in Europe was, as we have said, the discovery and colonization of America. From the day when the news spread far and wide concerning this great New World, where was neither master nor lord nor priest; where the land was free as heaven, and all were equals, the sturdy revolutionary element in Teutonic Europe, as well as to some extent in France, began to stream steadily westward. The people were thus diverted from the slow and bloody work of reconstructing the society in which they found themselves, to the easier and more hopeful path of emigration. For three hundred years a strong tide of the more enterprising spirits who leavened the lumpish mass of European peasantry poured into the Thirteen Colonies. A more perfect safety-valve for the revolutionary agitation of the Old World could scarcely be imagined.

In the logic of events these colonists, still haunted by the fear and hatred of oppression, could not do less than throw off forever even the formal suzerainty of Europe. The revolution of 1776 which brought into being the agrarian democracy of the United States, although it was instigated by the commercial classes was but the glorious culmination of the old peasant revolts of the fourteenth and fifteenth centuries in England and Germany. But the revolutionary fire did not stop there; it leaped back again to Europe, where it had been all but extinguished in earlier days, and blazed more gloriously still in the French Revolution, which drove the big land-owners from power, and established the beginnings of an agrarian democracy in France.

From the spirit of this great revolution — a classic example of the agrarian revolt, since at that time the industrial problem had not yet arisen to complicate the issue — there came forth a philosophy that was intensely expressed by the three principles that were to provide the battle-cry of the future revolutionary movements of the world: Liberty, Equality, Fraternity. This philosophy, crossing the Pyrenees into Spain, was quickly absorbed by the Intellectuals and applied by them to the ripe revolutionary condition of the Spanish people. In the upheaval that followed, the famous constitution of 1812 was proclaimed, the first in the history of Spain to recognize the power of the common people as the true governing force of the nation, and the first to reduce the King from his position as ruler in divine right to that of ruler in the name of the people.

Wrapped in the parchments of the Holy Inquisition itself, hidden in the leaves of prayer-books, the new doctrines rapidly spread from Spain to Spain's great colony — Mexico. Under the bitterest anathema of Rome they yet made their way to the seminaries and universities. The students learned the new doctrines in secret, and relishing the forbidden fruit, mixed them with the theological dogmas that were the only canons of the civil and economic life of the time. When, finally, these students left the discipline of the schools to enter life as priests, lawyers, teachers, and writers, they became the ardent propagandists of the new ideas. Particularly was this true of the poorer class of priests; for their daily routine, more than that of any other profession, brought them into close contact with the slavery of the common people.

CHAPTER IV

POLITICAL AND ECCLESIASTICAL CONSTITUTION OF MEXICO IN THE COLONIAL PERIOD

DURING the three hundred years of the Spanish régime in Mexico, the executive head of the government was the viceking, or Virrey — an appointee of the King of Spain. This Virrey was assisted by an Audiencia, or legislative body, and by a consultative body with judicial functions, which constituted the Supreme Court of Appeals. The provincial governments were similar in constitution, having as an executive head a corregidor, or governor, appointed by the Virrey, with the approval of the King, assisted by a provincial Audiencia. In political life, as in ecclesiastical life, the Church of Rome was omnipotent, and a majority of the Virreys were ecclesiastical officials. The few of them who were not, were army officers who represented the interests of the Church quite as efficiently as did the ecclesiastics themselves. Throughout the entire colonial period, terminating with the independence, no matter what interest the Spanish Government itself might take in the protection of the peasants, the colonial government worked solely in the interests of the big land-owners, of whom the Church itself was the chief.

Another characteristic feature of the Spanish régime in Mexico was the avaricious jealousy exhibited by the Spanish Government in regard to the Mexican colonial trade. Only Spanish vessels were allowed to visit the three ports in the Gulf of Mexico, the one exception being a vessel that came once a year to the port of Acapulco from China, laden with rich Chinese silks and general merchandise. In view of such a condition of affairs — an autocratic and unenlightened government, and complete isolation from the more advanced nations of the world — it is not surprising that we find Mexico, at the beginning of the nineteenth century, in much the same miserable condition as characterized the times of the Conquest.

Society was divided into three strata. At the top stood the privileged Spanish class of big land-owners, comprising the Church and Aristocracy. This class dominated the entire life of the country, and used the government and army merely as a means to maintain their supremacy. Far below them lay the small and insignificant middle class of mixed Spanish and native blood — the intellectuals, petty professionals, and merchants, who crawled at the feet of the wealthy in the ever-present fear of being trampled upon and flung into the common servitude. Nevertheless, the members of this class, ambitious, and eternally renewing the struggle to raise themselves to a loftier and more secure position, were nourishing in their bosoms the germs of a future revolution. Far below the middle class again, and in the deepest misery and degradation, were the toilers of the soil — the natives, Aztecs, Toltecs, Mayas, and other allied races — immensely outnumbering the two other classes, but powerless in their ignorance and disorganization.

The Church itself comprised the secular and regular clergy. The entire country was covered with convents and monasteries, filled with friars and nuns, for the most part living in idleness and debauchery on the labour of the wretched serfs. At the time of the Conquest the King of Spain had given to the various religious orders in Mexico great grants of land called "Mercedes," as ecclesiastical estates for the erection and support of convents and monasteries. The grant further empowered these religious orders to christianize and enslave the native population located on these lands. To enslave the body it is necessary first to enslave the mind. The Spanish priests found it an easy matter to inspire the fear of hell-fire in the superstitious na-

PRESIDENT DIAZ AND HIS CABINET

Standing (from left to right): Gen. Manuel Gonzales Cosio, José Y. Limantour, Olegario Molina, Justo Sierra Seated (from left to right): Justino Fernandez, Ramón Corral, Vice-President, Gen. Porfirio Diaz, Enrique C. Creel, Leandro Fernandez

THE COST OF THE BATTLE OF OJINAGA

Reminiscent of a bronze plaque of the flight of the children of Israel through the Red Sea is this remarkable picture of the flight across the Rio Grande of the peace-loving inhabitants of the little town of Ojinaga during the assault of the Constitutionalists

THE COLONIAL PERIOD

tives, and to inculcate a proper obedience to themselves as the sole representatives of God upon earth. The more vigorous or rebellious minds were taken care of by the Holy Inquisition, and in a comparatively short time the system, on which the Church in Mexico was to found her fabulous wealth and power, was in perfect working order. Not content with their enormous original land grants, the priests continually used their power to withhold extreme unction from the dying, as a means of obtaining deathbed inheritances. By these and similar practices, the Church during the three hundred years of the Spanish régime in Mexico became the supreme economic power and the chief land monopolist in the country.

"With the exception of a certain amount of land owned by the aristocracy, almost all the valuable lands of Mexico were in the hands of the Church, and even those not so owned were under heavy mortgage to her, or were crushed with tithings and taxes which went into her coffers." ("México á través de los Siglos," Vol. IV, p. 317.)

"The clergy, mainly the higher officials, had accumulated and taken out of circulation an incalculable quantity of riches. In 1809 the tithings of six bishops amounted to the sum of $2,500,000 — immense wealth in those days. There were bishops and archbishops whose salaries amounted to more than $100,000 a year. Indeed, a careful estimate of the revenue of the Church just previous to the War of Independence reveals the enormous figure of $50,000,000 a year." (*Ibid.*)

At the time of the Independence the number of friars, nuns, and secular clergy had reached such proportions as to constitute a deadly menace to society. Baron von Humboldt gave conservative estimate of no less than twenty thousand of them in various parts of the country, and of these, Mexico City alone held twelve hundred. Nor was the Church, as an offset to her enormous plunderings, performing any useful function in Mexican society. With the very rare exception of a member engaged here and there in philanthropic work, this vast army of parasites was delivered up to a life of selfish indulgence, and, to a large extent, of unspeakable vice.

"During the seventeenth and eighteenth centuries many secular clergy had come to Nueva España (the colonial name for Mexico) in search of fortune, having little prospect of success in their native country. These were, for the most part, mere adventurers, vicious, and a cancer in the body ecclesiastic. The natives among the seculars, with a few exceptions, had also been contaminated. Of this we have abundant evidence in papal bulls and royal orders, in the reports of several viceroys, among whom one was a distinguished prelate, and in the edicts of the Inquisition. Violation of the vows of chastity, impeding the administration of justice, trading against express prohibition, manufacturing prohibited liquors, collecting excessive fees, and defrauding the Crown were common practices; and, indeed, some of their deeds were so scandalous that decency forbids their relation. . . . But it must be confessed that the regular orders also contained unworthy members, men who shrank from poverty and discipline, some of whom were vain, covetous and profligate, and who looked upon their mission in the New World only as an opportunity to gratify their desire for a life of ease and pleasure. . . After the spiritual conquest of Mexico it was an easy matter for these ecclesiastics to have themselves assigned to parishes which became, in spite of an outward show of religion, mere hotbeds of vice, even the sacred act of confession being profaned. These scandals in morality were most noticeable in the eighteenth and early years of the nineteenth century, at the seats of some of the dioceses and small towns." (Bancroft, "History of Mexico," Vol. III, pp. 681-682.)

"With regard to the private life of the friars it cannot truthfully be said that it was in keeping with the abstinence required. The contrast between them and the earlier missionaries is striking. Many indulged not only in the pleasures and luxuries of the laity, but also in their vices. Instead of abstemiousness, feasting and carousing prevailed among them, as among the secular clergy; instead of humble garb and bearing, pompous display in embroidered doublets and silken hose of bright colour; instead of study and devotional exercises, dice throwing and card playing over which the pious gamblers cursed and swore and drank. Immorality too often usurped the place of celibacy, and murder that of martyrdom." (*Ibid*, Vol. III, p. 708.)

"While convents and friars thus multiplied, religious sisterhoods increased in a corresponding degree. Over four hundred were already established by the middle of the seventeenth century. It would be supposed that these religious establishments, designed as peaceful retreats for females, would be free from strife, but truth compels me to say that the nuns were as contentious as the friars. All the orders, in fact, incessantly endeavoured to shake off the control exercised over them by the provincial prelates and free themselves of their supervision." (*Ibid*, Vol. III, p. 710.)*

Second only to the Church in power and extent of land monopolization was the Spanish landed aristocracy of Mexico. For the most part this aristocracy consisted of the scions of the Spanish nobility, or their descendants, who had come to the colony bearing "Mercedes," or land grants, from the King. In course of time many of them married the daughters of the native chieftains, thus founding a genuine Mexican aristocracy of blood.

At the time of the Independence the basic wealth of the country — the land — was accumulated in a very few hands. Some families, descendants of the Conquistadores, were in possession of real estate as large as a province, ceded to them by the King of Spain, and entailed as the property of the Church. Wealthy merchants and mine-owners also bought vast estates and erected them into dukedoms, marquisates, and counties, entailed by the patents of nobility bought from the King. And

---

*We quote Bancroft somewhat more liberally than the Spanish and Mexican historians of this period, not only because he here shows himself impartial, painstaking and accurate, but because it will be easier for English speaking readers to verify the quotations made.

all these vast fertile estates were tilled by the wretched native serfs, whose wages never at any time reached the sum of twenty cents a day, but who were, nevertheless, heavily taxed both by Church and State.

To the parasitic Church and Aristocracy and Government must be added yet one more burden to the bowed back of the peon — the parasitic Army. Throughout the entire period of the colonial régime, lasting some three hundred years, the strength of the standing army remained in the neighbourhood of thirty thousand men. Yet Mexico was a very peaceful colony. The privileged classes were well contented with their condition, and the peons were too broken, ignorant, and depressed to give any trouble. The reason for such an absurdity as this army, with one officer to every two privates, is to be found partly in the determination of the Church to guard against any possible retaliation on the part of the people, and partly in the Spanish system of primogeniture, which sent all the younger sons of the Spanish nobility into Mexico to fasten themselves on the military pay-roll. With no war or possibility of war to absorb their energies, this military class outvied the clergy in debauchery and perversion.

Such was the condition of the Mexican people during the Spanish régime. A nation of only six millions supported a vast host of alien parasites and plunderers without relief or hope of relief. "The conquerors distributed the natives amongst themselves as serfs, and although the admirable 'Legislacion de Indias' tried hard to remedy such a state of affairs, it was impossible to prevent the Spanish priests from submerging the natives in superstition, or to prevent the Spanish land-owner from forcing the natives to work for wretched wages and under degrading conditions." (Gustavo Baz, "La Vida de Juarez," p. 14.)

"According to another authority, the unhappy Mexican people were distributed as slaves, used as beasts of burden, subjected to the most brutal treatment, and were often the food of their masters' dogs,

THE COLONIAL PERIOD

"In three years no less than four hundred thousand of them died through this iniquitous treatment. Our hieroglyphic scriptures, glorious monuments of civilization, in which are contained the records of our history and origin, were destroyed by the barbarous Bishop Zumárraga, emulous of Omar and worthy imitator of Cardinal Jimenez." (J. J. Baz, in a speech delivered in 1859.)

Much has been written anent the paternalism of the Church. "They made the natives toil for them without payment," says Bancroft. (Vol. 13, p. 704.) The whole history of the period, even when recorded by Catholic writers, goes to show that the Church exceeded the aristocracy and military in her brutal and cynical treatment of the unhappy native peons. For these toilers of the soil there were no schools. If they fell ill — and that was often enough — there were for them but two or three miserable hospitals in all Mexico, and in these they did but only die of starvation and mistreatment. Their sole pastimes and recreations were the Church festivals, where under cajolement or threat they yielded up their scanty savings to the priests for mass-payments. If they escaped from the priests with a few centavos, there were still the drinking-places, also kept by the priests where the vilest liquor was sold, and the peons sank in the mire at the end of their long-anticipated holiday, robbed and drugged.

Not only did the clergy enjoy this vast economic and spiritual power, but also certain privileges which protected them from the reach of such civil law as there was at the time. These privileges, which were termed "fueros eclesiasticos," exempted the priest, the friar, the nun, and the military from any retribution at the hands of the civil courts for any crimes committed by them. On the other hand, offences against the Church committed by civilians were punished with the utmost severity. We shall find these iniquitous fueros playing a prominent part in the history of Mexico.

CHAPTER V

THE REVOLUTION OF INDEPENDENCE

BY THE year 1808 conditions in colonial Mexico had become so intolerable for the great mass of people that revolutionary symptoms began to appear simultaneously in all parts of the country. The Intellectuals, as we have seen, were already deeply imbued with the doctrines that had emanated from the French Revolution — doctrines that in the presence of the desperate wretchedness of the common people pointed in letters of flame to the necessity of a radical change in the economic and political system of the times.

Some mild reformers of the wealthy class were already mooting the question of independence from Spain, prompted chiefly by their discontent with the unwritten law which preserved all the higher appointments in the colonial government for Spanish court favourites. The movement, however, lacked virility, and never gained strength until, at a later day and under very different conditions, the common people — rising in independent revolt, Aztec against Spaniard, landless peon against landlord — were tricked into giving it support. The Virrey Iturrigaray himself was in the conspiracy. He planned to call to Mexico City from all parts of the country such delegates as were known to be in favour of the step, and by the aid of this packed convention to proclaim the independence of Mexico and establish a new constitution. The conspiracy bid fair to be completely successful, for great care was taken that the delegates should include only those malcontents who resented the exactions of Spain and the exclusion of the native aristocracy from the higher official positions. The plot, however, was discovered before it

THE REVOLUTION OF INDEPENDENCE

had time to ripen, and the higher officers of the Church and Army who preferred the *status quo* promptly seized the Virrey and dispatched him under guard to Spain, at the same time arresting and imprisoning his fellow-conspirators. A number of army officers had joined the plot, but the moment it was discovered they were quick to recant their revolutionary faith, and to affirm their loyalty to Spain and the government. It was these same men who afterward fought zealously against the real Revolution of Independence.

Indeed, it is a law of the historical process, demonstrated again and again, that no genuine social revolution can be successfully carried out by a class whose material interests are not at stake in that revolution. The so-called revolutions effected by the moneyed and military classes so common in Latin-America are not revolutions at all in the social sense, but simply surface disturbances for the petty purposes of legalized plunder and reprisal. Never have such disturbances the real freedom of the masses for their object. The student must be careful not to confuse these affairs (termed "comic opera revolutions," and rightly, were they not so tragic in their effects on the country at large) with the grim, pathetic, eternal revolt of the common people against conditions intolerably brutal and degrading.

The failure of this conspiracy was directly due to the treachery of one of the conspirators — a lieutenant of the army, named Augustin Iturbide. We mention the fact chiefly because it suitably introduces us to a figure destined to play a notorious part in Mexican history.

Many who took part in this "parlour-revolution" later on took part in the genuine Revolution of Independence. Particularly was this true of the Intellectuals. These men, as we have seen, were for the most part members of the ostracized middle class, and ardent students of the virile philosophy of the French Revolution. The social unrest of the time gave them an excellent opportunity to arouse the people to a struggle with the oppressive power of Spain. The advantage of independence for the Intellectuals was clearly enough defined. For them it meant freedom to express their ideas, and to attain by merit the highest positions in the realm.

The Church, now thoroughly on guard, was the first to sound a warning against the coming revolution; and well she might, for the tocsin of Independence was about to be heard. But it was not now the parlour-revolution of disgruntled Aristocrats and Intellectuals with which she had to deal, but the spontaneous revolt of the native working class — the common people, in bondage for three hundred years, and now aroused to their might as a race and as a class.

At midnight on the 15th of September, 1810, at the rectory of the revolutionary priest, Miguel Hidalgo, in Dolores, State of Guanajuato, the call to arms of the real Revolution of Independence was sounded. Two young ex-officers of the army, Juan Aldama and Ignacio Allende, devoted to the revolutionary cause, had crept by night to Hidalgo's house to warn him that their plans for a popular uprising were already known to the government, and that all three of them were in immediate danger of arrest. The undaunted Hidalgo exclaimed: "Action must be taken at once. There is no time to be lost. We shall yet see the oppressor broken and the fragments scattered on the ground." He thereupon promptly summoned the street watchmen who were already in the conspiracy, and bid them arouse the workmen in the town.

Miguel Hidalgo, destined to become the dominant factor in the great struggle which once and for all time freed Mexico from the oppression of Spain, was a good type of the average Mexican Intellectual. Although a priest, the incumbent of the scanty curacy of Dolores, he was a man of liberal scholarship. Eminently practical in his attempts to ameliorate the wretched conditions of his parishioners, and a close student of economics, he established for their benefit a number of coöperative enterprises, including porcelain, pottery, and weaving factories, a blacksmith shop, and a silkworm farm. He was a brave and deter-

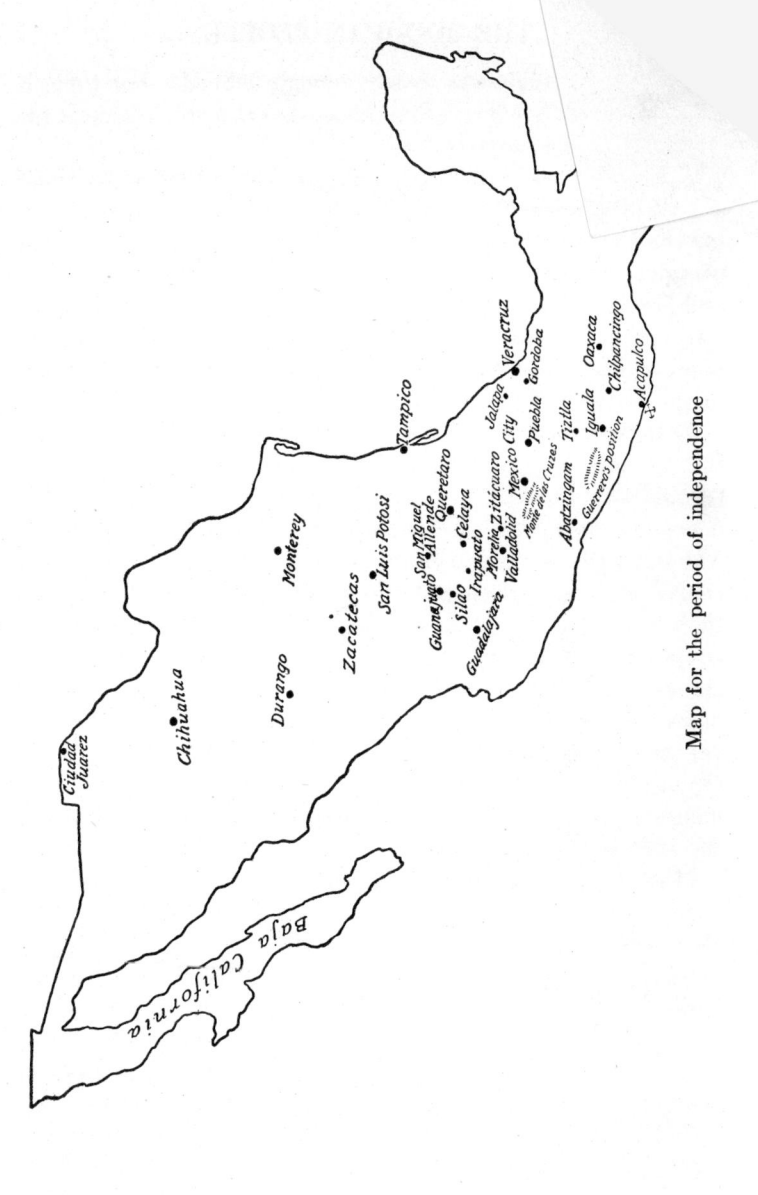

Map for the period of independence

THE REVOLUTION OF INDEPENDENCE

mined man, simple in his habits, quick-witted and humorous in conversation, and beloved of the people for the kindness which he invariably showed toward them. At this moment, when he first appears as the leader and organizer of the Revolution, he was about fifty-eight years of age; in physique, a man of medium height, robust proportion, ruddy complexion, and massive, well-modelled head.

The alarm once given, spread rapidly to all parts of the town, and peons and workmen, armed with weapons which they had themselves fashioned on the anvil, began to fill the streets without the parish-house. It was already three o'clock in the morning and the bells were ringing for the peons' mass. But there was no mass that morning.

"Hidalgo called the people into the church, and speaking from the pulpit said: 'My children, this day comes to us a new dispensation. Are you ready to receive it? Will you be free? Will you make the effort to recover from the hated Spaniards the lands stolen from your fathers three hundred years ago?'" (Bancroft, "History of Mexico," Vol. IV, p. 177.)

In this brief, momentous harangue stands crystallized the real issue of the Revolution of Independence. If the battle-cry of the insurgents was henceforth, "Down with the Gachupines" (a nickname for the Spaniards), this was not due so much to the fact that the big land-owners were Spaniards, as to the fact that they maintained their hold on the land only through the powerful arm of the Spanish executive. Supplementing this attitude toward the administration on the part of the native peons and workmen was the eagerness of the mixed-blood middle class to overthrow a régime that ostracized them from all the higher official positions in Church, State, and Army. But whatever advantage these Intellectuals may have hoped to gain, *the great mass of peons who shed their blood freely in the struggle had at heart no other idea than the ownership of the land. The Revolution of Independence was essentially an agrarian revolution.*

The harangue finished, Hidalgo stepped from the pulpit and,

placing himself at the head of the now armed and aroused insurgents, marched on the jail. The jails were filled with the sick and the more spirited peons who refused to bow down utterly to their masters. The first step of the Revolution was to give freedom to these men wrongly deprived of liberty. The guards of the jail were taken by surprise, disarmed, and their weapons handed over to the freed prisoners. From the jail the insurgents now marched on to the office of the Sub-Delegado, or Mayor of the town. This official was by law the collector and treasurer of the tithings wrung from the peons by the Church. Hidalgo promptly seized the entire treasure on behalf of the Revolution.

With men, arms, and money, the movement was already well under way. Since the previous night Hidalgo had dispatched messengers north, south, east and west, to arouse the peons of the haciendas. Soon they came marching in bands into the city. By noon more than six hundred of them were already enlisted in the Revolution. Scantily supplied with arms and untrained to war as they were, Hidalgo was reluctant to let them join the ranks. But they refused to withdraw. Their will was to stay, and at least to shed their blood for the cause of liberty, and Hidalgo acquiesced, in the hope that presently he might be able to find arms for them. For the first time in three hundred years the peons had imposed their will on the social process.

At last they were sovereign — so ran the minds of the native peons — they would work no longer for the enrichment of idle Spanish folk, but they themselves who tilled the land, planted the seed, and irrigated the crop, should garner the harvest and retain possession of it. No longer would they yield to soldier, and clergy, and aristocrat the fruits of their labour. Some of them would fight, while others at home would till the land to feed their brothers in action. Their masters would no longer be able to browbeat them; instead, they would have to flee and hide. The land henceforth would be the peons'. There should

THE REVOLUTION OF INDEPENDENCE 31

be no more peonage, no more taxes, no more tithings. To every peon should be given all the land he could cultivate, and the fruits of it for himself and his family.

This was the real issue of the Revolution. The bourgeois leaders endeavoured to confine the scope of it merely to territorial independence. But the great mass of peons who were doing the actual fighting were in the field not for mere political change but for the ownership of the land. Their ideas in the matter were not by any means communistic, as some have thought. On the contrary, they were strictly individualistic. The desire of the peon was that every man should own his own piece of land and the crop thereof.

At the first outbreak of the Revolution the Church promptly unsheathed her most terrible psychological weapon — the excommunication under the dread formula, "Si quis suadente diabolo." Under the careful tutelage of the priests the peasants had become incredibly superstitious, and no better idea can be given of the desperation and heroic abandon of this revolt than the fact that the excommunicatory thunders of the Church rolled over its head unheeded or derided. For these men the land was the thing. Religion was for the nonce submerged. Later in the campaign, when the hypnotism of centuries reasserted its power over them, they compelled the revolutionary priests in their ranks — and there were many of them — to perform mass in the camps and on the battlefields.

Contemporaneously with the Revolution of Independence in Mexico similar revolutions, aimed at the overthrow of the Spanish colonial régime, broke out in all Latin-America. Thus we see that the sturdy agrarian revolt which broke out in England in the fourteenth century had not expended its force at the beginning of the nineteenth century. We have seen it leap from England to Germany, from Germany to the United States, from the United States to France, from France to Spain, from Spain to Mexico, and from Mexico to all Latin-America. For a hundred years, not only in Mexico but in all Latin-America, this agrarian revolution has not slumbered an hour. Now smouldering and apparently dead, anon bursting forth in fitful gleams of flame, and, finally, during the last three years, culminating in the mighty Mexican conflagration, the struggle has been maintained for the land which is life and liberty and home. It must still be maintained. Eventually it must triumph. It is the struggle of the fourteenth century in England — the serf versus the feudal lord. The only difference in the two situations is that the feudal lord of to-day — the big corporation — is immeasurably more powerful and far more deeply entrenched than his ruffianly, picturesque prototype of an earlier age; while the peon is not only comparatively, but intrinsically more wretched, degraded, and incapable of resistance than the sturdy, bold, and comparatively well-fed serf of feudal Europe.

Within a few days of the fateful morning when Hidalgo from his pulpit aroused his people to the dawn of a new dispensation, the ranks of the Revolution had swelled to several thousand men. The government, at first skeptical of the importance of the affair, finally awoke to the necessity for action, and issued peremptory orders to the army to quell the "mob of bandits and marauders." At the same time the Virrey made a futile attempt to render the uprising abortive by issuing a proclamation in which he promised the peons relief from oppression and freedom from taxation. He was too late. The revolutionists had already tasted of success. Marching triumphantly through the State of Guanajuato, city after city, ungarrisoned and unprepared, fell into their power. Everywhere along their march they seized and imprisoned the Spanish landlords, holding them for hostage, or compelling them to flee into exile. Their lands were given over to the native peons who were working on them, and these latter found themselves suddenly possessors of the lands they tilled and the crops they harvested.

In five days the insurgent hosts had increased to thirty thousand men. Of these only about a thousand were in possession of muskets. The rest were armed chiefly with spears or weapons of their own manufacture. In their march across the state, the army passed through San Miguel el Grande, where they considerably increased their numbers; thence they proceeded to Celaya; and finally they laid siege to Guanajuato, the capital of the state, and the richest mining city of Mexico. The city's garrison consisted of only six hundred men, but the local government, assisted by the rich Spanish mine-owners and high clergy, succeeded in organizing a strong force of volunteers with which to oppose the revolutionists. The fiercest of the fighting raged about the city fortress called Alhóndiga de Granaditas. Here the defenders massed their principal forces and awaited events. The attack was opened by the insurgents, and so fierce was their onslaught that within a few hours the garrison, overpowered, and demoralized by the death of their commander-in-chief, surrendered. During the assault a priest within the fortress, seeing that the physical weapon was proving insufficient, decided to try the power of the psychological weapon, and marching forth from the fortress bearing aloft a large crucifix he commanded the insurgents to withdraw. Having neither steel nor ammunition to waste, the peons simply stoned him and smashed his crucifix without remorse. So fierce was the conflict that over two thousand of the unarmed insurgents lost their lives. The fortune of the day was decided by the heroism of an old insurgent peon known as Pipila. When the insurgents, even with a reckless sacrifice of life, found themselves unable to break into the fortress, this man placed a large, flat stone on his back and, taking fire and turpentine in his hand, crawled through a rain of bullets to the massive door of the fortress and, setting fire to it, tended the flames until an opening had been made for the assailants. More than four million dollars, mostly tithings and taxes extorted from the people by the Church, was discovered in the treasuries of Alhóndiga de Granaditas. This money was confiscated by the insurgents for the expenses of the Revolution. After the victory the insurgents sent emissaries to arouse the people to revolt in San Luis Potosi. Here, however, the vigorous opposition of well-disciplined troops frustrated the uprising.

The moment was opportune for the insurgents. Spain was at war with France, and the Virrey, fearing that the French Government might eventually dispatch an invading army to the shores of Mexico, was compelled to conserve the greater part of his military strength for the protection of Vera Cruz and the Gulf of Mexico. Thus the insurgents were able to make tremendous headway in the central and southwestern states, practically unchecked. And since the ill-gotten plunder of the Church was confiscated wherever the opportunity presented itself, the financial resources of the Revolution were soon considerable.

In possession of arms and money, Hidalgo now decided to march his revolutionary hosts on Valladolid (to-day Morelia), one of the wealthiest strongholds of the Church in Mexico, and for that reason a desirable source of supplies. When the news of the approaching insurgent army reached the city, the clergy themselves flew to arms and desperately endeavoured to put the town in a state of defence. The Bishop placed himself at the head of the garrison, and ordered the bells of the cathedral to be melted into cannon balls, while the friars stripped themselves of their monastical garments and donned the gay uniforms of the military. These ecclesiastics were generally exceptionally strong men. Feasting daily on the choicest of viands, living almost continuously in the open air, riding and hunting, untouched by the penalties of labour, they were physically quite fit for the fray. When the insurgents appeared before the town, however, the masses of the people within the gates arose in their favour, and the gallant ecclesiastics fled for their lives without firing a single shot. More than half a million dollars of tithings was confiscated from the Church treasuries and restored to the use of the people in their struggle for freedom, and the Canonical Chapter was compelled to repeal the sentence of excommuni-

THE REVOLUTION OF INDEPENDENCE 35

cation which had been laid upon the insurgents. The Virrey, at last recognizing that the insurrection was liable to prove a more dangerous enemy to his power than the French invasion, dispatched an army of six thousand men under the command of El Conde de la Cadena into the disaffected districts. However, when the royal troops arrived at San Miguel El Grande they found little food for their steel, as the revolutionists had already vacated the town to take possession of Valladolid. Instead of being welcomed with wild cheers, as they had expected, they found themselves received in silence and cold disapproval by the townsfolk, who only a few weeks before had opened their arms to the insurgents.

From San Miguel the discomfited El Conde de la Cadena marched to Dolores, and there joined forces with General Calleja. Having no insurgents to fight, they amused themselves with destroying Hidalgo's house. Meanwhile the insurgents had left Valladolid to begin their fateful march on Mexico City. Hidalgo strongly opposed this step, for he was well aware of the disorganized and unarmed condition of his forces, and foresaw clearly the result should they be obliged to engage the well-disciplined and heavily armed troops of the metropolis. The peons themselves, however, were anxious for the venture, and the chieftains associated with Hidalgo were as eager as their followers, the more that daily messages were being received from the capital promising a general uprising of the people within her gates in support of the revolutionary assault. All these circumstances combined to overcome Hidalgo's opposition to the step, and the insurgent host set forth.

The two royal generals, El Conde de la Cadena and Calleja, armed with the Virrey's authority summarily to execute not only actual insurgents but any one suspected of insurgent sympathies, were encamped at Dolores with seven thousand well-trained men and four pieces of artillery. At the same time General Trujillo was ordered by the Virrey to take another seven thousand picked men from the garrison of Mexico City to break up Hidalgo's march. At a place called Monte de las Cruces the two armies engaged. The insurgents, under Hidalgo, numbered eighty thousand, but not more than two thousand of these were well-armed; the larger number of them were boys and old men, whom love of liberty and a dream of heroism and martyrdom for freedom had drawn into the ranks. Hidalgo in vain endeavoured to hold them in reserve. They complained so bitterly against this restraint and pleaded so hard to be allowed to go to the front, that Hidalgo was compelled to let them have their way. On the 30th of October, at dawn, in the midst of the forest of Monte de las Cruces, on an altar of rocks, and in full sight of the royalist forces, Hidalgo celebrated mass. Scarcely was it finished before the battle began. All day and late into the night the carnage raged. When morning dawned the royalists were completely routed. But the victory had been bought at a terrible price — more than ten thousand half-naked, unarmed insurgents lay dead on the field, mowed down by the heavy musket and artillery fire of the well-equipped royal forces.

The psychological moment of the Revolution had arrived. If the people of the city and neighbourhood proved true to their promises and pledges, and rose to aid the advancing insurgent army, all resistance would be vain before their overwhelming hosts, and the military, beset on all sides, could do nothing but surrender. Emissaries were dispatched to the capital and surrounding country calling upon the people to rise. There was no response. Again and again messengers were sent by Hidalgo into the city to arouse concerted action on the part of the metropolitan insurgents with the invading army. Still there was no response. Whether cowed or cajoled it matters not. The men who had summoned Hidalgo to march on Mexico City now refused him the aid they had promised. The terrible slaughter of the insurgents showed him clearly the prematurity of his action in marching on the metropolis, and he fell back, effecting a detour to the north. A few days later he encountered Calleja and sustained a severe defeat at his hands. Now victorious, anon defeated, the insurgent hosts finally succeeded in reaching and taking possession of Guadalajara. Already, as we have seen, the southwestern portion of the country was in the hands of the revolutionists, while Zacatecas and San Luis Potosi had become centres of revolutionary activity.

At the beginning of the revolt, Hidalgo, using the power with which he was invested as leader of the insurgent forces, had uttered a decree abolishing slavery, peonage, and the taxation of the poor. Now, in Guadalajara, he issued a further decree restoring the land to the peons. At the same time he initiated the first form of an organized government by the appointment of a minister of state and members of the Audiencia, and by the nomination of Pascasio Letona as envoy plenipotentiary to the United States with instructions to make, if possible, a treaty of alliance and commerce with the republic. Meanwhile the first public organ of the insurrection appeared in Guadalajara under the caption *El Despertador Americano.** At the same time Hidalgo and his chieftains went forward vigorously with the important work of disciplining the troops and thoroughly training them in the use of arms, although of the latter there was still a very inadequate supply.

It is not our intention to follow step by step the course of Mexico's struggle to wrest independence from Spain. That has been done adequately elsewhere. Our object is to reveal the economic cause that lay at the base of this Revolution. We propose to show here and throughout this volume the eternal strife between the two main classes of society — the possessing class and the non-possessing class — and the tactics used by

---

*Perhaps it is well to mention here that the word Mexico, as the name for the country lying between the United States on the north and Guatemala on the south, was first used officially in the Treaty of Cordova (1820) by which Spain agreed to recognize Mexico's independence. Under the Spanish régime this country, which then extended much farther north and south than it does to-day was officially termed "Nueva España," or "New Spain." During the struggle for independence the name of America was adopted, and this is the name used in all the writings of the period.

them in the fight. At the base of this struggle, as at the base of all the succeeding struggles, lay the effort of the peons to obtain the land. For the rest — the middle class, Army, Aristocracy, and Clergy — united or divided on the various issues, according to the dictates of their material interests. For instance, in this particular struggle, native Intellectuals could be found in numbers on the royalist side, and Spanish Intellectuals on the insurgent side, showing that the question of territorial independence was the formal rather than the real issue at stake. As a general rule we shall find the Church and Army and Aristocracy presenting a solid and united phalanx, for their interests are generally identical; while the middle class is divided, as indeed are its economic interests.

Eventually, Hidalgo and his forces were driven forth from Guadalajara and were compelled to retreat into the north. Already, however, as an offset to this reverse, the Revolution had begun to gain ground in other parts of the country. But on the march from Coahuila to Chihuahua the insurgents suffered a defeat in an encounter with royalist troops, and Hidalgo, betrayed by one of his own officers, was captured, subjected to a war tribunal, and sentenced to be shot.

His speech before the tribunal remains, like the famous utterances of Abraham Lincoln, an inspiration to the political conscience of the people for all time. He said: "Our aim and purpose in arousing and furthering this Revolution was to effect a popular election of Congress in which would be represented every individual in this country, whether he live in town, or city, or village, or farm. It was our intention that this Congress should promulgate laws for the welfare and happiness of the people, and for the purity of religion in a spirit of humanity; for the people must be governed with the sweetness of fatherly commands. By these laws it was our intention to establish the brotherhood of man, the destruction of poverty and ignorance, the prevention of the ruin of the nation, the progress of the fine arts, industry, and commerce, recognizing in every one

THE REVOLUTION OF INDEPENDENCE

without exception the right to enjoy the bounteous production of our rich lands, and the right to be happy, thus obeying God's fatherly commands to this country."

In these simple words was enshrined a noble doctrine, but a doctrine that chimed ill with the economic interests of the privileged classes in Mexico. Hidalgo was not merely voicing his personal aspirations for the welfare of the people; he was voicing the aspirations of the entire Revolution. Herein lay the heinousness of the crime that destroyed his life.

Before daybreak, on the morning of the 31st of July, 1811, Hidalgo was led forth to the place of execution. Recollecting that he had left some sweetmeats under his pillow, he stopped and requested that they might be brought to him. These he distributed among the firing platoon. Being bound upon the seat of execution, he raised his hand to his breast without a tremor and reminded the soldiers that this was the mark at which they must aim. The signal was given, the platoon fired, and Hidalgo, one of the world's greatest heroes in the cause of liberty, lay dead.

The same fate was meted out to his three gallant lieutenants, Ignacio Allende, Juan Aldama, and Mariano Jimenez. By the order of General Felix Maria Calleja, their bodies were beheaded and sent to Guanajuato, where they were nailed to the four corners of the Alhondiga de Granaditas, beneath the following inscription:

The heads of Miguel Hidalgo, Ignacio Allende, Juan Aldama, and Mariano Jimenez, great bandits and chief leaders of the Revolution, who ransacked and robbed the treasuries of God and the treasuries of the King, who shed with great atrocity the innocent blood of faithful priests and good judges of the King our Lord, and filled with ruin, disgrace, and calamity, these faithful and royal parts of the kingdom of Spain. Here are nailed their heads by the orders of the Señor General Don Felix Maria Calleja Del Rey, illustrious vanquisher of Aculco, Guanajuato, and Calderon, and restorer of the peace in this America. Guanajuato, in the year of our Lord, 1811.

This summary execution of the capable and devoted leaders of the Revolution was a check to the insurgents, but it left the survivors undismayed. The Revolution had spread over the whole country, and those already in arms were only the more determined to carry on the struggle. Already vast stretches of land were in possession of the peons. For the first time in their lives they tasted of personal freedom; for the first time they could hold their heads high, free men, and lords of the soil. Not willingly would they surrender these precious conquests; rather would they die to a man.

Already the foul mists of superstition were beginning to lift from their minds in the exercise of free activities. They had seen the Church — ogre and master of their souls — made humble and impotent before their own might, its excommunications derided, its dread priests stoned, and its treasuries, supposed to be guarded by the avenging hand of the Most High, sacked with impunity. In the violation of the very code in which they had been crushed and enslaved, body and soul, they found — not the fearful punishments that they had been taught from infancy to expect — but, on the contrary, freedom, well-being, possession of the lands and of themselves. To the courage of desperation had succeeded the valour of hope and manhood — things not easily crushed whatever be the opposing forces.

As we have said, the entire southwest was practically under the control of the Revolution. In the west, J. Maria Morelos successfully held three or four provinces; in the south, Bravo and Rayon maintained large commands of insurgents; in the east, Matamoros was gaining ground; while in the north, Bernardo Gutierrez de Lara was driving the Spanish Government out of Texas.

This last revolutionary leader relinquished the fight for a time in order to seek moral and financial support for the cause at Washington. The insurgents were sadly in need of arms and ammunition; and the aid and countenance of the sister republic in this matter would have been invaluable. In the negotiations which ensued, James Madison, then President of the United

States, offered moral and financial aid to the Revolution on condition of receiving for such services substantial grants of Mexican territory. Bernardo Gutierrez de Lara indignantly repulsed these overtures and returned to his command.

In these early years of the nineteenth century revolution was rife in all parts of the Spanish Empire. In Spain itself the Liberal party, profiting by the national discontent and the subservience of King Fernando VII to Napoleon, had been able to enforce their demands for the summoning of a general Congress representing Spain and the Spanish possessions, for the purpose of framing a new constitution which should effectually express the will of the people. This Congress, known in history as Las Cortes de Cadiz, met in the city of Cadiz, where the new constitution was duly proclaimed on the 18th of March, 1812. This was the first constitution to fully recognize the equal rights of all Spanish subjects, whether natives of Spain or of the colonies. It likewise definitely wrested the sovereign right from the royal family and vested it in the people as a whole.

Principles radical as were these at that time, necessarily aroused tremendous opposition on the part of the Church and Aristocracy, not only in Spain, but in all the Spanish colonies, including Mexico. This opposition developed to a bitter hatred of the new order, when, in the following year, the Liberal party decreed the abolition of the Holy Inquisition. From that moment there sprang up in the minds of the privileged class in Mexico a spirit of rebellion against the Liberal home government which developed during the next eight years into open secession. For the nonce, however, the privileged classes of Mexico sorely needed the aid of the Spanish troops to suppress the growing agrarian revolt within their borders, and must needs dissimulate the real nature of their sentiments.

As a temporary measure they compelled the Virrey to proclaim that the new constitution was not suited to the conditions obtaining in Mexico, and consequently need not be obeyed. They realized, however, that the crisis was becoming acute. If, on the one hand, they refused to submit to the Liberal constitution, and, on the other hand, feared an open rupture with the home government, they saw that it was highly necessary for them to adopt some third course which, while safeguarding their own interests, would nevertheless have the appearance of conforming, if not to the spirit, then to the letter of the new order.

With this object in mind the privileged classes decided to call the election of a colonial Congress which would clothe their old dominance in a new garb. Meanwhile, in view of the fact that the Revolution was increasing in extent and power every day, they compelled the Virrey to issue a dummy proclamation, couched in terms of perfervid generosity, conceding to the people not only all that the most radical revolutionary had ever asked, but more than the most Utopian revolutionary had ever dreamed. This interesting document proclaimed that all the government land was to be divided among the peons, and that the peons were to receive likewise all the capital they needed for the development of these lands from the treasuries of the municipalities to which they belonged. The latter promise was the more amusing in that the treasuries of the municipalities at this time were invariably empty. The contempt of the privileged classes, however, for the peon intelligence was such that they felt quite sure this proclamation would put an immediate end to the Revolution. It had, of course, even less effect on the insurgents than had the excommunicatory thunders of the Church.

Throughout the whole period the press was merely another supplementary tool of the privileged classes. Under the constitution of Cadiz, it is true, the complete freedom of the press had been established by law, but when a few newspapers endeavoured to avail themselves of the privilege, the Virrey announced that such liberty was incompatible with the welfare of the country, and they were promptly suppressed.

We have seen that at the earliest opportunity which presented itself in the course of the Revolution, Hidalgo had endeavoured

THE CONSTITUTIONALISTS' AGRARIAN PLAN

General Blanco signing the titles to the confiscated 73,000-acre estate of Felix Diaz, near Matamoros. After its seizure this estate was surveyed and divided into tracts which were placed on sale to peons at nominal prices

JOSÉ MARIA MORELOS

Insurgent leader and the leading spirit in the framing of the constitution of Apatzingam. Morelos preferred the title "Serf of the Nation" to that of "Generalissimo"

to organize a revolutionary government. From Guadalajara, the temporary seat of his administration, he had sent Ignacio Lopez Rayon to the south to confer with the patriot leader Morelos on the advisability of establishing a republican form of government. Morelos had accepted Hidalgo's suggestions, and, pursuant to his wishes, had organized a committee which opened its session on the 19th of August, 1811, at Zitácuaro, in the state of Michoacan.

This Junta de Zitácuaro, as it was called, consisted of five members, among whom were José Liceaga, José Sixto Verdugo, and Ignacio Lopez Rayon, this last occupying the presidential chair. The junta formally appointed Morelos commander-in-chief of the Army of the Rebellion, with the title of "Generalissimo." Morelos, like most of the other great figures of the Revolution, a plain man of the people, expressed disgust with this title, which savoured so strongly of the gayly uniformed officers of the royalist army. He preferred, he said, to be called "The Serf of the Nation."

The establishment of this junta deeply alarmed the government, and their efforts to subdue the Revolution were redoubled. War raged fiercely in every part of the country, and the Church and government, panic-stricken before the now imminent danger of being overwhelmed by sheer force of numbers, began sending frantic appeals to Spain for troops. In the meantime, the junta called upon the people to elect representatives to a congress for the purpose of framing a constitution and organizing the country under its provisions.

On the 13th of September, 1813, in the city of Chilpancingo, to-day the capital of Guerrero, this justly celebrated Congress convened. Its first act was to declare the independence of Mexico from Spain. In the following year it framed the first Mexican Constitution. This remarkable document, generally known as the Constitution of Apatzingam, from the town where it was first proclaimed, was a triumph of Liberal statesmanship. It recognized the rights of citizenship of every male inhabitant of Mexico over eighteen years of age. It established indirect elections, the free ballot, and the liberty of the press. Although recognizing the Roman Catholic religion as the national religion, it provided, to some extent, for freedom of religious opinion; and while establishing tithings for the support of the clergy, abolished the land monopoly of the Church; and, furthermore, brought the Church under the civil tribunal by the abolition of the hated clerical and military fueros. In administrative matters the constitution adhered to the principle of the division of power, creating an executive, judiciary, and legislature. The appointment of the executive, called the "Supreme Government," was placed in the hands of Congress. This executive was uniquely constituted in that it consisted of three men who, during the period for which they were elected, succeeded each other in rotation, each holding the supreme power for four months. The Supreme Court of Justice was constituted to consist of five judges to be elected by Congress.

It may occasion the reader some surprise that this Congress, which represented the will of an avowedly agrarian revolution, should treat the land question so inadequately. It must be remembered, however, that this Congress gave expression to the immediate necessities of a social transition rather than to the reconstructive projects of an accomplished social revolution. The men who framed the constitution recognized that the immediate necessity of the hour was the establishment of a full republican form of government, by means of which — the Revolution once accomplished — the people might establish their will.

Many other admirable features were woven into the fabric of this constitution — among them laws aimed at the suppression of luxuries, abolition of poverty, and the adjustment of remuneration for labour to a higher standard of living. Personal taxation was abolished and provision made for placing *the burden of government support on capital alone.* The democratic control of legislation was further secured by a special declaration which *vested in the people the right to initiate laws* for the consideration of Congress. The whole document, indeed, constitutes a truly remarkable record of the political genius of the native Mexican common people as distinguished from the alien, perverted, and decadent ruling class. The United States has had a hundred years of democratic legislation since the Mexican Constitution of Independence was framed, and has only recently adopted the initiative in a few of her states, while her legislation, in respect of taxation and labour, appears hopelessly inadequate beside the provisions which mark this first effort of Mexican democracy.

"In comparing the final form of the constitution with the original draft of it, prepared by Ignacio Lopez Rayon, the influence exerted on the deliberations of Congress by the new Spanish Constitution, established at the Cortes de Cadiz, is clearly seen. *For the rest, the modern socialist will have no difficulty in recognizing his own concepts of social reconstruction in many of the principles, beloved of Morelos, which this document embodied in regard to taxation and the remuneration of labour.*"* (Zamacois, "Historia de Mejico," Vol. 9., pp. 303–304.)

If we consider for a moment the trying circumstances under which this constitution was framed we shall be amazed at the splendid accomplishment of these men of the revolutionary Congress. Often hiding in the mountains, fleeing constantly from retreat to retreat, always in imminent danger of their lives, their property confiscated, their wives and families at the mercy of the royal government, under sentence of death as traitors to the King, and under the awful excommunications of Rome for violating her altars, these men, upborne by the passion for liberty, carried their great task to a superb conclusion. Such was the spirit of the Revolution of Independence, and such is the spirit of the agrarian revolt which has shaken Mexico to her foundations in recent times.

The establishment of the constitution and the organization

---

*Throughout this work the italics in quotations are our own except where otherwise stated. — AUTHORS.

of government gave a mighty impetus to the revolutionary movement. Congress again endeavoured to establish international relationships and dispatched an envoy, José Pablo Anaya, to Washington to obtain recognition for the new nation. Little result attended this embassy, however; Anaya, happening to encounter Andrew Jackson at New Orleans, received from him many friendly promises and an offer of financial assistance in the purchase of ammunition for the insurgents. But neither the formal recognition of the Revolution nor the promised financial aid ever materialized.

By this time the Revolution had reached the zenith of its power; and, but for help from without, the dominance of the trinity of privilege — Church, Army, and Aristocracy — would have been destroyed from Mexico for all time. Unfortunately, however, at this critical moment, a counter-revolution broke out in Spain, which abolished the constitution of 1812, and made the King absolute ruler once more. He immediately responded to the frantic appeals for help received from the panic-stricken royalists in Mexico and dispatched an army to their assistance. Equipped with the best artillery, and numbering — if the troops already in action are counted — over a hundred thousand men, this army of Spain descended like an avalanche on the revolutionary forces. From that moment the cause of liberty began to lose ground. Before the opposing host the revolutionists suffered reverse upon reverse, culminating on the 22nd of November, 1815, in the capture and execution of the great Morelos. The loss of Morelos was an almost overwhelming blow to his followers. His powerful genius as a fighter and organizer had succeeded in maintaining more than sixty thousand soldiers in the field, and nothing short of the heavy reinforcements received by the royalists from Spain could have prevented his entry into Mexico City.

The Revolution was apparently crushed. This was only true, however, of that phase of it which found expression in arms. Other subtler but no less powerful forces were at work destroy-

THE REVOLUTION OF INDEPENDENCE

ing the old order and upbuilding the new. Prominent among these was the illicit free trade between the coast ports of Mexico and the countries of Europe, which had sprung up unchecked in the general social confusion. In a previous chapter we have referred to the tutelage in which Nueva España was held by Spain, and nowhere was this tutelage more stringently enforced than in the matter of trade. With Spain alone were the colonial merchants allowed to exchange their produce, and all commercial communication with the rest of the world was sternly repressed. Under the stress of the Revolution, however, the vigilance of the government weakened, and Mexican merchants were quick to seize the opportunity of trading with vessels from other European countries. In fact a kind of free trade was established. The great profit accruing from this new commercial freedom brought vividly to the consciousness of even the wealthy classes the decided advantage of Independence. It is true, their lands had been wrested from them by the peons, but this new trade bid fair to compensate them for the loss. Moreover, they cherished the belief that even a government based on Independence would restore their land to them, more particularly if they themselves should prove active in supporting its establishment. In view of these facts, therefore, it is not surprising that a number of the more enterprising land-owners and merchants began to transfer their support from the royalists to the revolutionary cause.

This breaking up of the monopoly of the Mexican trade held by Spain was a very genuine conquest of the Revolution. If in the year 1816 the cause of progress seemed to have lost ground on the battlefield, it had yet made an invaluable advance in this matter of opening the avenues of the country to the commercial currents and civilizing influences of the great outside world. It was not only foreign bales of goods that entered Mexican ports, under the new freedom, but new ideas, the great conquests of the human mind in science, and philosophy, and government, from which the Mexican people had been too long cut off. The importance of this intellectual contact to the cause of democracy cannot be overestimated. Thus the positive loss to the Revolution was more apparent than real. Even in the matter of the land — large areas of it had been confiscated already by the people — they might not be able to retain all that they had won, but they would undoubtedly be able to retain a portion of it. The hands of the clock could never go back to the old position.

There was another cause, however, less direct but more profound than the last, which, while mainly responsible for the final success of the Revolution, in so far as territorial independence was concerned, was equally responsible for its perversion from the program of economic reconstruction which had formed its base. This cause lay in the reconquest of power by the Liberal party in Spain. As we have said, a counter-revolution had broken out in Spain which had abolished the constitution of 1812, and made the King absolute ruler once more. The change had occasioned a series of sporadic uprisings throughout the whole country, which, however, were easily suppressed. Finding himself master at home, the King had proceeded to deal with the colonial situation. Already, as we have seen, a hundred thousand Spanish troops had been poured into Mexico to aid the royalist party against the insurgents. The King had then dispatched further reinforcements, and succeeded in so far mastering the situation that, of the mighty hosts which had swept the country under Hidalgo and Morelos, only a few thousand insurgents under the command of Vicente Guerrero remained to maintain the insurrection in the mountains of the south. At the same time the King had dispatched well-armed and numerically powerful contingents to several of the other Spanish-American colonies where revolutions had broken out. In this way, with a singular lack of foresight, he had practically denuded the home country of the military forces on whose support alone any absolutism can stand.

The Liberal party in Spain, which, since the overthrow of the constitution, had never ceased to plot in the secrecy of the Ma-

THE REVOLUTION OF INDEPENDENCE

sonic Lodges the downfall of absolutism, had been quick to perceive and take full advantage of the royal negligence. Suddenly revolution burst forth in all parts of the country. A portion of the army which remained in Spain had joined the movement, and the King, impotent without his troops, was compelled to restore the constitution of 1812, to abolish the Holy Inquisition, and to submit himself to the tutelage of a government junta organized by the revolutionists.

Thus, in a trice, the whole front of affairs changed, and the privileged classes who comprised the royalist party in Mexico found themselves once more, after a brief respite, under the dominance of a constitution as opposed to their psychology and inimical to their material interests as was the revolutionary constitution of Apatzingam. No longer could they look to Spain for troops and supplies to subdue the insurgents. For *them* now, rather than for the insurgents, independence from Spain had become an urgent necessity. Whatever hope they may have cherished that the Spanish Congress might prove reactionary, was dashed to the ground before the event. The Spanish junta, in due time, called for the election of representatives to Congress from all the districts of Spain and the Spanish possessions. When this Congress convened it proved to be overwhelmingly Liberal in sentiment. It not only upheld the radical provision of the constitution of 1812 but proceeded to enact laws for the suppression of a number of religious orders, including the Jesuits,* confiscating their wealth to the use of the government, and abolishing the hated ecclesiastical fueros, under which the clergy had been immune from the civil law. It is easy to imagine the state of alarm aroused within the Church by the promulgation of these measures. By them her power was practically de-

---

*In the year 1905, due to an understanding between President Diaz of Mexico, President Roosevelt of the United States, and the Catholic Church of California, the Tribunal of The Hague sentenced Mexico to support the Catholic Church of California by a payment of $1,420,682.67 cash, and a subsequent yearly subsidy of $43,050.00 — this in spite of the fact that in 1820 the Spanish Congress had suppressed the order of the Jesuits and had confiscated their estates.

stroyed, and it is not surprising that Church and King at once made common cause in an effort to start a counter-revolution against the Liberal party. In Mexico the Church, while secretly perfecting schemes for maintaining her power, was able to prevent the immediate effects of the new legislation by means of her censorship over the avenues of publicity. Such a state of affairs could not in the nature of things continue long. The representatives of Mexico, or, more correctly, Nueva España, to the Spanish Congress, headed by Ramos Arizpe, had succeeded in obtaining the dismissal of the Virrey Apodaca, and his successor, the Virrey Novella Azaball — both Mexicans and ready tools of the Church — and had secured in their place the appointment of one of the foremost leaders of the Spanish Liberal party, the able Juan de O'Donojú. The new Virrey was of Irish descent, a brilliant Intellectual who had endured the tortures of the Holy Inquisition for his religious and political convictions. Previous to his appointment as Virrey of Nueva España he had held the position of Jefe Politico of the city of Sevilla, in the province of Andalucia, where, on assuming office, he had earned the fear and hatred of the Church by expelling all the ecclesiastics from the city as undesirable citizens. His appointment as Virrey of Nueva España, under the recommendation of the revolutionary representatives, meant the endorsement of the principles of the insurgency in Mexico, the downfall of the privileged classes, and the triumph of the people. Such a crisis demanded quick action. As soon as the facts became generally known, the Church and Aristocracy, acting as one man, embraced the cause of Independence. For them, of course, independence bore no relation to the economic reorganization demanded by the regular insurgents. For them it meant territorial independence merely, an independence which implied for them the right to continue to suck the life-blood of the country in the way that seemed to them most convenient and effectual.

This sudden change of front naturally aroused the suspicions

THE REVOLUTION OF INDEPENDENCE 51

of the insurgents; but in a country where free speech and freedom of the press were unknown, at a time when few among the lower classes could even read, it was impossible for them to peep behind the scenes. Consequently, tired of fighting, hoping at least some relief from the now assured Independence, but still suspicious, they, for the most part, allowed themselves to be drawn into the meshes of the Church and used once more as blind creators of their own enslavement. The insurgents in the field, it is true, at first held sternly aloof from the movement, but, as we shall see, even they were finally seduced into the required acquiescence.

The Revolution for Independence and Privilege, as opposed to the people's Revolution for Independence and the Land, gained headway with great rapidity. It was so clearly to the interests of the privileged classes of Mexico to free themselves as speedily as possible from the dominance of the new Liberal power in Spain that even the highest magnates of the Church, the Army, and Government threw their weight into the movement without hesitation. At a series of meetings held in Mexico City under the chairmanship of Father Tirado, president of the Holy Inquisition, the high prelates of the Church, chief officers of the Army, leading government officials, principal merchants and aristocrats — gathered in joint session — rapidly formulated plans for the establishment of Independence. The Army, of course, was the principal object of their attention. With the aid of the 100,000 royal troop already in the country, the success of their plans was assured. The chief officers were leaders in the plot, and the conspirators were confident that with the exercise of some diplomacy and bribery they could bring the entire rank and file to their side. Once fully assured of military support, their utmost desires would be fulfilled. With such a force at their disposal, these aristocratic revolutionists could defy Spain, crush any local revolt, and establish a government that would effectually safeguard their system of feudal exploitation of the toiling masses.

To carry out this preliminary step of seducing the Spanish legions, an officer was chosen in every way fitted for the task. This man was Augustin Iturbide, the same who betrayed the previous conspiracy aiming at Independence. By the exercise of a superior ferocity against the insurgents he had gained high favour with the Church and privileged classes. He was now rewarded with the delicate and important twofold mission of seducing the Spanish legions, and establishing a government in entire conformity with the financial and social interests of the Church and Aristocracy.

Entirely ignorant of the plans of the conspirators, and completely under the influence of the Church, the Virrey Apodaca walked blandly into the net spread for him. At the instigation of his ecclesiastical advisers, he duly appointed Iturbide commander-in-chief of the army, and ordered him to lead a contingent southward against the guerilla bands of Vincente Guerrero and Pedro Asencio, the last bulwarks of the people's Revolution. The exigencies of the recent warfare had distributed the royal army in widely sundered parts of the country. Consequently Iturbide was able to mobilize at first only a comparatively small force of some five thousand men. A few days after leaving Mexico City, however, in accordance with the prearranged plans of his fellow-conspirators, he began sending urgent messages to the Virrey, requesting substantial reinforcements and money for supplies. The Virrey innocently complied, as far as the necessities of the case permitted, and thus by the time Iturbide reached Teloloapan in the State of Morelos, in December, 1820, he commanded an army of nearly ten thousand men. Here he lavishly banqueted his troops, and taking advantage of the festive spirit of the moment, suddenly unfolded to them his plans for proclaiming the independence of Mexico. The Spanish mercenaries knew only the Paymaster and the Priest. The Paymaster treated them handsomely and filled them with glowing promises of the future. The Priest warmly supported these promises with fierce anathemas for those who should continue

THE REVOLUTION OF INDEPENDENCE 53

to remain loyal to the impious and Liberal power of Spain — and the trick was done. Iturbide's proposals were enthusiastically received, and the main purpose of the conspirators was accomplished. Similar scenes occurred at every military post in Mexico. The priests had carefully prepared the ground and the entire army fell into line, as had been anticipated, without a protest. The Virrey was still in complete ignorance of the conspiracy; for the Church had acted throughout with that profound secrecy which has always characterized her political methods. Indeed, so far from suspecting himself betrayed, he considered himself loyally served, and gladly complied with the suggestion of the Church that he should increase Iturbide's power.

The new movement, now gathering tremendous momentum, was naturally fostered with particular zeal by religious orders whose suppression had been decreed throughout the Spanish Empire by the Liberal Congress of Spain. In Mexico City the very backbone of the revolutionary conspiracy was the order of Jesuits; while in Vera Cruz, Father Fra José de San Ignacio, general of the Order of Betlemitas, exhibited extraordinary activity in organizing all the influential people in his district under the banner of the Revolution, in obtaining supplies of money, and in lauding Iturbide as the "Saviour of religion and the Liberator of the Fatherland."

If it was an easy matter to sway the allegiance of a mercenary horde, it was a quite different affair to win over the stubborn revolutionaries of the south. Again and again Iturbide dispatched messengers to Guerrero, offering him wealth and a high position in the army for himself, and positions in the ranks for all his followers. Guerrero refused. He mistrusted this man who spoke so glibly of the sacred ideal of human liberty, and in the same breath offered him bribes. His was an extremely difficult position. Ignorant of the great change which had placed Spain and her possessions under a constitution as enlightened and humane as the revolutionary constitution of

Apatzingam, ignorant of the dark conspiracy of the Church which aimed to destroy this enlightened rule and to set up an independent despotism in Mexico, he was unable to grasp the true position of affairs. Hitherto, the only policy he had known was to fight to the death; if not in the open, then in the fastnesses of those mountains which he had made the last stronghold of the cause of liberty. He and his followers were prepared to wait, if need be, for years for that odd chance which should enable them once more to take the aggressive in the glorious struggle for freedom. It was no easy matter, therefore, to trick, bribe, or cajole these men into surrender; for Guerrero was a man of the purest principles, a real revolutionist in whose heart burned the deepest passion for human liberty.

Iturbide cherished the secret intention of proclaiming himself Emperor of Mexico when the opportune moment should arrive, and he recognized in this stubborn native farmer, Guerrero, a serious obstacle to his plans. Failing to cajole him into surrender, he endeavoured to attack him in his mountain fastness. The position of the insurgents, however, was impregnable, and Iturbide retired, discomfited. Cajolery and force had both failed. Time was precious. Iturbide resorted to strategy. With the sanction of his fellow-conspirators he delivered his master-stroke. On the 24th of February, 1821, from the town of Iguala, in the State of Guerrero, he issued a manifesto which he caused to be distributed broadcast over the whole country. This manifesto, generally called El Plan de Iguala, proclaimed the following principles:

I. The establishment of the Roman Catholic Apostolic Religion as the national religion, without toleration for any other.

II. The absolute Independence of Mexico.

III. The establishment of a monarchical form of government, tempered by a constitution suitable to the country.

IV. The summoning of Fernando VII, or some member of his

THE REVOLUTION OF INDEPENDENCE

family, or of some other royal family, to the throne of Mexico, to reign as emperor and establish a dynasty.

V. The establishment of a junta to carry on the government until the meeting of the Cortes.

VI. Said junta to rule in virtue of an oath of allegiance to the King until the duties of government could be assumed by the monarch in person.

VIII. That in the event of Fernando VII being unwilling to accept the throne of Mexico, the junta to continue the functions of government until such time as a suitable ruler be chosen.

IX. The government to support and maintain the three warranties (Independence, Unity, and Religion, symbolized on the national flag by the colours red, white, and green).

. . . .

XIII. The maintenance of the present institutions of property.

XIV. The endorsement and protection of all ecclesiastical fueros, privileges, and possessions.

In addition to the articles quoted there was a number of provisions dealing with the constitution of the army and judiciary, but we have sufficiently indicated the drift of the document. It would be difficult to find a more clear-cut expression of the class struggle in society than his manifesto affords us. In its entire scope, the peons, the Intellectuals — in fact, the whole body of the useful and vital element of the nation are completely ignored. The despotism of the Church and big land-owners, on the contrary, is affirmed as the supreme ruling factor of the nation. Not the collective intelligence, but the army, is made the support of the functions of government. The people are again nailed to the cross with the spikes of religious intolerance, military despotism, and economic absolutism.

The necessity of a monarchical form of government was very clearly defined in the minds of the conspirators. Reaction and monarchy are good yoke-fellows, while the republican form of government — even a pseudo-republican form of government — is by no means as amenable to control by the forces of Privilege. The manifesto was widely distributed over the whole country, blessed by the bishops, and promulgated by their agents. To the illiterate masses it was made to represent not only the salvation of their country but their own future redemption from poverty and wretchedness.

Iturbide's scheme proved successful beyond his dreams. When Guerrero and his followers saw the people dazed in the glare of the false revolution, and blindly following it to their destruction, they surrendered. Of what use was a revolution which had lost the support of the great mass of the nation? Freedom was not yet — later perhaps. These unsophisticated leaders even hoped some benefit might accrue to the common people from territorial Independence; and for the rest, they saw that they must leave to the future the accomplishment of their revolutionary plans.

"Guerrero and Iturbide met in the town of Teloloapan. The new hero of Mexico solemnly assured Guerrero that the land would be distributed to the people as soon as peace was restored. With this understanding the entire body of insurgents joined the ranks of the army, thus adding a very decisive strength to the movement." (Zamacois, "Historia de Mejico," Vol. X, pp. 671, 675.) Guerrero's example in joining forces with the false revolution was promptly followed by all the old insurgents scattered over the country. Naturally they saw in his action full warranty that Iturbide was honest in his motives. Thus the complete success of Iturbide's military masquerade was assured.

From Iguala the combined force of insurgents and royalists now marched to Valladolid, where their ranks were further augmented by the local garrison. At the same time in Guadalajara General Pedro Celestino Negrete, acting in concert with the Church, proclaimed his adherence to the Plan de Iguala. A great celebration was held at the cathedral, where the people were harangued by the noted theologian, Doctor San Martin. "The War for Independence," said he, "is a war for religion. Every one of us ought to be a soldier in its cause — the clergyman, secular, and regular; the aristocrat, the plebeian, the rich and the poor, the child and the adult — every one should shoulder a gun and march under the commands of our military chiefs, to fight and die, if need be, for honour and religion. O God! save the American Mexican Church, and save the Army, the protector of our Church!" (Zamacois, "Historia de Méjico," Vol. X, p. 741.)

During the course of the summer of 1821 the garrisons of Queretaro, Monterey, Coahuila, Tamaulipas, and Durango had declared themselves in favour of the new movement. On August 2d, 1821, Iturbide entered Puebla at the head of his army amid universal acclamation. Two days later a great Te Deum was celebrated in the cathedral, and Bishop Perez placed the climax on the mock-hero's career by publicly suggesting his enthronement as Emperor of Mexico. The Plan de Iguala, as drawn up by Iturbide himself, called for the placing of Fernando VII, or some other member of European royalty, on the throne of Mexico. Neither Iturbide nor the Church had ever seriously contemplated such a step. Iturbide had long ago definitely determined to become emperor. With so large a personal following as he now had, an attempt to thwart him in his ambition would have been fatal to the plans of the Church.

At this juncture the new Virrey, Don Juan de O'Donojú, the chief exponent of the Liberal policy in Spain, arrived at Vera Cruz. In face of the entirely unsuspected condition of affairs which he found confronting him, the new Virrey was utterly at a loss. He had been appointed by the new Liberal Congress not only to enforce the brilliant and humane constitution of Cadiz in Mexico, thereby suppressing the power of the Church and laying the foundation of a real democracy, but had likewise authority to recognize Mexico's independence as the best means of carrying into execution the common ideas of the revolutionists of both countries. He now found himself confronted, not by the real Revolution of the people which he had been led to expect, but by a counter-revolution, a mere military uprising for the purpose of erecting an independent despotism in Mexico in defiance of the Constitution of Spain.

In view of the power attained by the new Revolution, compromise was the new Virrey's only possible course. Accordingly, after an interchange of notes with Iturbide, he agreed to meet him at Córdova, in the State of Vera Cruz. Here, on the 24th of August, an agreement was entered into between Iturbide, representing Reaction in Mexico, and Don Juan de O'Donojú, representing Liberalism in Spain. Its provisions read as follows:

I. It is agreed that this America be recognized as a sovereign and independent nation with the name of the Mexican Empire.

II. That the government of this empire be organized as a constitutional monarchy.

III. That Fernando VII, or failing his acceptance, some member of the European royal families be invited to the throne of Mexico. In the event of such invitations meeting refusal, that the Cortes of the empire elect an emperor.

IV. That the emperor hold his court in Mexico City, which is to be regarded henceforth as the capital of the empire.

V. That a committee of two be appointed by His Excellency Señor O'Donojú to be dispatched as an embassy to the court of Spain to place a copy of this treaty in the hands of Fernando VII.

VI. That, pending the organization of government, a provisional governing junta be established, consisting of the foremost men of the country.

THE REVOLUTION OF INDEPENDENCE

VII. That His Excellency Señor Don Juan de O'Donojú be a member of the junta.

VIII. That the provisional governing junta appoint its chairman and a regency of three persons to hold the executive power until the assumption of office by the monarch.

Like El Plan de Iguala, this treaty aimed at the speediest possible enthronement of the privileged classes, and the consolidation of their power. Backed by Iturbide's powerful army, and the old insurgency duped into coalition or scattered to the winds, the privileged classes felt themselves to be amply secure at last, and able to dictate with assurance to all their enemies. It is interesting to notice the diplomatic clauses in this treaty referring to the summoning of Fernando VII to the throne. Too bold an announcement by Iturbide of his intentions of assuming the royal purple himself would have been highly impolitic at that moment, even if it had not thrown the Aristocracy, who were natural worshippers of royalty, into strong opposition. The conspirators were now well in the saddle. Independence and the dominance of Privileges were already accomplished facts. Insurgency was dead. To maintain the admirable *status quo*, however, it was necessary to keep the Army in high good humour.

Absolutism depends — as indeed every form of class rule depends — everywhere and at all times on two forces for its support: the psychological and the physical. The first bends, the second breaks. The first, under the guise of religion, seeks to bind the spirit and stultify the intelligence of the people; the other, under the guise of patriotism, is constituted to destroy physically those who will not be bound or stultified. In the present case the power of the Catholic religion had suffered severely at the hands of the insurgents, even had not the spread of the philosophy of the French Revolution almost entirely discounted its doctrines among the Intellectuals. It was the more necessary, therefore, that the physical force represented by the Army should be well groomed and petted. To this end its officers were promoted wholesale, while the primitive love of the soldier for gewgaws was fed by the lavish distribution of cordons and medals and badges. Military vanity was further flattered by the creation of the "Imperial Order of the Mexican Eagle" for distinguished service. To crown the content of the Army, the Church, in one long week of celebration, consecrated it to the service of the Most High under the title of "Army of God."

Let us glance for a moment at the other side of the picture. In the fields toiled the peons, still tilling the land from dawn till dusk, under the lash of the master, still enduring the pangs of hunger and the darkness of ignorance — and now, sunk in unspeakable despair before the wreck of all their high hopes. The blood of comrades called from the ground: "Was it for this we died?" And the peon could find no answer. Away in the city thousands of Spanish soldiers, themselves the sons of the hungry, ignorant Spanish peasantry, were being fêted and pampered, degraded to the level of sleek brutes — their highest office to perform the ferocious will of the master class; their highest ambition to beat back their oppressed brothers, should they arise once more out of their darkness and despair in cohorts battling toward the light.

CHAPTER VI

THE FIRST EMPIRE

WERE we to compile a text-book of the Science of Government by a ruling class, for the use, for instance, of some young modern aspirant to power, the testimony of all history, from the most remote times, would compel us to divide our work into three main chapters: the first, on the necessity of religious instruction for the people; the second, on the necessity of patriotic instruction for the people; the third, on the necessity of diverting the revolt of the people by instituting a campaign of foreign aggression, or by inviting the invasion of the home country by a foreign army. Herein lies the entire science of government by class rule.

Far deep in the history of the race, in times so remote that only archæological research is able to piece together the social records, arose the practice of trading on what is termed the "religious instinct" of man on the part of the priest class. This term "religious instinct" is in reality but another name for the deep, obliquely expressed desire of the partially awakened man to become initiate in that science of mind which he dimly divines will emancipate him from the fear which is ignorance, eradicate the reflex matter-impulses which he calls his passions, and make him altogether human, the supreme master of himself and his environment.

To toy with, to pervert, to trade upon, to debauch, and to frustrate this pure central instinct of life for the purposes of oppression and plunder has been the work of priestcraft in all ages and climes.

The first despotism, a despotism that was worldwide before Egypt was born, was built upon the skilful and unscrupulous manipulation of this sacred fundamental instinct. The same despotism persists to-day. From the profound craft of the prehistoric Druid to the polished cynicism of the mediæval Jesuit, and the vulgar cunning of his modern exemplar, the process of manipulation persists, identical in essence, differing only in form. Nothing less than univeral scientific education, such as might subsist under a Collectivist administration of society, can ever destroy it. This, the Church knows well, and herein lies the secret of her fierce rage against the modern movement toward Collectivism, and against the sociological analyses generally grouped under the name of the Socialist Philosophy.

Again, it seems a truism to say that a country can belong only to the people who own it. Yet this fact has not yet been perceived by the great majority of the propertyless workers. Under the careful patriotic instruction of the master class, millions of men have shed, and are still ready to shed, their life-blood, fighting for what they have conceived and still conceive to be "their" country, when few of them can show title to so much as a square foot of it. They do not yet perceive that the country they fight for is the master's country, and that they fight only because they are hypnotized by the pulpit and press and hired orator into the insubstantial belief that it is their "duty and glory" thus to fight. Least of all do they perceive that in nine cases out of ten they are induced to fight simply to divert their energy from its legitimate function of enforcing economic reform.

The third chapter of our text-book, we said, should deal with the necessity of diverting domestic revolt by instituting a campaign of foreign aggression, or by inviting foreign invasion. A ruling class in deadly peril from the revolt of an oppressed working class, and unable to cope alone with the conflagration it has invoked, has, in the final analysis, only three possible courses before it: First, to abandon its power to the people, and by sufferance, if not by actual coöperation, to permit the inception of a true democracy; second, to inflame the people through the medium of the pulpit, press, and platform, with a false patriotism, and betray them into conflict with another nation, thus diverting their collective will and strength from economic reform to so-called national glory; third — and this last method we wish to emphasize somewhat, since it is the one chiefly favoured by the decadent ruling class of Mexico — to invite the invasion or assistance of a foreign army.

Such assistance as is predicated in the last alternative is never far to seek. The ruling classes of the world readily support one another in the subjugation of proletarian revolts, for here their interests are entirely mutual. A successful proletarian revolt in any country of the world, however remote from the centres of civilization, is a tremendous menace to every other ruling class. There remains, of course, a yet more immediate reason for such ready assistance — the pay is good. Be it in the form of mythical claims which are allowed by the assisted nation in favour of the assisting, or in the form of secretly ceded territory, or commercial strangle-holds, the pay is always sufficiently attractive for its own sake.

If to the uninitiated mind there seems an element of incredible treachery and ruffianism in this violation of national integrity and shedding of innocent blood on the part of the ruling class in order to head off the march of the people toward freedom and light, it can only be said that the unswerving testimony of history — and by history we mean the systematized researches of unbiased investigators, and not the official or inspired chronicles of the master class — amply attests the constant use of this method. To the sophisticated mind and blunted moral sense of the oppressor such methods are neither good nor bad — they are expedient. Any ruling class will waste seas of blood, and drag the national honour in the dust, rather than relinquish its grip on the throat of its victim — the people. By the law of its being it must preserve its dominance, or cease to be.

We have not yet dealt with the first possible course which presents itself to the ruling class when confronted with the growing power of the people — i. e., abdication. History bears no record of any such abdication; its possibility is purely theoretical. But the last two alternatives with which we have dealt above constitute the *raison d'être* of nearly all the conflicts of history. Behind war is found at last the terror of the master class before the advancing Spectre of Democracy. Occasionally, indeed, the various ruling classes quarrel among themselves over the division of territory and then, before the lust of imperial expansion and commercial supremacy has been satisfied, hundreds of thousands of working women mourn their sons. But this cause of war is far less potent than the others mentioned above.

The unsophisticated mind of the working class is, and has been, throughout the centuries, but clay in the hands of the skilful potter — the master class. By the aid of judicious religious and patriotic instruction, coupled with the final appeal, in case of revolt, to the methods of foreign aggression, or invited home invasion, it has been possible for an insignificant minority to reign as supreme lord and master of the great majority, systematically robbing them — through the evolving economic systems — chattel slavery, feudalism, and capitalism — of the fruits of their labour, and maintaining them in a state of bovine ignorance and acquiescence during the process. This is the entire Science of Government by class rule.

In the course of this history we shall see the weakened and debauched ruling class of Mexico taxing the three great expedients of government to the utmost. Now thundering excommunications against the popular revolt through the mouth of the Church, anon leading an army of peon-patriots from their proper work of economic reform into an infamous attack on Texas; again, inviting a French, a Spanish, and later, an American invasion, to head off the march of democracy.

That the mills of the gods were grinding surely, albeit exceeding slowly in Mexico, is indicated by the fact that the Revolu-

THE FIRST EMPIRE

tion which had given Spain a modern Constitution had brought a new and permanent factor into the political field. This was the Liberal party which henceforth both in Spain and in Mexico was destined to carry on the struggle of the people against the reactionary forces of the Church, Army, and Aristocracy, represented by the Conservative party.

The new nation was now fairly launched on its independent career. Thanks to the adroitness of the Church and Iturbide's Spanish mercenaries, the privileged classes were as firmly entrenched in power as before the Revolution. The junta, which under the provisions of Article IV of the Treaty of Córdova was to assume the functions of government *ad interim*, consisted entirely of bishops, generals, and aristocrats to the number of thirty under the presidency of Iturbide. The junta had scarcely taken office before its sole Liberal member — the noble Don Juan de O'Donojú, came to a sudden and mysterious end — poisoned, it is strongly suspected, by Iturbide at the instigation of the Church.*

According to the provisions laid down in the Treaty of Córdova this junta exercised the functions of a consultative body, with legislative powers, electing from among its own members an executive, or regency of five. Of this regency Iturbide was likewise president. We see him, therefore, in supreme control of both government and army. The first step of the junta on exercising office was to summon the people to elect members to Congress. In order safely to exclude any candidate of Liberal ideas an ingenious system of triplex indirect elections was devised. Under this system the people were instructed to elect delegates from each town; the municipal councilmen were then to exercise the right of deciding in secret session which delegates received the majority vote; finally, these delegates were to elect the representative to Congress. To make assurance doubly sure these municipal councils were to act under the chairmanship of the curate of the town; while in order to further refine the

*See Zamacois' "Historia de Méjico," Vol. 11, p. 20.

process of selection it was decreed that a delegate must be a clergyman, a soldier, a lawyer, or a land-owner. Meanwhile, the press was effectually throttled by the establishment of a rigid military censorship. The destiny of the new nation had fallen into the hands of those least fitted for rule — the Soldier and the Priest, ever to be found hand in hand, opposing with brutality and ignorance every attempt of the people toward progress.

The Liberals, unable to fight openly, strove as well as they could under the cover of the Masonic Lodges, to save the nation. Among other activities they endeavoured to found secular schools on the Lancasterian or mutual instruction system. Hitherto all education had been carried on in Catholic schools and seminaries, where the mind of childhood and youth had been necessarily perverted and dwarfed to the exigencies of ecclesiastical dominance. By the establishment of these secular schools the Liberals sought to remedy this abuse, and to lay the foundation for a more enlightened generation. Meanwhile, the old insurgents who had joined Iturbide's army had begun to realize how completely they had been duped. Instead of the distribution of the lands and the economic readjustments they had been promised, they were compelled to witness that great democratic spirit which had found voice in the Congress of Apatzingam utterly betrayed at the hands of the new ecclesiastical and military despotism; and the old spirit of revolt began to brew among them.

The new administration was already seriously embarrassed for funds. While the upkeep of a vast army and an avaricious military caste necessitated enormous expenditure, the disorganization of the times had emptied the treasury. The Church, therefore, as matter of self-protection, agreed to furnish the government a loan of two million dollars, without interest, taking as security the revenues derived from the seaport customs. By way of reward, the governing junta agreed to recognize the Pious funds of California as a national indebtedness to the Church in spite of the fact that this fund, amounting to nearly two million dollars, had been cancelled by the Virrey in colonial times in compliance with the royal pragmatica of Charles III of Spain for the suppression of the Jesuits. Thus was laid on the backs of the people a load of indebtedness merely to bribe the services of an army in which officers outnumbered privates.

On the 24th of February, 1822, one year after the Declaration of Independence, the new Congress, consisting of one hundred and two delegates, met in Mexico City. When — the inevitable celebrations and Te Deums ended — Congress at length settled to the serious business demanded by the critical conditions of the hour, it proceeded to waste day after day in the minute consideration and discussion of such matters as the indulgences granted to the Mexicans by the Pope of Rome for their loyalty to the Church, and the authorization of papal decrees in matters of feasting and fasting. From such deliberations as these it finally turned to more earthly affairs, and decreed the maintenance of a standing army of seventy thousand men — to maintain peace in a country of only seven million population!

In spite of the elaborate precautions of the Church a certain number of representatives of Liberal ideas had succeeded in being elected to the Congress; and their spirited opposition to the clerical *bloc* was instrumental, at least, in giving wide publicity to the conspiracy which was being perpetrated against the people in the name of government. These fighting tactics of the Liberal party, backed by the rising discontent of the old insurgents, kept the administration in a state of constant alarm. Finally, when the Liberals proceeded bitterly to criticize Iturbide in person he accused them before Congress of treachery to the country and had them imprisoned.

It will be remembered that in the Treaty of Córdova provision had been made for the appointment of a member of the royal family of Spain to the throne of Mexico. So far Congress had made no effort to carry this provision into execution. The reason for its inertia in the matter is not far to seek. Congress knew perfectly well that the Spanish royal family was quite averse to such a proposal, and that the ecclesiastical and military designs necessitated the appointment of Iturbide as Emperor of Mexico. Indeed, Iturbide's well proven fanatical devotion to the Church, and his false prestige as "Liberator of Mexico," and Commander-in-chief of the "Army of God" marked him out as preëminently the man best fitted for the position. This matter of appointing a sovereign had now thoroughly matured and the moment was ripe for action.

In order to give a veneer of popular election to Iturbide's nomination, the soldiers were induced to go through the farce of proclaiming him emperor. On the night of the 18th of August, 1822, a sergeant of the army headed his company in a parade through the streets of Mexico City shouting: "Viva Augustin the First, Emperor of Mexico!" The entire garrison of the city immediately joined in the parade. In a few minutes the streets were crowded with soldiery, and hoodlums hired for the purpose, who lustily shouted the same cry. The following day similar scenes were enacted, and the excited hordes, directed and inflamed by the priests and friars, stormed the hall of Congress, where only a few representatives already in the plot were in session, and demanded, in the name of the nation, that Iturbide be proclaimed Emperor of Mexico. The "Rump Congress" complied, and Iturbide was duly appointed.

The first act of the new Emperor was to reward his soldiers. Again the army delivered itself up to a general Saturnalia of feasting and drinking, beneath a fresh shower of gaudy cordons, medals, and decorations. In order to give the new court the aristocratic leavening so beloved of the parasites, a new order — "The Knights of Guadalupe" — was created, and in the official gold-trimmed dress of the order — short trousers, and broad-brimmed hats lavishly adorned with ostrich plumes — the new knights displayed themselves with the utmost content. The capital and entire country indulged in festivities, in which William Taylor and General Wilkinson, the envoys of the United States, took part in an official capacity.

VINCENTE GUERRERO — PRESIDENT OF MEXICO IN 1827
The "Great Commoner of Mexico" who decreed religious freedom, and abolished chattel slavery and peonage

GENERAL CARRANZA ADDRESSING A CROWD OF CONSTITUTIONALISTS

Carranza has frequently said: "The first necessity is the fair and free election of a President. We Constitutionalists refuse to recognize any President who may be returned by a fraudulent election"

THE FIRST EMPIRE

It was at this juncture of affairs that the most fascinating character in Mexican history appeared on the scene in the person of Fra Servando Teresa de Mier, better known as the Bishop of Baltimore. Although a member of a religious order, so radical were this priest's ideas that the Holy Inquisition, deeming him in need of discipline, imprisoned him, and finally dispatched him to Rome as a penitent. The Pope was greatly impressed with the vast learning and radiant wit of this strange penitent, and punished him by appointing him Bishop of Baltimore in the United States, a city in which he was already well known and greatly loved. Instead, however, of proceeding to his new diocese the Bishop joined the Revolution in Spain. Here he was arrested by the royalist authorities, but finally escaped to the United States, where he learned that during his absence the people of his native state of Nuevo Leon had elected him a representative to Congress. He immediately set out for Mexico City, but was again arrested by the captain of a Spanish war cruiser. Once more, however, he managed to effect his release, and arrived in Mexico City in time to take his place in the councils of the nation, just after Iturbide's scandalous seizure of the imperial throne.

His natural genius, tempered by deep learning and cosmopolitan culture, made him at once the leader of the fighting Liberal minority in the House, and the highly unwelcome opponent of the clerical *bloc*. Before his polished wit and searing satire the Emperor was entirely discomfited, and the great mass of the people, disgusted as they were with the recent unscrupulous *coup d'état* took fresh heart. The Bishop comprehended the situation at a glance, and through the columns of the Liberal press, in the hall of Congress, on the public platform, and in the private conclave, poured such a stream of ridicule upon this absurd Emperor, his Knights of Guadalupe, his tinselled soldiery and tawdry court, that even those who had helped to place Iturbide in power felt abashed before their handiwork. It was a case of "those who came to pray remained to scoff," and the witty Bishop, by giving the empire the real colour of comic opera, contributed very materially to its downfall.

As we have previously mentioned, the political struggle was mainly directed from the secret conclaves of the Masonic Lodge. In Mexico at that time Masonry was divided into two factions — the Scottish Rite, Catholic in personnel, and the York Rite, Liberal in personnel. In these two factions appears the division of a society in which the main executive power was the Army. Here we have a decided rearrangement of forces. Under the Spanish régime the Church, in virtue of her enormous wealth and psychological control of the people, was the supreme ruling power. The Revolution of Independence, however, had substituted for the economic and psychological control of the Church the brute force of arms. Henceforth the Army was the real commanding power of the nation. The Church, now only able to maintain her privileges by the use of armed force, and unable herself to take the field, was compelled to depend on the military support. In this wise was established the "Pretorian" system of "cuartelazo,"* as it is called in Spanish. For the last hundred years this system has been the one great obstacle in the struggle of the Mexican people toward democracy. We shall find it being invoked again and again to the utter wreckage of all civil institutions.

The attacks of the Liberal party in Congress on the administration had become so formidable that Iturbide, on the 26th of August, 1822, ordered eleven of them to be arrested and imprisoned. A few days later, foreseeing that even the remaining Conservative members might oppose his imperial will, he ordered the complete dissolution of Congress, thus constituting himself the sole ruler of the nation. It is at this juncture that the sinister General Santa Ana makes his first appearance in Mexican

---

*Cuartel is the Spanish equivalent for the English "barracks," and "azo" an affix indicating repetition of action. Cuartelazo, then, is a term of contempt for a military uprising, destitute of civil foundation, and culminating in a military despotism devoid of respect for civil law. The military uprising by which Iturbide seized the imperial throne was a typical "cuartelazo."

THE FIRST EMPIRE

history, supplicating Iturbide for the honour of suppressing Congress by military force — a fitting entry, indeed, for a man who was destined to deluge his country in blood and drag the national honour into the deepest disgrace.

Congress was dissolved, but before the dissolution had been accomplished the Conservative *bloc* had been instructed to enact a law authorizing the government to issue a foreign loan of $30,000,000, secured on the entire national revenues — this, also, to feed the voracious maw of the Army. The insurgents and Liberals were now thoroughly aroused. They had never forgiven Iturbide his royalist activities against the insurgents; they had seen him wrap himself in the mantle of Independence only to impose a worse despotism upon the people; they had laughed in bitterness before his farcical assumption of the imperial purple; they now beheld in his cynical dissolution of Congress the complete demolition of their last hope for the betterment of the people. Soon, however, they were to witness the downfall of the false hero at the hands of the very faction that placed him in power.

The student of Mexican history is often surprised and bewildered by the apparently inexplicable inconsistencies of the clerical policy. It would seem, at first glance, that the high prelates of the Church were men of weak, vacillating minds. The act of to-day is reversed to-morrow; the favourite of one hour is the victim of the next. On a deeper view of the matter, however, this extravagance reveals itself as the necessary sinuosity of a deep, tenacious purpose — the protection at all costs of the material interests of the Church. As we have indicated, from the time of the Independence to the present day the Church in Mexico has been compelled to use the Army for her own protection and the organization of government. The military, however, are egotistical, vain, and profoundly ignorant of the principles of sociology. Discipline makes them mechanical, and thus tempered they are the less potent for evil. When, however, freed from discipline, they assume the leadership of society, their unsocial training, ignorance and egotism, coupled with a sense of the basic immorality of their position as the tool of a faction, make them not only thoroughly unfitted to rule, but often make them positively dangerous to the faction which employs them. Thus, subsequent to the Independence, the Church was compelled to enter the race for power, mounted on a horse which, none too well broken, often refused to run straight, and sometimes bolted off the course: hence the apparent inconsistencies of her policy. Could the Church have ruled directly, matters would have had an entirely different aspect; but Mexico, backward as she was in comparison with the rest of the civilized world at that time, was yet too far advanced to permit a theocratic rule. Prætorianism, therefore, was the Church's sole recourse.

The bitter hatred with which Iturbide was regarded by the Liberals and insurgents, and his increasing unpopularity with even the Conservatives themselves, showed clearly to the astute prelates of the time that he must be sacrificed if another disastrous popular revolt was to be averted. They accordingly decreed his downfall. To dethrone the emperor of a day the same tactics were adopted as were used to enthrone him. A cuartelazo was invoked against him under the leadership of that same Santa Ana who had shown such eagerness to aid in the dissolution of Congress.

Iturbide realized the situation at a glance — and accepted it. An emperor, spawned by the Church and cuartelazo, he was too familiar with the tactics of both to offer a futile resistance. When he found himself deserted by his adoring army he summoned the Congress he had dissolved, and endeavoured to effect a dignified retreat by formally presenting them with his resignation, merely requesting his salary for service in the Revolution of Independence. Congress repudiated his resignation and banished him to Italy under pain of death. Later, in obedience to the secret summons of the Church, he returned, landing at Sotol a Marina in the state of Tamaulipas. Here he was arrested by the local authorities under the direction of the Liberal governor, Gutierrez de Lara, convicted of defying the decree of the National Congress, and executed.

Thus ended the comedy known in Mexican history as the First Empire.

CHAPTER VII

THE REPUBLIC

THE PRESIDENCY OF GUADALUPE VICTORIA

THE Liberal party was now about to enjoy a brief period of power. Taking vigorous advantage of the confusion of the Church and Army, occasioned by the downfall of Iturbide and his subsequent execution, it forced Congress formally to declare Mexico a federal republic.

The Church, momentarily demoralized by her recent disastrous experiment, and seeing no immediate possibility of establishing a monarchy of royal blood in Mexico, accepted the situation for the nonce. Her discontent was the less bitter in that the new federal system was not essentially antagonistic to her immediate interests. Certainly, by the large measure of autonomy with which it endowed the provinces, federalism paved the way for a possible piecemeal demolition of her power; but for the present it left intact her spiritual monopoly, privileges, fueros, and general material interests. The Church acquiesced, and bided her time, confident in her power to overthrow the new order at a more convenient moment.

On the 4th of October, 1824, the constitution establishing the federal system which had been drafted by Congress was proclaimed. It provided that:

"Each state be granted the right to frame its own constitution, in conformity with the republican principles of general popular election, and the division of power into executive, legislative, and judiciary.

"Each state be granted the right to protect freedom of speech and of the press, and to carry on all its affairs with complete independence, as a sovereign entity.

"Representatives and Senators in each state be chosen by direct popular election.

"The President and Vice-President of the nation be elected by the state legislatures, each legislature to have the right to vote for two different candidates, the National Congress to appoint as President the candidate holding the majority of votes, and as Vice-President, the candidate polling the largest minority."

Such, in brief, were the political concessions gained by the people. The Catholic religion, however, was recognized as the national religion to the exclusion of every other form of faith, the Church property and privileges were fully respected, and the iniquitous clerical and military fueros were upheld. Under the circumstances, the gain to the common people was more apparent than real. Power in the last analysis is always economic power, and this still remained, and was bound to remain, under any political system short of Collectivism, in the hands of Privilege. It was under such conditions that General Guadalupe Victoria became first President of the Republic.

As we have previously mentioned, the last act of the Rump Congress before its final dissolution by Iturbide was to authorize the flotation of a foreign loan to the amount of $30,000,000. Under that authority, President Victoria now proceeded to contract a first loan of $20,000,000, and English bankers furnished the entire amount, at 8 per cent. interest secured on the national revenue. During the preliminary negotiations, the Church and Monarchists managed to force a stipulation on the President, entitling the Church to receive from the first disbursements of this loan, the original sum of $2,000,000 loaned by her to the administration of Iturbide. In addition, they demanded that the sum of $8,000,000 should further be recognized as the national indebtedness to Spain for her services against the insurgents.

The United States, which had viewed Mexico's imperialistic experiment with mixed feelings, promptly recognized the new Republic, and dispatched B. Joel Poinsett as Minister to Mexico City to represent her interests. At this time, the struggle in the United States between the feudal aristocracy of the South and the industrial *quasi-democracy* of the North, which later was destined to deluge the nation in blood, had reached only the stage of political intrigue. In the enormous industrial development of the free Northern States, the Southern States, sunk in the stagnation which attends chattel slavery, saw the impending doom of their political and economic dominance. With a view to correcting the balance of power, they had already begun to cast envious eyes on Texas — at that time a Mexican state, populated largely by slave-holding American colonists. Could Texas by force or fraud be wrested from Mexico, her slave-holding representatives in the United States Congress would materially help the South to maintain her cherished supremacy.

Minister Poinsett's particular mission in Mexico,* therefore, was to insinuate himself into the Mexican political intrigue of the time with a view to bribing the discontented factions, likely at any moment to regain power, with the promise of recognition and support from the United States in return for the concession of Texas. Greatly aided in his mission by his standing as a Mason, he was enabled to enter actively into the intrigues of the Masonic rites — the real parliament of Mexico — and to lay the foundations for the embroglio which finally made Texas a part of the United States.

For a time, the new Republic, under President Victoria, seemed to be prospering. A more or less troubled peace had succeeded to the wild disorder of the past. The privileges of

---

*See G. L. Rives' "The United States and Mexico, 1821–1848," Vol. I, pp. 161–170.

the Church were fully respected: the exchequer held sufficient funds for the regular payment of the army; and the Liberals, in the brief enjoyment of a certain tolerance, were contentedly busy in the propagation of their ideas. Even the peons, though as poor as ever, and still bearing on their backs the entire burden of the national production, were now free from the excessive taxation of the past. For them, also, there seemed some faint gleam of better things on the horizon.

In order to understand the immense influence of the Church in Mexico at this time, it is necessary for us to glance for a moment at the question of education. Throughout the colonial régime and up to the presidency of Victoria, the clergy had entire control of the rudimentary school system, the seminaries, and the colleges. Under this system, superstition took the place of ethics, and a fanatical admiration for militarism took the place of history, science, and art; while the entire plan of instruction and discipline was carefully calculated to bind the student in physical, intellectual, and moral slavery.

To quote the brilliant author of the "Life of Juarez":* "The life of the seminaries was a tiresome one. The monotony of the classes, the corporal punishments, the incessant fasting, the same daily routine of prayer, repeated again and again, the lack of healthful recreation, and the gross ignorance of the superiors in matters of physiology and hygiene, degraded the students to the practice of secret and debasing vices. Nothing was taught in these seminaries of social intercourse, of good manners, or practical life. Education was deliberately used, by those who controlled it, as a weapon wherewith to break the spirit and subdue the conscience."

The seminaries afforded education, such as it was, only to the children of the wealthy. The millions of the toilers of the soil were left in utter illiteracy. Such native intelligence as they possessed (and as a class the peons are possessed of good ability) was twisted and stunted by the inculcation of superstition and

---
*G. Baz, "Vida de Juarez," p. 28.

cowardice at the hands of the priests. Particularly was the prospect of hell-fire, as a punishment for disobedience to the Church, held continually before them. Indeed, only thus could this vigorous and imaginative peasantry be successfully subjugated to the will of their masters.

The Liberal party was by no means slow to use the opportunity for aggressive educational propaganda against the Church which the tolerance of the new régime temporarily permitted them. Nor was the Church slow to retaliate. Discouraged by the failure of the empire, and disgusted with the administration of the federal constitution, which, while it respected her own privileges, respected also the rights of others, the Church in desperation turned to Spain — the Spain she had but just betrayed — as a means of salvation. In the secrecy of the Masonic Lodge of the Scottish Rite — the rite of the aristocrat and ecclesiastic — a conspiracy to restore the colonial régime was strenuously carried on. So well did it succeed that the Spanish King was finally persuaded by the envoys of the conspirators to believe that, were he to land in Mexico, the entire nation would rise as one man to welcome him, and that a mere handful of soldiers would be sufficient to quell the resistance of the few malcontents who still desired independence.

The principal leaders of the conspiracy were the fathers: Joaquin Arenas, Francisco Martinez, Hildago Tordesillas, and Amat, all of them members of the Royal Order of Santo Domingo de Guzman. In spite of the preliminary success of the plot, its final execution was delayed for some time by the inertia of the Army. Indeed, although many of the generals were prominent in the conspiracy, the main body of the soldiery proved to be too contented with the easy life and regular pay to make good material for another cuartelazo.

The Liberals promptly took advantage of this weakened control of the Church over the Army to force several anti-clerical measures through Congress. They were not very violent, it is true; indeed, every dictate of reason and morality was on their side; but in the eyes of the Church they constituted a formidable precedent. One of these measures cleverly pitted the material interests of the military and clergy against each other by proposing the suppression of the revenues of the friars of Alta and Baja California, and their appropriation to the use of the Army. When debated in the hall of Congress, it was clearly shown that these large funds had been diverted from the purpose for which they had been originally extorted from Mexico, and were used by the friars, not to convert the Indians of California, but to enslave and exploit them. Nevertheless, the Church, enraged and unabashed, threatened to provoke a military revolt if the measure were executed.

Such a threat would have fallen impotent had the balance of the loan of $30,000,000, amounting to $10,000,000, promised by the English bankers, materialized. It did not, however, and the matter requires some explanation. The Church saw clearly that the Army, well and regularly paid, and therefore contented, was not amenable to her will; that with the arrival of the last instalment of the loan, the new administration would be more powerful than ever, the Army more content than ever, and that consequently all her own schemes for supremacy would miserably fail. Curiously enough, at this juncture, the negotiations in the matter of the English loan began to weaken, and presently they failed altogether. In his "Leyes Fiscales," p. 28, Luis G. Labastida reveals the fact that the agents — good Clericals all of them — deliberately ruined the negotiations. The nation faced bankruptcy and disorganization, but the Church was saved!

It was at this *impasse* in affairs that President Victoria's term expired. The failure of the London loan had created a financial panic in Mexico, and the Church, unable to control the situation, was completely outgeneralled in the ensuing election by the Liberals. The vigorous propaganda carried on by the latter during the tolerant régime of President Victoria now showed its fruits, and Vicente Guerrero was elected President

— that same Guerrero who had so faithfully maintained the fight for freedom in the southern hills until duped into submission by Iturbide. In the presidential race, the Church fell into the second place with the election of General Anastasio Bustamante, an old officer of the royalist army, as Vice-President. A little later we shall see this Bustamante playing a conspicuous rôle in the machinations of the Clerical party.

The result of the elections took the Church altogether by surprise. She recognized with bitter chagrin that Guerrero in power would use his utmost efforts for the welfare of the common people; but she was not seriously alarmed. She counted fully on the loyalty of the new army to her interests, and particularly in view of the financial embarrassment under which the new administration had come into power. She argued, correctly enough, that as soon as pay fell into arrears, and the Army became discontented, it would be a simple matter to invoke another cuartelazo and restore a military despotism. Or, indeed, if that plan failed, was there not the still flourishing conspiracy for invoking the return of the Spanish colonial régime?

On the first of April, 1829, Guerrero was inaugurated President, with Bustamante as Vice-President. It would be difficult to find a more ill-matched pair, or better exemplars of the characteristics of the two contending factions. On the one side, the liberal-minded, magnanimous patriot; on the other, the fanatical and unscrupulous tool of the Church. On the day following the inauguration, the Church instituted a fierce campaign of vilification against the new President.

Guerrero — as we have seen — was the Great Commoner of Mexico, a man of the people, one of the remnants of the old guard who had fought in the ranks of Hidalgo and Morelos. Duped into the army of Iturbide by his simple good faith, he had lived among bigotry and corruption and remained clean; he had lived among the pampered and corrupt military, and had retained his high ideals of the rights of the people. Such a man was a fit mark for the intrigues of the Church. Such as these she has ever crucified.

In the struggle which followed, the entire forces of the Army, Church, and Monarchists were lined up against Guerrero and the party of the people. To quote Zavala: "No misrepresentation or falsehood was left unused by the Clericals against a man who was the personal representative of the people. Every day new falsehoods were uttered to sap the moral strength of the government, and undermine its power. The decrees of the cabinet were not met with justified censure, nor with accusations containing some semblance of truth, nor with the legitimate satire to which the abuses of bad government may be subjected. They were opposed by the lowest calumnies, the most impudent fabrications, and the most obscene accusations which wrath, rancour, and insolence could produce." (Zavala, "Historia de las Revoluciones de Mexico," Vol. 2., p. 183. *Also see* Bancroft's "History of Mexico," V, pp. 77, 78, 79.)

Scarcely had Guerrero assumed the reins of power when the conspiracy to restore the Spanish colonial régime began to assume dangerous proportions. Says Zavala in speaking of this period: "If we judge from appearances, we are forced to believe that the Spanish Government had spies all over the country, as well as a host of hired writers and agitators busily at work provoking disorder and civil war." ("Ensayo Historico de las Revoluciones en Mexico," Vol. I, p. 183.)

Behind the Spanish activities lay the conspiracy of the Church in Mexico. At all costs Guerrero was to be harassed, and prevented from giving his attentions to the reforms so urgently required for the country's welfare. Here, we see the ruling class following the precedent of the ruling class of all time and of all countries, in diverting domestic reform by inviting a foreign invasion. Such an invasion must be met, and reforms, even such as are fundamental to the national existence, must be laid aside for the nonce, and an undivided front presented to the enemy.

The trick worked on this occasion, as it had worked a thousand times before, and as it will continue to work so long as society is divided into possessing and non-possessing classes. The news suddenly arrived at the Mexican capital that the Spanish fleet had been sighted off Tampico. At once the business of domestic reform receded to the background, and Guerrero had to summon the people to the defence of the country. Lured by the representations of the Church into the belief that his invasion would meet with little resistance, the King of Spain had at last consented to dispatch an armed force against Mexico. It landed at Tampico in 1829, but instead of the ready welcome it had anticipated, it was forced to face the furious onslaught of the unorganized insurgent peasantry of the old revolutionary states of Tamaulipas, Nuevo Leon, and Vera Cruz. In spite of the deliberate bungling and interferences of a number of corrupt army officers, who appeared on the scene, ostensibly to take charge of the defence, but in reality to hamper it, the Spanish troops were swiftly swept into the sea.

The fighting had been done almost spontaneously — with scarcely any direction — by the people of the locality, most of whom were small land-owners. The enemy defeated and dispersed, these sturdy farmers returned to their homes and thought no more of the matter; but the partisans of the Church, the army officers who had arrived on the scene for the purpose of treacherously coöperating with the invaders, executed a nimble volte-face, when they found their plans had miscarried. They now boldly took the entire credit of the expulsion to themselves, and returned to Mexico City, the self-announced liberators of the country, and the mock heroes of the hour, with Santa Ana as the chief "hero." The Church promptly took the cue, and covered her chagrin and terror at the abortion of her treachery by enthusiastically welcoming the victors and celebrating elaborate Te Deums in the cathedral. In all of this, President

Guerrero was studiously ignored; and to the simple folk, unlearned in treachery, intrigue, and cabal, it seemed that the Church and her Army, and not the rugged insurgents of the coast, were the real saviours of the country.

The tactics of the Church and Army could repress the political expression of the new ideals, but they were unable altogether to repress the propaganda of these ideals among the people. Under the freedom and security of Guerrero's presidency, the Liberals continued the good work begun in the days of Guadalupe Victoria, and by press, platform, and book, proclaimed far and wide the great principles of the French Revolution. That the leavening was beginning to work became evident when whole bodies of the peasantry began to refuse to pay tithings.

In the meantime Guerrero had abolished the last vestige of chattel slavery which still persisted in Mexico. The influence of this abolition went far to break up the bondage of peonage and serfdom. From this time the peons began to move from estate to estate as opportunity beckoned; and the government accorded a moral if not legal sanction to this slackening of the toilers' bond.

In addition to these measures, Guerrero interpreted the constitution in regard to religious matters, with characteristic liberality, declaring that if official sanction was withheld from any form of faith other than the Catholic, this by no means implied that the holding of another form of faith constituted an offence in the eyes of the law — an interpretation that was tantamount to the proclamation of religious liberty.

If the abolition of slavery and the undermining of peonage infuriated the great land-owners, this practical proclamation of religious liberty aroused the Church to frenzy. She foresaw clearly that for every independent religious thinker there would be a corresponding loss of tithings and Church taxes.

Guerrero had held office scarcely twelve months. The Church had not wasted her time; already her plans were ripe. Suddenly she struck. Vice-President Bustamante, obedient to his orders, started a cuartelazo in Jalapa to overthrow the President. In his harangue to his troops he declared: "The government has entirely neglected to uphold the privilege and welfare of the Army, while all its activities are given to the benefit of the lowest class, which has never given to the country the glorious services of the soldier." Bustamante's command alone numbered ten thousand men, and its traitorous example was speedily followed by the garrisons in Campeche, Yucatan, Tampico, Vera Cruz, and Mexico City. With scarcely a word of warning and within a few hours, Guerrero found himself deserted by the entire army, and forsaken even by his personal followers.

Stricken to the heart, not so much by the onslaught of his enemies as by the desertion of those whom he had deemed his trusted friends, Guerrero left Mexico City with a few hundred soldiers to seek support among the peasantry. A few days later these soldiers also deserted him, to join the main army in rebellion. Meanwhile Congress, obedient to the Church, formally deposed him from office, declaring him to be insane, and unfitted to hold authority.

On the 1st of June, 1830, the Church and Army, acting in consort, declared Bustamante President of the Republic, with Lucas Alaman, a powerful, subtle, and devoted friend of the Church, as Minister of Foreign Relations and of the Interior. By this one masterly stroke the powers of reaction were again triumphant.

We shall divine, rather than see, a great deal of Alaman during the ensuing period of Mexican history. A man of great ability and deep learning, but obsessed with an unscrupulous and fanatical devotion to the interests of the Church, he remained for years the unobtrusive but all-powerful executor of the Clerical policies. His immediate task in this instance was the crushing out of the spirit of revolt among the peons, and to this he set himself with the same energy and pitiless zeal that characterized all his evil career.

Copyright by Underwood & Underwood, N. Y.
NATIVE MAYA GIRLS
Typical scene in the "tierra caliente" (hot country) in southern Mexico. The Mayas are one of the original Mexican tribes, whose antecedents date back as far as the Aztecs and Toltecs

Photograph by Brown Bros.

ORE SORTING

At one of the rich mines at Guanajuato, central Mexico. Though sympathetic to the revolution the labourers in these industrial communities are not its mainstay, as are the toilers in the soil

NATIVE SILVER SMELTER

A small smelter in the interior in which all the crude, old-time methods of the early Spanish miners are still used

THE REPUBLIC 85

Guerrero retired to Titzla, in the State of Guerrero, but upon receiving warning that six cutthroats had been unleashed from the Mexico City jail to murder him, he removed to Chilpancingo. Here he was met by Juan Alverez, an old insurgent chief of 1810, who had already raised a force of several thousand peasants. Soon a series of peon uprisings occurred in the old revolutionary states of Michoacan, Nuevo Leon, San Luis Potosi, and Coahuila, against the hated usurper, and in favour of the ex-President.

Unorganized and ill-equipped, the revolt had no chance of success. Indeed, the great land-owners, filled with blood lust against the man who had abolished slavery and loosened the bond of peonage, organized armed expeditions of their own against the insurgents. To these activities, rather than to the efforts of the government, was due the final suppression of the revolt and the destruction of Guerrero's followers. Guerrero now removed from Chilpancingo, and established his revolutionary headquarters at the seaport of Acapulco. It was here that the patriot fell a victim to a ruse of his arch-enemies, Bustamante, Alaman, and the Minister of War, Facio.

Lured on board a brig in the harbour by a certain Picaluga whom he regarded as a trusted friend, he was set upon by the crew, seized, bound, and taken to the port of Huatulco. Thence he was removed to Oaxaca, where, after a mock trial at the hand of the most reactionary members of the Army, he was sentenced to be shot as a traitor on the ridiculous charge of having conspired with Minister Poinsett to sell Texas to the United States! On the 14th of February, 1831, the patriot Guerrero fell, like his noble comrades, Hidalgo and Morelos, before the firing platoons of the reactionaries.

It has been charged against the administration of Guerrero that he endeavoured to rule in a democratic spirit a people ignorant and inexperienced, and devoid of democratic training and traditions. The criticism is altogether illogical. Everything must have its beginning. How shall a nation acquire democratic training and tradition save by the exercise of democracy? Do we forbid the child to walk because at first it totters and falls? Such criticisms as these have their foundation not in the facts of the case, but in self-interest. Guerrero tried nobly to found a democracy, but such a democracy was essentially inimical to the material interests of the ruling class. The people, in spite of their backward condition, were equal to the task, but Privilege was more powerful than they — and Privilege triumphed.

CHAPTER VIII

THE PRESIDENCY OF BUSTAMANTE

BY THE murder of Guerrero, the government calculated to quell the revolt of the people, sufficiently, at least, to enable it to prepare more thoroughgoing measures. The great struggle for Independence had planted deep in the hearts and minds of the peons the dream of democracy, of personal ownership of the land, and of freedom from oppressive taxation. The Church, out of her age-long experience as the arch-oppressor of the nations, well knew that these ideas, once aflame, could never be extinguished, and that presently the people would rise again with renewed might.

At all costs, this stream of patriotic energy must be diverted. To continue to oppose it merely by the upkeep of an enormous standing army, voracious, and demoralized by inactivity, had already proved a cumbersome and unreliable method. There was but one expedient suitable for the situation — the oft tried and invariably successful one of inviting foreign invasion. Such an invasion must be, in this instance, a much more serious affair than the unsuccessful Spanish expedition. It must be sufficient not only to engage the activities of the army, but to arouse the entire nation to arms: above all, it must be sufficiently disastrous to insure the wholesale massacre of the more spirited peons, who, at the first alarm of national danger, would be foremost to relinquish their insurgent activities and flock to the government standard. To bring about such a happy consummation was now the settled determination of the Clerical party. And her new appointees, President Bustamante, Minister of War Facio, and

Minister of Interior and Foreign Relations Lucas Alaman, proved suitable tools for her purpose.

The first step of the new régime was the complete suppression of the freedom of the press, followed immediately by the bitter persecution of the leading men of the Yorkino, or Popular party. "The shooting of Guerrero was a legal murder; but thereafter the new clerical administration wasted no time in the farcical processes of law. The governors and other officials of high position, suspected of popular sympathies, were summarily deposed: prominent citizens were exiled or executed, and the jails were filled with the political opponents of the administration, and with Liberal suspects denounced by paid spies." (Rivera, "Historia de Jalapa," p. 11.)

"Puebla, Morelia, and Mexico were states which witnessed savage executions. Military courts, denunciations, dungeons, the insolence of the Army, and protected tyranny of the Clergy, were the characteristics of the Bustamante administration. It made of Congress an assemblage of lackeys, and spread the terror of the gallows over the whole country." (Gustavo Baz, "Vida de Juarez," p. 37.)

The federal system proclaimed by the constitution of 1824, conservative as it was, had yet given a certain breathing space to Liberal aspirations. The next activity of the Clerical administration, therefore, was to destroy this federal system, and replace it by the central system of government. Under this latter, the autonomous, constitutional home government hitherto enjoyed by the state was subordinated to the authority of military chieftains with despotic powers. In this way the requirements of civil governments were rendered entirely subservient to the arbitrary demands of military force. A more despotic governmental machinery seldom has been devised. The public act of the people and the private act of the individual alike were subjected to the rigid examination of this military autocracy, and any merely suspected antagonism to the established order was savagely punished without process of law.

THE PRESIDENCY OF BUSTAMANTE

The first clash of the impending struggle between the civil and military elements occurred in Guadalajara, in the State of Jalisco. A man named Brambila, having published a pamphlet criticising the military commander of the state, General Ignacio Inclan, was arrested by his orders, and summarily sentenced to be shot without civil trial. The governor of the state, a man of Liberal ideas, elected under the late federal system, peremptorily demanded the delivery of the prisoner to the civil authorities for just and proper trial, according to established judicial procedure. Inclan curtly refused, and by way of protest the local legislature and state government left the city together with the larger part of the population. Inclan, alarmed at the seriousness of the situation, and in spite of the support given him by the national government, delivered up his prisoner.

From that moment the struggle recommenced with added bitterness. The times had changed. On the one hand the spread of the doctrines of the French Revolution and the long war of the people against Privilege had rendered them more class-conscious and more defiant in their attitude; on the other hand, the Church and Army in their efforts to maintain control had grown more despotic and brutal than ever. The whole country was soon aroused to resistance, and the old revolutionary states of the south and west — Jalisco, Zacatecas, Nuevo Leon, Coahuila and Texas, Tamaulipas, Sonora and Sinaloa — were already in open rebellion.

The immediate object of this uprising of the people was the reëstablishment of the federal system. This conservative and narrow demand on the part of an oppressed people constitutes a good example of a social phenomenon of common occurrence, frequently misunderstood by sociologists. As according to the fundamental law, "action and reaction are equal and opposite," which is as true — dialectically interpreted — for social dynamics as for physical dynamics, the extreme reaction of the privileged classes should have called forth, in this instance, an extreme counter-action on the part of the people.

However, we find merely the demand for the federal system. But behind this moderate claim smouldered a spirit of fierce rebellion which presently was to sweep the military despotism of the central system from power, and in a few brief months reëstablish, not merely the federal system, but a larger measure of liberty and constitutional government than Mexico had ever known — eloquent proof enough of the soundness of the law. In every struggle, the outpost must be taken first. The change of political systems was the immediate necessity of the movement, the requisite precondition of all future progress.

It was on this, then, that the Revolution concentrated its attention for the moment. Social evolution furnishes many similar instances — e. g., the great movement of Scientific Socialism, in its advance among the nations, frequently is compelled to narrow its fundamental issue — the socialization of the means of wealth production — to such immediate measures as the procuring of an eight-hour law, or the establishment of the initiative, referendum, and recall.

The states of Zacatecas and Guanajuato were foremost in the effective organization of the revolt. In the former state, a contingent of some three thousand armed civilians called "civicos,"* was quickly mobilized, while in the latter the revolutionists had already routed the government forces. The radical decrees of Guerrero's administration had given immense impetus to the revolutionary agitation all over the country, and the work of the great patriot, too speedily underestimated by his enemies, was now beginning to bear fruit.

"There was," says Navarro, in his "Historia de Méjico," "in Mexico at this time, a social body, numerous and energetic, who eagerly sought to place in the front of affairs those

---

*The "civicos," who afterward played such an important part in the history of Mexico, were first created under the constitution of 1824, which established the federal system. Democratically constituted, electing their own officers, and consisting for the most part of the old insurgents, these armed civilian bodies performed the function of state guards, and afterward became the bulwark of civil institutions against the depredations of the regular army.

THE PRESIDENCY OF BUSTAMANTE

who believed in the abolition of fueros, the confiscation of the estates of the Church, the dissolution of monasteries, and the suppression of the army."

The fierce resistance offered to the establishment of the despotic central system greatly embarrassed the plans of the Church and caused her to resort to an astonishing stratagem. It will be remembered that a certain General Santa Ana had wooed notoriety under the empire by soliciting Iturbide for the honour of dissolving Congress by military force. A little later we saw this same fortune hunter heading the cuartelazo on behalf of the Church against Iturbide, and finally entering Mexico City as the "Liberator" after the rout of the Spanish expedition by the peasants of the coast. It was this man that the Church now employed to outwit and confound the revolutionists by starting a military revolt in favour of that same federal system whose establishment was the main object of the people's revolution! The stratagem was abundantly successful. Pressed hard by the regular army under Bustamante, nonplussed by the sudden accession of the powerful and popular Santa Ana to their cause, the insurgents abandoned the fight, and while waiting for the situation to resolve itself, threw all their strength into the impending presidential election.

During the recent years of political struggle and armed conflict between the people (represented by the Liberal party) and the Church, Army, and Aristocracy (represented by the Conservative party), the former had gained a partial or complete control of most of the provincial legislatures. But if the latter had suffered a corresponding diminution of prestige among the people, they had by no means lost their economic power, at all times the dominant factor in the social process. The Conservatives now nominated Santa Ana for President. It was an appropriate selection. Not only had Santa Ana proved himself again and again the admirable and ingenious tool of reaction, but his reputation as the saviour of the country and the hero of the Republic, coupled with his recent spectacular stand for federalism, practically insured his election in spite of the powerful opposition of the Liberals.

The Liberal candidate was Dr. Valentine Gomez Farias. In opposition to the military masquerader, Santa Ana, Gomez Farias was the very type of the citizen Intellectual who believes that society should be for the organized security and advantage of all, and not for the organized pillage of the mass by the few. According to the constitution of 1824, the state legislatures were empowered to elect both President and Vice-President. In the ensuing elections the Conservative party, representing the Church, Army, and Aristocracy, using every resource in their power, succeeded in placing their candidate, Santa Ana, at the head of the poll; while the Liberal party, with a very large minority, succeeded in electing Gomez Farias as Vice-President. In the national legislature elected by the people the Liberals had full control of both houses. Under such circumstances a terrific struggle was imminent.

On April 1, 1833, the first Liberal Congress of Mexico opened its session, and Santa Ana and Gomez Farias assumed their respective offices. The Church at last had begun to realize the tremendous gains made by her adversaries. Completely overpowered in the lawful administration of government, she abandoned the political field entirely, and turned with venomous energy to the plotting of another cuartelazo. Her purpose, however, lay deeper than the accomplishment of merely another *coup d'état*. The power of the people had become such that a mere military uprising was foredoomed to failure, unless immediately supported by the diversion of the whole force of the nation from domestic reform to national defence. To the invitation of a foreign invasion to supplement her premeditated military uprising, the Church, therefore, turned her entire effort.

Thus followed one of the most significant, but to those uninitiated in the subtleties of the Church one of the most mystifying steps in the history of the Clerical policy in Mexico. Santa

Ana, under instructions from the Church, asked Congress for leave of absence, placing his power temporally in the hands of the Liberal Vice-President, Gomez Farias!

To relinquish voluntarily to her enemies the last vestige of control in the government of the country at this particular moment seems at first glance the work of sheer despair or insanity on the part of the Church. A little deeper insight, however, will show us that it merely indicated her supreme contempt for constitutional methods in class warfare, and her cynical confidence in her own intrigues. Of what use to retain Santa Ana as the impotent President of a government overwhelmingly Liberal when he could be employed to immense advantage in the work of organizing the intended cuartelazo? Of what use to take the present political situation too seriously when at the first alarm of the planned foreign invasion the power of the people and all its brave handiwork must be sunk in the struggle with the intruder?

The Liberals, whether conscious or not of the mines which the Church was sinking beneath them, took immediate and vigorous advantage of their power. The attack was opened by the legislature of the State of Mexico with the passage of a thoroughgoing revolutionary measure which struck directly at the roots of the existing social evils. Its main provisions were as follows:

I. The estates in the province of Mexico that pertain to the support of the mission of the Holy Rosary in the Philippines, are hereby confiscated in favour of the said province of Mexico.

II. The government shall divide the said estates into small farms, each one large enough to support a family, and shall cause these farms to be appraised by experts.

III. The government shall sell these farms to the people at a price equivalent to 5 per cent. of their value, and the money thus received from the sale shall be used for the purpose of building roads and constructing irrigation works.

Following this law, another enactment was made, prohibiting the immigration of members of religious orders. In several other states of the country the local legislatures were adopting similar measures, while Vice-President Gomez Farias, at the head of the nation, was surrounding himself with progressive and capable citizens to the exclusion of the clergy and military.

In the national Congress there now followed a torrent of legislation of such sanity and clear vision that one wonders what bright example Mexico might have set to the world had she not been halted in her splendid re-birth by the Texas war.

The congressional decrees of the 19th and 24th of October, 1833, established non-sectarian education throughout Mexico, and suppressed the privileges of the Church in the matter of opening schools and granting diplomas. Exasperated by this vital blow at her psychological control, the Church instigated a military uprising of the troops garrisoning Mexico City. Gomez Farias, however, with the aid of an armed body of civicos, promptly suppressed the revolt and disarmed the soldiers. Following the suppression of this premature cuartelazo, laws were passed in rapid succession abolishing the yearly subsidy from the national treasury to the Church, abolishing the compulsory payment of tithings and taxes to the Church, and releasing the members of all religious orders from their vows.

These terrible blows, levelled at the very heart of the material and moral power of the Church, were inflicted amidst the most dramatic surroundings. Cholera was raging throughout Mexico. In Mexico City alone two thousand bodies were buried in a single day. A black pall of mourning darkened the land, rent from border to border with the convulsive cries of victims and the lamentations of those bereft. The Church, cool and calculating amid the national agony, quickly seized the opportunity to turn the sufferings of the people into political capital. Priestly processions paraded the streets, praying and wailing in a loud voice, and calling upon the people to repent, for God had sent

THE PRESIDENCY OF BUSTAMANTE

this plague upon them to punish them for the iniquitous acts of the Liberal government.

To the machinations of the Church, Congress answered by a decree appropriating the estates of the missions of upper and lower California to the use of the government. The same decree was also applied to the other estates of the mission of the Holy Rosary in the Philippines, thus completing on a national scale the expropriation initiated locally by the legislature of Mexico state. This marked the climax of the people's brief but fecund reign of power. One step more, and the Mexican nation would have achieved democracy.

Congress had already intimated its intention of confiscating the entire property of the Church and applying it to the use of the people. It now proceeded to aim the deathblow at the supremacy of Privilege by decreeing the suppression of the Army, and creating in its stead a permanent bulwark to the liberties of the people by the organization of bodies of civicos — free citizen militia — with the right of electing their own officers.

The moment for the decisive grapple had come. The Church was fully prepared, and in a flash the long premeditated cuartelazo burst forth. In the State of Mexico a certain Colonel Unda headed a military uprising, calling upon Santa Ana to seize the dictatorship. The moment was not yet ripe for the President to show his hand. With admirable aplomb he appeared to be much enraged, and gathering all the available troops in Mexico City marched against the rebels. When, however, he seemed about to engage Unda, his troops revolted, arrested him, and joined the rebels! Needless to remark, the arrest and defection were only parts of a clever scheme arranged by Santa Ana himself. A few days later he returned to Mexico City, having successfully escaped from his self-imposed imprisonment.

The first part of the plan had been accomplished, Mexico City was defenceless, and her garrison with the rebel forces. The cuartelazo now became general throughout the country. In the south, Nicolas Bravo headed his troops in rebellion against the Liberal administration, calling upon Santa Ana to assume the dictatorship, and declaring that he and all his men were prepared to die as martyrs in the defence of the Christian faith and the freedom of the fatherland. In the State of Michoacan the garrison, under the command of Ignacio Escalado, followed suit with a similar uprising and proclamation. From all parts of the country came tidings of revolt.

The psychological moment had arrived for Santa Ana to declare himself. His leave of absence had expired and he was already due at the capital to resume his duties as President. Suddenly he appeared in Mexico City, not, however, as the lawful executive of the country, but at the head of the rebellious troops, proclaiming the abolition of the federal system and the restitution of the central system. Before the Liberal party could prepare a defence, he had dissolved Congress by military force, and had promulgated a decree repealing all its recent enactments against the privileges and power of Church and Army.

With one foul blow the great constructive work of the people had been destroyed. Although demoralized for the moment, by the swiftness of the onslaught, the Liberals, backed by the overwhelming power of the people, undoubtedly would have swept the cuartelazo, and with it, both Church and Army, from Mexico forever. But scarcely had they gathered themselves for the fight, scarcely had the eager multitudes throughout the land unstacked their rifles for the reconquest of democracy, when out of the north, as scheduled by the Church, came the cry of international war.

In the face of national danger the revolt died at birth. Reaction was triumphant. The rifle loaded for the heart of Privilege, in defence of the freedom of the people, was now hurriedly turned against the foreign enemy — an unwilling enemy, goaded into attack only by the persistent barbs of the Church.

The rebellion of the American colonists in Texas, fomented

THE PRESIDENCY OF BUSTAMANTE

by every device known to intrigue, had come to snatch from the people the fruits of their victory.

With the arbitrary dissolution of Congress, Santa Ana had caused the no less arbitrary deposition of Gomez Farias. Not content with his deposition, Santa Ana ordered him out of the country on pain of death. It is interesting to note in this respect the comment of *La Lima de Vulcano*, the inspired organ of the ruling class, in its issue of September 9, 1835: "Yesterday the hated Gomez at last left this capital under the most justified condemnation of the whole country. He has brought upon the nation cholera and poverty, immorality and tyranny, spying and treason, ignorance and sacrilege, the uplifting of crime, and the repression of honesty, the victory of the low and vulgar people, and the casting down of the select, terror, and mourning families' proscription, tears and death, in a thousand horrible ways." In direct opposition to this let us quote from Bancroft's "History of Mexico," Vol. 15, p. 127: "Gomez Farias left the executive office without a stain on his character."

The Clerical party was now busy throughout the length and breadth of Mexico celebrating the accession of Santa Ana to power, and endeavouring to arouse a spirit of enthusiasm among the people on his behalf. Some glimpse of the means employed for this purpose can be gained from the following manifesto, issued by the Archbishop of Mexico City and Canon of the Holy Metropolitan Church:

A thousand times blessed is the man [Santa Ana] who, with his firm hand, has returned to God His legitimate heritage. His memory will be eternally blessed to the end of the centuries, and his crown of glory will shine in heaven for all eternity. His name will be remembered with gratitude by generations to come, and the prayers of old and young, of virgins and children, will go up to him as the elected son of God. His victorious sword has come to the protection of religion and, through his true Catholicism, we have regained the peace, liberty and everlasting power of our Church. . . . We were in fear that God's mercy was denied to us, but God himself, looking upon us in kindness, compassionated our sufferings. At the end of last April He caused to appear on our national horizon a shining star whose beauty, gleaming in splendour, announced as in the ancient days of the Wise Men, that justice and peace were about to descend upon our land. This was the coming to this capital of our beloved, His Excellency the President, Don Antonio Lopez de Santa Ana, to take once again in his hands the command of our republic. In him, our deepest religious and patriotic feelings will eternally recognize the glorious hero who deserves the love and gratitude of our nation.

It is significant of the depths to which the Church had fallen that she no longer proudly dictated her will but must needs fawn upon an intriguer, beg from a charlatan, and bribe a scoundrel, in order to maintain her hold on the wealth of the nation.

Forty thousand dollars a month was the bribe which the Church offered Santa Ana for his services, a bribe which he was cynical enough publicly to accept. His Minister of Justice announced in the official organ: "His Excellency the President, according to the wishes of several ecclesiastical bodies, has accepted from them the donation of $40,000 a month for the next six months for his expenses." ("México á través de los Siglos," Vol. 4, p. 342.) This was the "thirty pieces of silver" paid by the Church as the price of her salvation, and the betrayal of the nation. Never before in the history of the Church in Mexico had she opened the money bag with such prodigality, and never before according to her own records and documents had she greater need.

Santa Ana having dismissed the Liberal Congress, President, and cabinet, appointed as his premier the Bishop of Michoacan, Juan Cayetano Portugal. Meanwhile the Texas revolt successfully held the attention of the people from the consideration of domestic reforms. For them the affair was not merely a local uprising against the national authority, but a war with the United States, dangerous in the extreme, to Mexican integrity. The Church had accurately calculated the effect of her plot, and so eager had she been to thwart the intended uprising of the Liberals against the cuartelazo that she had announced the armed revolt of the American colonists in Texas *two months before it broke out*.*

When the news had spread throughout the country, the **armed**

---
*Bulnes, "Las Grandes Mentiras de Nuestra Historia," p. 354.

bodies of civicos, organized by Gomez Farias in Mexico City, Zacatecas, Guadalajara, San Luis Potosi, Oaxaca, and other parts of the country, who were preparing a vigorous revolt, found themselves compelled to desist in view of the threatening national danger.

CHAPTER IX

THE TEXAS WAR

I. THE INTRIGUES OF THE CHURCH IN MEXICO

IN CONSIDERING the war with Texas it will be necessary to bear in mind several important basic facts:

I. *The Church in Mexico wanted war.* A war with some foreign country was at this time absolutely necessary to the ruling class in Mexico for the preservation of its powers.

II. *The Southern States of the United States wanted war.* A war with some foreign country was at this time beginning to be highly desirable for the ruling class in the Southern States, for the diversion of national attention from the conflicting issues of the North and South, and for the preservation of the planting interests in Congress.

III. *The Southern States wanted Texas for political, not territorial, reasons.* In view of the rapid development of the industrial North, the feudal South recognized that unless it could strengthen its numerical representation in the Senate by the acquisition of additional slave-holding territory, such as Texas, it would soon lose its economic and political dominance in the country.

IV. *The Texans were loyal to Mexico.* The Texan colonists were heartily opposed to secession from Mexico, and not until the last moment, when harried to desperation by bands of hired American outlaws and bodies of Mexican regulars, did they take any hand in the matter themselves.

V. *A tacit understanding existed between Andrew Jackson and Santa Ana.* Although thousands of lives were sacrificed, and a legacy of race-hatred bequeathed to the contending peoples which endures to the present day, never at any time was the conflict viewed seriously by either of the ruling classes, American or Mexican, who invoked it; never at any time did Lucas Alaman, the Mexican Minister of Foreign Relations, and Santa Ana, the Mexican President and commander-in-chief of the Army (both of them mere creatures of the Church), act in conflict with the desires of Andrew Jackson and his Cabinet in Washington.

VI. *The interests of the Church in Mexico and of the Southern planters were identical.* The interests of the two contending parties were identical: the one robbed to preserve its internal supremacy, the other consenting to be robbed for a like reason. Only the peaceful and industrious Texan colonists, the volunteers and hired gunmen of the United States, and the deluded Mexican soldiers, were the immediate sufferers in the conflict.

VII. *Religious fanaticism was used by both parties to fan the conflict.* Texas was one of the most ardent supporters of the federal system in Mexico, although perfectly willing to accept the central system for the sake of peace and it was at least half Protestant in faith. The Church in Mexico, therefore, obtained an additional zest from its torture, and utilized the cry of "heretic" to make of the affair a "holy war." On the other hand, the Protestant fanaticism of the United States was readily utilized by the paid agents of the South to inflame the North into coöperation in the war which could boast for its ostensible purpose the deliverance of Protestant American colonists from the persecution of Rome.

Bearing these seven basic facts in mind, the seeming wantonness of the Texas tangle ceases to embarrass the mind, and the affair resolves itself into a simple and classic illustration of well-accepted principles in class rule.

In the year 1819, while Mexico was still under the colonial régime, Moses Austin, a sturdy pioneer from Connecticut, sought permission of the governor of Northern Mexico to establish a colony of three hundred families in Texas. The Virrey at that time, Juan Ruiz de Apodaca, to whom the request was referred, readily gave the desired permission, and authorized the military commander of that region to choose a location for the settlement of the colony, on the right bank of the Brazos River, ninety miles from the Gulf of Mexico, The concession stipulated that the colonists be natives of Louisiana, Catholics of approved behaviour and morality, and that on taking possession of their land they swear allegiance and obedience to the Spanish Government. In April, 1822, Austin visited Mexico City, and remained there a year, arranging the final terms of the concession with the government, now no longer Spanish, but Mexican. In the course of these negotiations he not only obtained liberal modifications of the original conditions, but was honoured with the brevet of colonel of the Mexican Army, and accorded full powers to use his discretion for the welfare of the colonists. In the following year the colonists, under his direction, took definite possession of the land allotted them by the government.

Later in the year, when the new constitution established the federal system, the Texan colonists entered the federal family under the official designation of the "State of Coahuila and Texas." Under this new constitution, which gave autonomy to the provinces, the local government had power to make such land concessions as it deemed fit; and Moses Austin made good use of the opportunity to establish hundreds of new settlers on the land. The Liberal administration no longer upheld the conditions requiring the profession of the Catholic faith on the part of the colonists, and in consequence, many of the new settlers were Protestants. Under the tolerant national and local régime of the time the devotees of both religions worked side by side in perfect amity, and there is no record of any serious friction between them, in spite of the insincere accusations of persecution flung back and forth during the so-called Texas War, between the Mexican clerical intriguers on the one side, and the Southern Protestant intriguers on the other.

The fertility of the land thus freely given, the seven years of exemption from taxation which the new settlers enjoyed, and the rising prosperity of the colony, attracted a steady stream of immigration into Texas, and by the year 1826 the western side of the Brazos and Colorado rivers, as far as the Nacogdoches River, was fairly well populated. Not only was there a friendly feeling manifested between the Catholic and Protestant settlers, but also between the Mexican residents and this incoming tide of new population. Amid the general prosperity mutual good feeling was general, while the government of the state gave every facility for the welfare of all. Thus the colony would have become a strong, harmonious, and richly productive society — a new state in the Mexican federal family — had it not been for the hands which were laid upon her to save the supremacy of the Mexican Church and a slave-holding aristocracy.

Under the federal system, established by the constitution of 1824, the new colony shared in the privileges of autonomous government granted to all the states of the Republic. Of inestimable service to the prosperity of the country, this federal system proved highly inconvenient to the Church. For her it meant that the struggle for supremacy in the affairs of the nation must be carried on in thousands of different and widely sundered seats of war instead of in Mexico City alone, thus entailing the entire readjustment of her own essentially central and hierarchical organization. For this reason the Church bitterly fought the introduction of the federal system, and in the conflict which ensued between the Clerical and Liberal powers the colonists took their full share.

As we have seen, when Bustamante seized the control of government from the hands of President Guerrero, he at once obeyed the dictates of the Church and established the central system. He knew well enough, even as his Minister Alaman knew, that the people would never surrender to such a disastrous change without a bitter struggle. There was but one possible method of averting the coming conflict — to embroil the nation in a foreign war. It was to this well-worn expedient, then, that the Clerical party, represented by Bustamante and Alaman, turned. In this connection the brilliant writer of "Las Grandes Mentiras de Nuestra Historia" — Francisco Bulnes — says, p. 757: "For the government of Bustamante, as for any government established by the cuartelazo, foreign war was the only possible method of avoiding civil war; for, in the face of national peril, patriotism unites all factions under its flag."

The plot, which made the unwitting colonists the victims of political intrigue, had begun to assume shape when Bustamante, immediately after his accession to power, abolished the federal system in Texas, and established the central system, accompanied by brutal military rule. Says Doctor Mora, a Mexican historian of recognized worth, in speaking of this phase of the situation, in his work, "Mexico y sus Revoluciones," (Vol. 1, p. 414): "The new military commanderies in Texas were a fruitful source of trouble and disorder. The determination of the military class to overawe the civil government, and the disrespect of the soldiery for the lawful authorities, constituted a ready weapon for the throttling of civil liberty and the shedding of citizen blood."

The military class, when charged with despotic power, were, at their best, well calculated to irritate the most peaceable community into revolt; what they were at their worst, when tacitly prompted and supported in their acts of outrage by the supreme authority of the nation, can well be imagined.

"The natural animosity of the peace-loving colonists toward their turbulent soldiery was further intensified by the hideous crimes of some of the officers of the army stationed in the colony, which were allowed to pass quite unpunished." (Blas Filisola, "Guerra de Texas," Vol. 2, p. 86.)

Stephen Austin, a man who exercised a great and beneficent influence among the colonists, and who opposed the independence of Texas to the last moment, wrote, in a letter addressed to General Mier y Teran: "I have informed you many times, and I inform you again, that it is impossible to rule Texas by a military system. I am convinced that the more the army is increased in Texas the greater will become the danger to the country's peace and tranquillity. . . . From the year 1821 I have maintained order and enforced the law in my colony simply by means of civicos, without a single soldier, and without a dollar of expense to the nation. . . . The situation of the colonists is a very delicate and unhappy one, and I trust you will not be offended with the frankness and clarity with which I express myself in regard to military power. Upon this subject of military despotism I have never hesitated to express my opinion, for I consider it the source of all revolutions, and of the slavery and ruin of free peoples. I firmly believe that until the reduction of military authority and the abatement of military privilege is accomplished, no peace, stability, or progress can be expected in Mexico. This, and the establishment of religious liberty, are the two remedies most sorely needed, and the man who will bring them to pass will deserve the honest name of 'Washington of Mexico.'"

One can readily imagine what a bad effect this noble letter had on the clerico-military intriguers who had decreed the revolt of Texas.

The fact that more than half of the colonists were Protestant Americans, and that the Protestant faith was beginning to gain ground even among the Mexicans, furnished the Church with yet another weapon for provoking the required strife. Proclaiming a "holy war" against "the dissolute and sacrilegious enemies of God in Texas," the priests used every artifice in their power to arouse the prejudice and passion of the Mexican people against the colonists, calling upon them as the modern Israelites, and Chosen People of God, to go forth and destroy the Philistines of the north. In all of these harangues the priests were careful to confound the Texan colonists with the whole American nation in order to give to the local friction the significance of an international war.

As a matter of history the United States as a whole was profoundly ignorant of the wretched imbroglio, and only the Democratic clique immediately surrounding Andrew Jackson exhibited any sign of active interest in it.

In order to keep the exasperation of the colonists at fever heat, President Bustamante had dispatched General Mier y Teran to Texas with instructions to suppress all trace of civil government. Teran executed his orders with zeal, and not only suppressed the civil courts and trial by jury established by the colonists, but even declared null and void all contracts and land concessions made by the federal government prior to April, 1830, thus violently depriving the more recent colonists of the farms and homes which they had established in perfect good faith.

Not content with these measures, Teran permitted a tricky politician, named Francisco Madero, who had accompanied him from Mexico, to set himself up as a distributor of land concessions under the supposed authority of the central government; and many of these land concessions included the cancelled concessions already homesteaded. In addition to this, on the 6th of April, 1830, the national Congress of Mexico passed a measure prohibiting the further colonization of Texas by American immigrants; and General Teran, in enforcing the law, interpreted it in such fashion as to deny the right of any man of Anglo-Saxon extraction to hold Texan land concessions, giving to this unwarranted and mischievous interpretation a retroactive effect against the land concessions already recognized by the law. If history bore no further evidence to prove that the revolt of Texas was deliberately invoked by the Clerical party in Mexico, this utterly brutal and inane assault on the legitimate possessions and elementary rights of the colonists would alone amply prove the contention.

From the moment General Teran set foot in Texas the country was given over to the lawless ruffianism of the Mexican military. "Colonel Nicolas Condelle entered upon his duties in Goliad by holding up the Mayor of the town at the point of the gun, and forcing him to deliver up the funds of the municipal treasury to the amount of five thousand dollars. He then proceeded forcibly to disarm the citizens of the district of Bejar, who more than any other of these colonists were open to the attacks of the Indians. In addition to these measures, he impressed the best of the citizens into the army, and finally compelled every family to support five soldiers." (Yoakum, "History of Texas," Vol. 2, p. 13.) It would be tiresome to detail the innumerable outrages practised against the colonists by the military commanders with a view to driving them to revolt, but mention should be made of a particularly goading measure which forbade Anglo-Saxon colonists to engage in retail trade, under the pretext that this was the prerogative of native-born Mexicans — this, in spite of the fact that by the original decree which gave them their land concessions, the colonists had become fully enfranchised Mexican citizens.

In the month of April, 1835, President Santa Ana was preparing to strike the final blow at the revolutionary movement of the Liberals under Gomez Farias, and it is a matter of the highest significance that at this time "it was announced in the lobbies and government offices of Mexico City, in the cafés and places of fashionable resort, that in the year 1836 an expedition would be dispatched against the Texan colonists, not merely to enforce their obedience to the law, but to punish them severely with extermination or expulsion." (Blas Filisola, "Guerra de Texas," Vol. 2, p. 137, 138.) At the time when this sanguinary threat of extermination was already openly uttered in Mexican clerical and military circles the Texan colonists were not in revolt at all. It is true that in the general Liberal uprising against Bustamante in 1832, which abolished the central system and established the federal system, the Texans had naturally taken part at the invitation of the other states of the federation, but since that time they had remained peacefully loyal to the government. The colony, indeed, now numbering 21,000 souls, had good reasons to be contented, for it was probably the most prosperous and best organized society in Mexico.

On the 31st of August, 1835 (a matter of forty-one days before the first actual uprising in the colony), a circular, couched in the following terms, was addressed to all governors and municipal authorities at the instigation of the Church: "The colonists established in Mexico have shown unequivocally to what extremes they are prepared to go in their perfidy, ingratitude, and treachery. Forgetting their duty to the Supreme Government and to the nation which had so generously given them a place in her bosom, with fertile lands for cultivation, and all the natural resources necessary for their bountiful living, they have revolted against this nation under the pretext of sustaining a system, a change in which has been desired by the majority of Mexicans; in this way hoping to hide their criminal ambitions to dismember the Republic." (Colección de Leyes Decretos y Circulares. Dublan y Maza tomo que comprende los años de 1835 a 1840.)

The effect of this circular distributed broadcast throughout the country, coupled with the persistent agitation set up by the pulpit and press, was successful in arousing the deluded people of Mexico to the desired war fever, and in causing them to lay aside for the time all effort to remedy their own bitter wrongs. Thus was the Church again triumphant. In spite of all this deliberate antagonism, however, the great bulk of the colonists still remained loyal to the government. This large loyal faction was divided into two wings, the one loyal to the government, but opposed to Centralism; the other, loyal to the government unconditionally. Indeed, so closely were the economic interests of the colonists bound up with the economic interests of Mexico that even at a later day, when the exasperating actions of the government had passed all bounds to which honourable men may submit, they still remained fatuously and stubbornly loyal, hoping that the great Liberal party, at whose hand they had received so large a measure of autonomy and civil liberty, would again come into power and reëstablish the federal system.

The population of Texas as a whole at this time was divided into three parties: The Annexationist, the Independent, and the Mexican. The Annexationist party comprised only a weak and uninfluential group organized by the paid agents and political adventurers maintained in Texas by Andrew Jackson, then the President of the United States.* The Independent party, another comparatively weak and uninfluential minority, wished to erect Texas into a separate independent republic. They were strongly opposed to the policy of the Annexationists, for they clearly discerned that annexation to the United States meant annexation to the already jeopardized slave-holding interest of the South. The Mexican party, on the contrary, which included in its ranks the great majority of the wealthier and better educated colonists, and of course the Mexican residents, upheld the policy of loyalty to Mexico at any price. It opposed annexation for the same reason that the Independent party opposed it, and it opposed Independence on the just grounds that it would prove a very costly matter for so small a population as Texas then held to maintain a separate system of governmental machinery as well as the large standing army which her exposed position would render imperative.

The Mexican party was loyal to Mexico, because in this loyalty they divined the best warranties for their peace and prosperity. It is true that the prohibitive tariff erected against them by the centralist government would have given them economic reason for relaxing their adherence to Mexico had the tariff ever actually taken effect. In reality, however, it worked

---

*For a somewhat favourable view of Jackson's intrigues to get possession of Texas, see Rives' "The United States and Mexico, 1821–1848."

no hardship upon them at all; for the Mexican customs service was quite inadequate to the task of patrolling such an enormous extent of border, even if it had not been readily bribed and corrupted into coöperation with the contraband trade.

Again, in the matter of chattel slavery, the interest of the colonists was clearly best subserved by loyalty to Mexico. Quite a large number of the wealthier colonists were slave-holders, and although by the decree of President Guerrero slavery had been abolished in Mexico, the decree had never been enforced as far as Texas was concerned. The central government which had superseded Guerrero had continued to overlook breach of the law in this respect, and the Texan slave-holders had come to consider the matter as practically settled in their favour. Indeed, even had the central government taken cognizance of their disobedience to the abolitionary decree, they had good precedent for expecting rich indemnity in the shape of land grants for their confiscated slaves. On the other hand, they foresaw the rapidly approaching doom of slavery under American rule. Thus every dictate of their material interest cried aloud to them to remain loyal to Mexico and hope for the best.

"I say it again," says Bulnes, "the great majority of the Texas colonists were willing to accept Mexican rule, even the hated Centralism, so long as it was unaccompanied by military ruffianism." (Francisco Bulnes, "Las Grandes Mentiras de Nuestra Historia," p. 361.)

Similarly, says the American historian: "This Peace party which had so much to lose by any change in the political *status quo*, in fear lest the intolerable insults and prætorianism of the soldiery under General Teran might exasperate the less politic of the colonists into open retaliation, issued an energetic appeal to the people, lamenting that the interest of the great majority who stood for peace was being threatened by the temerity of the few, rebuking the disquieting attitude of the agitators and calling attention to the recent circular issued by General Cos and the *jefe politico* of Bejar, which contained full assurance on the

THE TEXAS WAR

part of the Mexican authorities that the political and civil rights of the colonists would not be injured. This peace manifesto went on to affirm that there could be no reasonable doubt but that the Supreme Government would listen with the utmost good-will to the appeals of the colonists, and that it would undoubtedly do whatever lay in its power to promote the progress and welfare of all the citizens in the Republic. It further expressed the firm determination of the Peace party to promote by all honourable means the union of the colony with Mexico, and due obedience to Mexican law on the part of the colonists, and to sternly reprove any acts or attitudes which could involve conflict with the central government. In conclusion it announced that the Peace party were ready to sustain the government in enforcing the law, in the hope that its present objectionable features might be presently eliminated; that they regarded the efforts now being made to destroy the harmony between Texas and the rest of the Republic with profound disapproval; and that they called upon all friends of order to support the present authorities, not only because it was to their material interest to do so, but because inviolable obligations, moral and legal, prompted them to sustain the government with their property, honour, and lives." (Conclin, "A New History of Texas," p. 147.)

Julian Travis, who afterward played a conspicuous part in the Texan Revolution, a man of admirable qualities and gallant courage, as he proved in the battle of the Alamo, in writing to a friend about the condition of the colonists at this time, said: "The truth is the people are much divided here; the Peace party, as they style themselves, I believe are the strongest, and make much the most noise. Unless we could be united had we not better be quiet and settle down for a while? There is no doubt but that a central government will be established. What will Texas do in that case? Dr. J. H. C. Miller, and Chambers, of Gonzalez, are, I believe, for unqualified submission. I do not know the minds of the people upon the subject; but if they had a bold and determined leader I am inclined to think they would kick against it. General Cos writes me that he wants to be at peace with us; Ugartechea does the same. God knows what we are to do! I, for one, am determined to go with my countrymen; right or wrong, sink or swim, live or die, survive or perish, I am with them." (Yoakum, "History of Texas," Vol. 1., p. 343.) And Travis was no enemy of Mexico, but simply a man of large heart, willing to share the fortunes of his people for good or ill.

We trust we have conclusively proved to the reader the first half of our contention: that the Texas revolt was not the spontaneous work of the colonists themselves, but the result of the deliberate machinations of the Clerical party in Mexico. We now hope to throw some light on the other half of our contention: that Andrew Jackson and the planting interests of the South were equally guilty with the Mexican Clerical party of inciting the colonists to revolt.

II. INTRIGUES OF ANDREW JACKSON AND THE PLANTING INTERESTS

In the year 1830 America was divided into two well-marked and antagonistic factions — the free, industrial, and rapidly developing North, the slave-holding, agricultural, and stagnant South. The psychology and material interests of the North were those pertaining to a society in process of rapid transition from agrarian and industrial quasi-democracy to fully developed capitalism, with its monopoly of Privilege on the one hand, and wage-slavery on the other. The psychology and material interests of the South, on the contrary, were those pertaining to a society in a state of arrested feudal development. In 1830 the Democrats of the South were the dominant economic and political factor in the United States; but they already foresaw the day rapidly approaching when their supremacy would pass irrevocably to the North. To avert such a catastrophe they were ready to go to any extreme. Foreign war, secession, or the acquisition of additional slave-holding territory, were the only possible alternatives before them.

Texas was already largely American and Southern in personnel. Slavery was one of its established institutions. Its territory when divided properly would be sufficient to return no less than eighteen additional Democratic Senators to Washington. Was it not then eminently fitting that Texas should be wrenched away from Mexico and added to the South? Andrew Jackson thought so, and the whole planting interests of the South thought so. A willing partner at the chess-board appeared in the Clerical party of Mexico, desperately bayed by the rising Liberals. It was a case of now or never with the South, as with the Church; and the Texan embroglio began.

When Andrew Jackson had come into power as successor to John Quincy Adams it had been with the understanding that he was to use all the powers of government to protect the planting interests who were responsible for his election. The South had judged its man rightly. A slave-holder himself, unscrupulous, determined, and with pronounced dictatorial proclivities, Jackson, more than any other president of the United States, succeeded in imposing his will on the American people. His own interests were at stake, as well as the interests of the faction he represented. He gathered about him a cabinet agreeable to his purpose, and determined never to rest until Texas had been added to the South. His first act in power was to instruct American Minister Poinsett at Mexico City to open negotiations at once for the acquisition of Texas at a cash price of $5,000,000! Needless to say, the Liberals who were at that time in power in Mexico wasted little discussion on such a proposal.

A little later Poinsett was succeeded at the Mexican legation by Butler — a close friend of Andrew Jackson, and a slave-holder.* Shortly after his arrival in Mexico City in 1829 Butler

*The citizen of the United States who is surprised at the low character of the diplomatic representatives of his country in Mexico, and the depths of intrigue to which they descended, will do well to read the great work by their fellow coun-

wrote to Jackson the following illuminating note: "I have not lost sight for one moment of the Texas question in which you have such a great interest, not only because I know your wishes about it, but because I know the great advantage to our country to obtain it. But the public opinion of this country is so strongly opposed to the acquisition of Texas by the United States that I believe the Government will never be willing to entertain a proposition in this respect, and much less the cession of Texas. Any time that the press try to arouse the fire of the opposition against President Guerrero, articles appear in the papers charging him with being willing to sell Texas to us, and that for this one crime alone he deserves to be thrown out of office." (*Revue des Deux Mondes*, 15 July, 1844, p. 239.)

When Jackson recognized that the Mexican Liberal government was not to be bought into the cession of Texas he changed his tactics; and by making known the failure of his overtures turned the attention of the South toward more drastic measures.

In the beginning of 1830 the *Arkansas Gazette* published an inspired editorial opening with these words: "According to information received from a *source entitled to the highest credit*, it appears that we are not to have any more hopes of the acquisition of Texas while there is not in Mexico a party more friendly to the United States." ("Biblioteca Nacional," Dirección, Vol. 17, Primera Serie de Documentos de la Historia de Mexico.)

Henceforward Jackson abandoned his intrigues for the acquisition of Texas by diplomatic methods, and bent all his energies

---

tryman, Mr. G. L. Rives, "The United States and Mexico, 1821–1848," Vol. I. On page 236 this author, writing of Butler as a "diplomatic" representative, says: "Some of Butler's correspondence is insolent and even scurrilous in tone; and all of it betrays the author as vain, ignorant, ill-tempered and corrupt." Rives states that Butler was a speculator in Texas lands, that Jackson knew it and became interested in his schemes to get Texas for the United States, that shortly after Butler began negotiations with Jackson, the latter declared the time had come to acquire, or to attempt to acquire, Texas, that Butler was ready to resort to bribery and violence in Mexico while there as a "diplomat," that, although Jackson apparently objected to express bribery, he was willing to approve it in veiled form (Rives, Vol. I, p. 258), and that after Butler was proved to be a scoundrel Jackson stood by him (p. 258).

toward inciting the colony to revolt. To this end he dispatched to the scene of operations his friend, Sam Houston.* Houston had been governor of the State of Tennessee, a representative to Congress from the same state, and having taken a very active part in Jackson's election, he seemed destined to a high and remunerative position in the Government. It was a great surprise, therefore, to the uninitiated when this favourite of fortune suddenly left the unsickled harvest at Washington to come to Texas, where he had neither agricultural, financial, nor political interests. The surprise, however, changed to a deep understanding when he announced upon his arrival that he had come to Texas commissioned by President Jackson to arouse the colony in revolt and annex it to the United States. The *Journal de la Louisiane*, in speaking of Houston's departure for Texas, announced with a cynical frankness which showed how completely the President's psychology dominated the press of the time: "He has gone to Texas to start a revolution in favour of its independence with the purpose of annexing it to the United States. We may expect shortly to hear of his raising his flag." (*Ibid.*)

To obtain the tacit sanction of the American people to this intrigue required some diplomacy and genuine effort, for the spirit of the Independence still lived among them, and not knowingly would they have lent it their countenance. The South, of course, was solid for the acquisition of Texas, by fair means or foul; New England, having no interests to be served in the matter, was largely antagonistic, but many parts of the North were under the imperialistic glamour created by the Slavocracy. To create the right atmosphere for the projected plot, there was

---

*Mr. Rives states that Houston was "known to the Indians as the Wanderer or Big Drunk, or Drunken Sam," and was at the time of his "diplomatic mission" to Texas described by a contemporary as "very much of a broken down sot and debauchee." ("The United States and Mexico, 1821–1848," Vol. I, pp. 292, 293.) A Mexican may be pardoned if he suspects that a President "restrained by an honourable sense of what the international obligations of the United States demanded" would hardly have appointed a sot and a drunken adventurer to conduct delicate negotiations involving the honour of the United States in Texas.

immediately to hand, of course, the zealous services of the great army of federal employees. To supplement their efforts the South engaged a host of newspaper men, political orators, Protestant preachers, lecturers, cheap politicians and ward-heelers, and dispatched them into the enemy's camp — the North, there to work upon the ignorance, passions, and prejudices of the people in favour of the Southern shibboleths — slavery and the annexation of Texas.*

The tricks of the ruling class, whatsoever its nationality, are ever the same. While in Mexico the Catholic priests inflamed the people by preaching a "holy war" against the heretic Texan, the Protestant clergy of the North preached a precisely similar "holy war" against the idolatrous Mexican, while the ruling classes of both sides rejoiced in the outcome of their scheming.

Apologists for the part played by the United States in the annexation of Texas have professed to believe that the South was compelled to the step it took by the urgent need of territorial expansion for the support of its growing population, and as an outlet for its surplus capital. It is true that the spirit of modern commercial imperialism readily sanctions territorial rape urged by such necessities, but unfortunately for the apologists, the facts of the case lend no support whatever to their contention. In 1830 the South produced 5,600,000 bales of cotton; in 1902 the same area of territory produced 34,575,000 bales of cotton. In 1830, then, at the time when Andrew Jackson was preparing to annex Texas, *the South had already enough fertile land to produce seven times more than she was producing.* Clearly it was not economic necessity of this order that influenced the South. An economic necessity there certainly was; not the need of more territory, but the need of more voters for the maintenance of slavery and Southern interests in the national policies. In this respect the Mobile *Advertiser* of January, 1830, spoke with perfect truth when it said: "The South wishes to have Texas ad-

*F. Bulnes, "Las Grandes Mentiras de nuestra Historia," p. 145.

MEXICAN TYPES
Federal Soldiers. A native girl of pure Indian (Aztec or Maya) blood.
A peon — his complete wardrobe

Copyright by Underwood & Underwood, N. Y.

CHAPULTEPEC CASTLE

Dining-room in the castle, where President Diaz entertained so lavishly, where Madero reigned briefly and uneasily, and where Huerta stands fighting with his back against the wall

Copyright by Underwood & Underwood, N. Y.

MEXICO PENITENTIARY

Tier in the Mexico City Penitentiary where President Huerta kept his 150 rebellious deputies imprisoned. It probably has entertained as many gentlemen for purely political reasons as any prison in the world.

THE TEXAS WAR

mitted to the Union for two reasons, and the first of these is to equalize the South with the North."

That the Texan revolt was not in the slightest degree a matter of Texan initiation, but the result, under the guidance of the Church in Mexico, of the intrigues of the Planting interests of the South, is demonstrated beyond a doubt when it is considered that in 1828, seven years before the question of revolt was even mooted among the Texans themselves, the following questions were put to Mississippi candidates to the national Congress: "What is your opinion of the acquisition of Texas? Should it be acquired by force or treaty? If Texas decided to secede, should we give the secession military assistance? What would be the effect of the acquisition of Texas upon the Planting interests?" (J. William, "A Review of the Mexican War," p. 17.)

Between the years 1830 and 1835 the intrigues of the plotting factions, Mexican Clerical and Southern Democratic, were vigorously prosecuted. The power of religious fanaticism to sway the good judgment of the people was well recognized by both parties; and if the cheap politicians and prostituted press performed yeoman service in the rape of Texas, no less valuable were the efforts of the Catholic priests on the one side and the Protestant clergy on the other. Indeed, Conclin (p. 105) rates the religious agitation as more effective than the political: "Great as was the result of the political agitation, the effect of the working of the agents amongst the influential and wealthy churches and religious societies produced even greater results by the pitiful pleadings that Mexico was oppressing the conscience of the colonists."

In 1835 matters reached the climax. In that year the lawfully elected governor of the State of Coahuila and Texas, Agustin Viesca Fonseca, was forcibly dispossessed of his office by General Santa Ana. The state legislature at once supported the Governor, and passed a measure in April, 1835, empowering him to organize bodies of civicos, to sustain by force the civil sovereignty. In view of the threatened advance of the army under Santa Ana, Viesca Fonseca deemed it wise to move the capital from Monclova to Bejar. While effecting the change he was arrested, together with the legislature, by General Cos, who immediately assumed the commandership of the state, and established military rule.

This outrage on the civil prerogative was the immediate cause which led the patriotic Julian Travis to start his revolt with a small body of men, none of them, however, colonists. Desperately as the honour of the state had been wounded the Peace party were still loath to countenance open revolt. In their hopeless efforts to maintain peace they not only publicly repudiated the uprising under Travis, *but offered to arrest him and deliver him to the Mexican authorities.*

Under such circumstances it would have been an easy matter for Santa Ana to have suppressed the insurrection with leniency. That, however, was the last thing contemplated by the Clerical party. Had they not laboured zealously for five years to achieve just this result, and were they now to miss the opportunity of fanning the promising spark of revolt into a respectable and serviceable flame?

Accordingly Santa Ana's Minister of War, General Tornel, issued drastic orders on August 1, 1835, to arrest and punish with the extremity of the law all the leaders of the insurrectionary movement, Lorenzo Zavala, José Maria Calvajal, and Juan Zambrano, together with the colonial leader, Travis, and the agents of Andrew Jackson, Houston, Thompson, Williamson, Baker, and William Moore, and all others connected with the revolt. The order, of course, was made simply to fan the flames. The actual force dispatched by General Santa Ana to carry out the threat and quench the activities of the revolutionists consisted of *two hundred and fifty men!*

A large and competent force, not fully understanding what was required of it, might have taken the situation seriously, and ended the revolt in a few days. Such a thing would have been

THE TEXAS WAR

disastrous to the plans of the conspirators. The comedy had to be played to more purpose than this.

Accordingly, the rebels, urged on by the American agents, were permitted to gain strength and organize their forces. A company of Mexicans, numbering four hundred men, under Juan N. Seguin, were already in the field, and by the 19th of October Austin had in his command an additional force of six hundred men. A few days later two filibustering companies, called the "Grays," arrived on the scene from New Orleans, followed immediately by a similar company from Mississippi.

Then the mockery of war began. Neither the hired gunmen on the one side, more interested in pay and loot than in fighting, nor the underfed and brutalized Mexican regulars on the other side, had much heart in the campaign, and desertions on both sides were of daily occurrence. It must be remembered that the vast majority of the colonists held entirely aloof from the fray. Even at the most acute stage of the revolt the colonial contingent scarcely mustered 10 per cent. of the revolutionary forces. Indeed, but for the hired gunmen from the United States there could scarcely have been enough opposition to the Mexican forces to create even the illusion of a war. In the siege of Bejar, Austin lost six hundred of his twelve hundred men by desertions in a few days, and, after the town had fallen, such colonists as had remained in the ranks to the end returned to their occupations. Before disbanding, however, they organized a legislative committee to maintain the insurrection in favour of — not Independence, not annexation to the United States, *but in favour of the Mexican Constitution of 1824!*

At this stage of affairs General Santa Ana arrived in Texas to take personal charge of the Mexican forces. His appearance infused fresh life into the farce that of late had fallen into imminent danger of being hissed off the boards, and the colonists were at last goaded out of their determined efforts to keep the peace into something like serious revolt.

The first notable engagement of the new campaign was the

insane massacre of Alamo. In this action Captain Travis with eighty-three men was compelled to give battle to Santa Ana with an overwhelming force of fourteen hundred men. History has no record of a more cynically initiated or more bloodily executed encounter than this action of Alamo. Before the day closed every rebel had perished, while the Mexicans had lost seventy killed and four hundred wounded. The one bright spot in this day of infamy was the gallant courage of the patriotic but deluded and doomed Travis.

Much wretched jingoism is taught in American schools in regard to this battle of Alamo in pursuance of a policy on the part of the educational authorities as narrow as it is vicious. The valour of the combatants on both sides is incontestable. If the American volunteers exhibited a fortitude worthy of a better cause, a fortitude no less admirable was exhibited by the Mexicans, for it is an army of the first class that will lose a third part of its strength in an assault.

The only comment possible on this incident is not one of credit or discredit to either faction, but one of profound pity for all the deluded men, American and Mexican, who in their ignorance fell a prey to the machinations of the planting interests of the South, and the intrigues of the Mexican Church.

After the massacre of the Alamo, Santa Ana, obeying instructions of the Church, entered upon a ruthless policy of extermination, and hundreds of prisoners and wounded were mercilessly murdered at his orders. It was not that the necessities of the case demanded the "iron hand," nor that Santa Ana himself had any particular antipathy to Americans — at least if he had, he was careful to conceal it on the occasion when he was fêted by Andrew Jackson — but because it was necessary to arouse enough opposition to sustain the illusion of an international war for the embarrassment of the Mexican Liberals.

Finally, in a cowardly and clumsy encounter with the rebels, Santa Ana was made prisoner and compelled to sign a treaty recognizing Texan independence in return for his life.

CHAPTER X

CLERICAL PRÆTORIANISM AND THE SUPREME CONSERVATIVE POWER

"BY THESE presents be it known to all the army that on the 21st of April, 1836, the President of the Republic, General Don Antonio Lopez Santa Ana was made prisoner on the battlefield while fighting to save his country. Be it further known that while His Excellency the President of the Republic remains in prison, the flags and pennants of the army will be in mourning with crêpe, and that the national flag will be flown at half-mast in the fortress, in the barracks and in the navy." In these words the Clerical government of Mexico wrote the epitaph of the Texas disaster. The colony was lost to Mexico forever. The real cause of its loss we believe we have established. "The truth is that we owe the loss of Texas to the militarism imposed upon the colonists by Lucas Alaman, a leader loyal and faithful to the Clerical interests, and a man of the greatest credit with the Church — a militarism personified in the vices, ambition, corruption, and degradation of its General, Santa Ana." (Francisco Bulnes, "Las Grandes Mentiras de Nuestra Historia," p. 651.)

The affair had served its purpose, and the Clerical party in power promptly relegated it to the limbo of forgotten things. Not so the people, however. They had been worked up to a high state of war-fever by the persistent harangues of the priests, and when the War Minister, José Maria Tornel, refused to send a regular army, they themselves organized a body of 8,000 volunteers for the purpose of retrieving the lost territory and wiping out the recent reverses to Mexican arms. Tornel permitted the volunteers to reach the northern deserts, and then in spite of the war-fund freely contributed by the citizens for their support, refused to send them either food supplies or ammunition, and they were compelled to return amid severe suffering, having accomplished nothing.

On the 29th of December, 1836, the Clerical party in Congress took advantage of the national confusion to proclaim a constitution establishing the central system of government. The constitution likewise created a Supreme Conservative Power, consisting of five men with authority to veto or censor any law passed by Congress, or any measure adopted by the national executive, or the governors of the states, or any decision of the courts, or any election of representatives. It likewise had power to dissolve Congress or impeach the President of the Republic or any other government official; while any disobedience to its orders, dispositions, or declarations was to be treated as a crime of high treason. The constitution further provided that no one possessing an income of less than thirty thousand dollars a year could be eligible to the Supreme Conservative Power, that the clerical and military fueros be reestablished, that state governors be appointed by the President of the Republic for a term of eight years, and that the home rule of municipalities be superseded by the appointment of municipal political chiefs with executive powers, and finally that the state legislatures be wholly suppressed. To the establishment of this iniquitous constitution the Liberal party, demoralized by the recent war with Texas, was unable to offer any effective resistance.

Meanwhile Santa Ana had gone to Washington where he was royally entertained by Andrew Jackson. When at length his visit terminated and he returned to Mexico on board the American warship *Pincer*, courteously placed at his disposal by the United States President, it was with that perfect understanding of the mutual interests of the Church in Mexico, and the Southern planters in the United States that enabled him afterward in the war with the United States to play — with President Polk as partner, and with the bodies of men as pawns — a game of chess which surpassed the Texan affair as the work of masters surpasses the work of amateurs.

Conditions in Mexico at this time were at their darkest. Special taxation had been decreed by Congress, from which, of course, Church property was entirely exempted; while nearly all the coin in the country was the debased product of counterfeit mints owned and operated by officers of the army. Protected by the military fueros, the counterfeiters wrecked the public credit with impunity, and with scarcely an effort at concealment.

On the 17th of April, 1837, Anastasio Bustamante, that faithful watch-dog of the Clerical interests, was elected to the Presidency of the Republic — *appointed* to the Presidency of the Republic would more accurately state the case, for the exercise of the franchise was so hedged about under the central system that all trace of popular will in the election of representatives was destroyed. Meanwhile Santa Ana remained quietly in the background, but close at hand to be ready for any emergency requiring his services.

By this time the Texan war-fever was beginning to abate, and the people had reached the stage of hesitating between supporting the government, and attacking it with a view to reëstablishing the federal system. Indeed, one or two sporadic rebellions of no great importance broke out in the states of San Luis Potosi and Nuevo Mexico, but they lacked general support and were readily suppressed. With the passing of another year, however, the old impulse of the people toward freedom began to gather way, and when on the 18th of February, 1838, the great Liberal and ex-Vice-President, Valentin Gomez Farias, returned from exile to Mexico City, he was given a tremendous welcome by the masses. The Clerical party was not slow to recognize the signs of the times, and unable to revive much interest among the people in the Texan affair, decided to resuscitate a former plot conceived by Lucas Alaman during the first presidency of Bustamante for embroiling the nation in a war with France. In accordance with this policy some mild and entirely justifiable claims made by France against Mexico were repulsed with the utmost insolence by Bustamante, and on the 28th of March, 1838, the French Minister, Monsieur Le Baron Deffaudis, found himself with no recourse but to deliver his ultimatum to the Mexican Government. In speaking of this incident, Zamacois, a Catholic, a conservative, and an ardent defender of Bustamante, says: "The Mexican Government had no right to procrastinate on a matter so readily settled when France was so easily satisfied." (Zamacois, Vol. 12, p. 129.) Congress fully supported the action of Bustamante, and in a great outburst of patriotism, calling upon the Mexican people to fly to arms in the defence of the national honour, proclaimed a war with France.

In order to arouse the French, whose genuine desire for a peaceable settlement was well known to the government, all French citizens were ordered out of the country. At the same time Bustamante, in order to inflame the fighting spirit of the people, ordered the remains of Iturbide to be disinterred and brought from the State of Tamaulipas and paraded through the streets of Mexico City amid every conceivable martial display. The inevitable masses were sung, and priestly harangues delivered, and the crumbling bones of the one time "emperor," were escorted to the cathedral through streets lined with troops and decorated with lavish splendour. Enormous sums were expended in this farce, while on the west coast of the country an earthquake had left thousands of families destitute and starving.

However the populace of the capital — always the ready prey of any Clerical ruse — might be dazzled by these childish tactics, they had little enough effect on the sturdy federalists of the old revolutionary State of Tamaulipas. Undaunted by the threat of French invasion, these men rose in revolt, seized the port of Tampico and endeavoured to control the entire state. Meanwhile French warships were hovering off Vera Cruz, and the French diplomatic representatives who accompanied the naval demonstration were straining every effort to effect an amicable settlement of outstanding disputes with the Mexican Government. Indeed, Admiral Baudin as special envoy of King Louis Philippe went so far as to request the Mexican Government to appoint a committee to meet him, to the end that an invasion of the country be avoided and the contention of the two nations be settled in peace. This committee was duly appointed, but with rigid injunctions to refuse every overture made by the French. At the same time Bustamante issued a theatrical manifesto to the Mexican nation in which he proclaimed that he was determined to defend even at the sacrifice of his own life the honour of the nation and the rights of the Republic against any foreign nation which should dare to besmirch the clear lustre of the fatherland; that his determination was shared by the Supreme Conservative Power and by the national Congress; that the government had omitted no effort to arrive at a decorous and honourable agreement, but that in view of the haughty attitude of the French, who showed themselves unwilling to withdraw their insolent demands, he had no hesitation in choosing the hazards of war to dishonourable peace. To this, Admiral Bazoche, commodore of the French navy in the Gulf of Mexico, retorted by a public declaration to the effect that all diplomatic relations between France and Mexico had ceased, that Mexican ports were already in blockade, and that the war had been uselessly invited, and would be sustained, not against the Mexican people as such but against their corrupt administration.

Immediately following this declaration the war began with an attack by the French forces on the port of Vera Cruz. At the critical moment Santa Ana, with his genius for the spectacular, appeared on the scene to take charge of the Mexican army, and to restore the splendour of his prestige as the saviour of the nation. The encounter that ensued was the sheerest farce. The only serious casualty was the loss of a leg by Santa Ana. With admirable aplomb, and no whit dismayed, he managed to make good capital out of the incident by posing now as the blood-stained martyr in the cause of liberty. At this juncture in affairs Mr. Pakenham, the British Ambassador to Mexico, used his influence to dissuade Bustamante from further opposition to the French demands. Accordingly a simple agreement was drawn up which the French consented to accept, and the war ended. Quite as strong, probably, as the arguments of Mr. Pakenham in influencing the Mexican Government to abandon their military flirtation with France, was the urgent necessity of suppressing the insurgents of Tampico, who unseduced by the siren-calls of Bustamante to come to their country's aid, were, on the contrary, using every effort to arouse the other states to join them against the government. Santa Ana, temporarily disabled, was unable to proceed against the rebels in person, and when Bustamante asked permission of Congress to lead the army himself, his request was granted, and Santa Ana was appointed President in his place.

The exchange was highly satisfactory to the Church, for Santa Ana was a much more energetic and facile man of affairs than the stupid and often wilful Bustamante. The first act of the new President was to arrest and throw into jail every newspaper man of the Liberal party, and every one suspected of holding Liberal opinions. This measure was immediately followed by the suppression of the Liberal Journals, *El Cosmopolita*, *El Restaurador*, and *El Voto Nacional*, and the destruction of their plants.

Finally Gomez Farias was arrested and thrown into prison. Mexico was again under the iron heel.

The necessity of keeping the attention of the people from domestic affairs compelled the Clerical party once more to resuscitate the idea of a war with the United States for the recovery of Texas; and the Catholic press and cheap politicians

CLERICAL PRÆTORIANISM

vied with each other in their efforts to inflame public sentiment in favour of the plan. The ruse succeeded immediately in so far as it gave the government sufficient strength to suppress the revolutionary movement for federalism in Tampico and Puebla. Later it was to find perfect fulfilment in a long and bloody campaign.

Santa Ana, having suppressed the insurrection, again showed his theatrical genius by resigning while the plaudits and acclaim of the populace still resounded. His place was filled in the interim by Nicolas Bravo, who resigned a few days later when Bustamante returned to resume his presidential duties.

At this period Mexico's condition was appalling. Revolt and war, coupled with a fatuous disregard for the economic welfare of the country on the part of those in power, had reduced the nation to utter exhaustion. The Church alone still remained prosperous. She was exempt from taxation, paid nothing for the support of the government, and the dire poverty of the people enabled her to exploit them with the lowest possible compensation.

Her selfishness and short-sightedness, indeed, went so far as to let the Government and Army, on which her own salvation depended, flounder on the verge of ruin for lack of sufficient funds. Such avarice would have provoked a prompt revenge had it not been that neither the official nor the military caste could have carried on their own particular depredations without the moral support and sanction of the Church. The Church and Army, moreover, were bound together by the common interest of maintaining the fueros, so necessary to their welfare, against the onslaughts of the Liberals.

Needless to remark, we can find in the Church no trace of common humanity — much less of that sublime humanity which alone is religion — nor in the Army any trace of patriotism. Both were merely predatory organizations for the purpose of appropriating the wealth produced by the toil of the common people.

The policy of the Church as the largest land-owner in the country was to exploit the wretched peons to the limit of human endurance in return for a pitiful pittance which mostly returned to her own coffers in Church taxes, forced donations, or payments for prayers and masses.

The generals and high officers of the Army, on the other hand, under cover of the fueros, supplemented their handsome salaries by operating counterfeit mints, gambling hells, and gaudy brothels; while the lesser officers contented themselves with mere blackmailing and open highway robbery. Occasionally the Army went into business for itself on a large scale and instituted farcical revolts and uprisings for purposes of loot and rape, submitting itself, when satisfied, to the government, and invariably receiving pardon and reinstatement. In some of these uprisings the rapacious military even went so far as to pose as federalists, and on one of these occasions, the 19th of March, 1840, they besieged President Bustamante in the national palace for two days and looted the entire city, only consenting to abandon their frolic at the urgent entreaties of the archbishop.

As for the common people of the time, they might be divided into three sections: those who, having succumbed to the malevolent hypnotism of the Church, had lost their spiritual birthright and had come really to accept the debauching doctrines of the holiness of poverty and obedience; others who believed in neither but were cowed into submission; and still others who repudiated the Church and all her works, and, conscious of the bitter wrongs of their class, struggled to recover for themselves their lost position as human beings.

Of these latter some were still duped by the persistent alarms of foreign war into delaying their activities, while a small but courageous minority refused to care whether the fatherland were invaded or not, and kept up a ceaseless struggle for liberty.

Since the Church had plotted the Texas revolt all her plans had been successful in confirming her power; but she had by no means reached the summit of her ambitions. She now proposed

CLERICAL PRÆTORIANISM

to embroil the nation in a war with the United States, and to take advantage of the national distraction in order to establish a monarchy by divine right. Such a monarchy, coupled with the central system of government, would give her again an unlimited despotism such as she had enjoyed under the colonial régime. The general misery and wretchedness of the country offered a good field for the agitation in favour of a monarchy. Moreover, President Bustamante, the government officials, the aristocracy of big land-owners, and the blackmailing, gambling, counterfeiting military were fully in favour of a plan which bid fair to perpetuate and consolidate their power.

Accordingly on the 25th of August, 1840, José Maria Gutierrez Estrada, a prominent Clerical politician and a close partner of Lucas Alaman, opened the campaign by publishing an open letter, suggesting to the government and the people the establishment of a monarchy.

"The Republic is death-struck by its own apostles," so ran the letter; "it is dying of inanition. We have seen the vitality of its moral life exhausted in sterile and cruel efforts. None will admit more readily than I the advantage reaped by other countries from a republican form of government, but no one will lament more sincerely than I that Mexico at the present time is not in a position to enjoy these privileges. Judging by her recent unhappy experiences with this form of government, we are compelled to believe that the time has come when this country should make the effort to found a real monarchy in the person of a foreign prince."

This letter, written to test the public sentiment of the time, created a storm of wrath and indignation throughout the country, and even some of the generals of the army felt themselves compelled to protest as republicans. Among these protestants was Juan Nepomuceno Almonte. Twenty-four years later this very man, in company with the Gutierrez Estrada mentioned above, took a prominent part in the plot which made Maximilian the Emperor of Mexico. Immediately after the publication of this letter Gutierrez Estrada left Mexico for Europe for the purpose of interesting one of the European royal families in this matter of founding a monarchy.

By the year 1841 the long-continued Clerical and military rule had crushed the people to such depths of poverty that even Bustamante had to take cognizance of the matter in his message to Congress, for the government itself was hard pressed by the general financial exhaustion. In the same message to Congress, Bustamante not only claimed that the resources of the common people were utterly depleted, but also that it would be necessary to look elsewhere for funds, and went so far as to complain of the importunate interference of the Supreme Conservative Power in the administration of the country, protesting that it hampered every act of the Executive, of Congress, and of the Courts.

It was a bold step for a President, spawned by the Church and a cuartelazo, to criticise the Supreme Conservative Power; for it was the purpose of the Church which created this oligarchy of five men presently to reduce its number to one man with absolute dictatorial powers, and later to transform this dictatorship into an unlimited monarchy. This undiplomatic utterance of Bustamante, coupled with several other blunders (one of which was the lenient treatment of a French citizen suspected of selling the works of Voltaire), convinced the Church that her tool had outlived the period of his usefulness.

Accordingly the inevitable cuartelazo was again invoked, and Santa Ana, always at hand for emergencies of this nature, was given charge of it. As a preliminary step the Church, through the instrumentality of Juan Mariano Paredes Arrillaga, one of her many myrmidons, issued a manifesto in which it was proclaimed:

I. An Extraordinary National Congress will be elected for the sole purpose of reframing the constitution.

II. The Supreme Conservative Power will elect a man possessing its confidence as chief executive with dictatorial powers,

CLERICAL PRÆTORIANISM

who will give an account of his acts to the first Constitutional Congress.

III. The present Congress will convene to declare that the present President is unfitted for his high office, and the Supreme Conservative Power will enforce the decree.

IV. The chief executive will have the power to decide the date of the meeting of the Extraordinary Congress, the method of the election, and the time of its duration.

The manifesto concluded with a series of accusations against the government and a declaration of the dismissal of President Bustamante. It is interesting to note that it was President Bustamante who in 1820, when he was Vice-President, had started the cuartelazo which overthrew the great President Guerrero on the plea that he was insane and unfitted for his position.

The military uprising began in the State of Vera Cruz, where Santa Ana was in command of a large force; and similar uprisings immediately followed in Mexico City and in all parts of the country. When Bustamante found himself deserted he promptly appealed to the Liberal party in the fatuous belief that the men whom he had persecuted for years would now support him. His overtures were repulsed with scorn. Hysterical at the idea of losing power, he then played completely into the hands of the Church by proclaiming the federal system, with himself, of course, as federal President.

"This sudden proclamation of the federal system had no connection whatever," says the historian, "with any one of the Liberal leaders, and none who was a Liberal would give his name to this performance." ("México á través de los Siglos," Vol. 14, p. 47.) The Liberal party clearly foresaw that the day would come when the Supreme Conservative Power would have so utterly discredited itself in the eyes of the people that there would be a unanimous and spontaneous revolt against it. That moment, they recognized, would be the political opportunity of the Liberal party, and they were too good tacticians to spoil such an excellent chance by any premature action at the bidding of such a mere adventurer as Bustamante.

Bustamante's hopeless *faux pas* was received with joy by the Clerical party, and Santa Ana immediately addressed a note to the Supreme Conservative Power couched in the following terms: "Sir: The federal constitution having been proclaimed by General Bustamante, or under his auspices, he has thereby become a rebel and bereft himself of the power which, according to the constitution of 1836, had been placed in his hands. Consequently the Supreme Conservative Power is in a position to dictate the measures which the constitution accords it in order to dismiss him from power, and I, myself, and my army are ready to give to you all the protection which you may require." In this note we see that Santa Ana makes no effort to conceal his intention of becoming dictator, and his cool assurance in offering to protect the Supreme Conservative Power shows how confident he was in his ability to impose his will on Clericals and Liberals alike.

Bustamante, after making a fatuous resistance in the national palace, was overpowered by Santa Ana and exiled to Europe, while the victor was overwhelmed with messages of congratulation from the chapter of every cathedral in Mexico. It is significant of the depths to which the Church had fallen that she found herself no longer able to command, but was compelled to bribe and beg the support of one military adventurer after another. The first act of the new dictator was to organize a large army, and to this end he ordered tens of thousands of peons to be impressed, while for the equipment and maintenance of this vast host the Church authorized him to sell those of her estates whose revenues were used for the support of the missions in California.

On the 5th of March, 1842, the elections for Congress were held; and in spite of the fact that the franchise under the central system was so limited and beset with restrictions as to render

CLERICAL PRÆTORIANISM

any expression of the popular will almost impossible, when Congress convened it proved to be strongly Liberal.

In its first deliberations it proceeded to pass measures depriving Santa Ana of his dictatorial powers, and establishing the freedom of religious belief and of the press. Santa Ana found himself out-generalled on the political field, and resorted to his usual tactics of asking for leave of absence for the purpose of plotting another cuartelazo. Nicholas Bravo was appointed as his substitute. The Church, realizing that nothing advantageous to her own interests was to be expected of Congress, supported Santa Ana, and the War Secretary himself, José Maria Tornel, addressed secret orders to all the garrisons of the country to prepare for another uprising.

On the 18th of September the plot came to a head. Congress was prorogued by military force, and Santa Ana returned to Mexico City to complete his plans for the future. Money was the prime need of the hour. The demoralization of the government and the terrible poverty of the people made it impossible to replenish the exchequer by the usual taxation, and the Church and aristocracy were compelled to supply the funds required.

Having reorganized the army, Santa Ana again took leave of absence in order to conspire more freely with the Church, and on the 6th of October, 1843, General Valentin Canalizo, an old officer of the royal army, was appointed as his substitute.

At this time another calamity fell upon the impoverished and oppressed people. The savage Indian tribes of the north, in a series of raids, swept down on the states of Sonora, Chihuahua, Coahuila, Nuevo Leon, and San Luis Potosi, leaving behind them a terrible trail of smoking ruins and slaughtered villagers. The Clerical government required the services of the army for its own intrigues, and refused to send aid to the stricken people, who were compelled to defend themselves as well as they might.

Meanwhile the upkeep of the army was beginning to prove a source of great annoyance to the Church and Aristocracy.

Although recognizing the necessity of maintaining a large and well-equipped force for the furtherance of their interests, they could not reconcile themselves to the expense it entailed, an expense hitherto borne by the common people. It mattered not that the common people had been already reduced to the depths of poverty, and were unable to contribute another centavo, nor that the army was used, as indeed every army since class rule began has been used, purely to promote the interests of the ruling class and to oppress the toilers, they still found Santa Ana's repeated requests for money highly provoking, the more so because it was well known that he embezzled the larger part of these funds for his own private use.

The new dictator thus soon fell into deep disfavour with Clericals and Liberals alike. The time, however, had arrived for the presidential elections. Santa Ana had long been scheduled for this position, and it was too late to elect another man. Accordingly on the 6th of January, 1844, Santa Ana was duly elected President by the House of Representatives, which by this time had been permitted to reconvene. The pending trouble with the United States kept the Liberals from indulging in armed action, but they were quick to seize any advantage which the situation offered for gaining ground in the political field; and on this occasion they readily coöperated with the disgruntled Clericals against the hated Santa Ana.

At first conditions seemed favourable to the new administration. The United States had recently annexed Texas, and the United States warships were anchored in the harbour of Vera Cruz. Santa Ana at once took advantage of the situation to ask Congress to authorize him to raise a loan of four million dollars to fit out an expedition for the recovery of Texas. Congress, however, refused; the Clericals, because they feared the money would be taken from their own coffers, and would most probably be used by Santa Ana himself; the Liberals, because they were utterly opposed to Santa Ana and to a war with the United States.

CLERICAL PRÆTORIANISM

When Santa Ana realized that his demands were not to be granted, he asked for his customary leave of absence to plot with his confederates another forcible expulsion of Congress. As interim President in his place General José Joaquin Herrera was appointed during the temporary absence of Canalizo, the real appointee.

Now followed another period of confusion in which cuartelazo followed cuartelazo. Finally, Santa Ana was crushingly defeated by the Clerical forces and exiled on parole. On his way to Vera Cruz, however, he endeavored to make another stand. Again he was subdued, and after much begging was permitted, in June, 1845, to leave the country for Havana.

The anarchy which the Church and Army imposed upon Mexico at this time is not a matter for surprise. Both organizations wherever and whenever they exist are by virtue of their nature incapable of assimilating or acting upon any idea of social order or development. In this instance, relieved by their cunning intrigues from effective opposition, they gave to the nation, for government, the cabal; for order, wild riot; for economic administration, the cuartelazo. This was the sum of their activities, and wherever given unrestricted sway the sum of their activities is invariably the same. If we read the history of the military rule in Rome when the Prætorian Guard was making and unmaking emperors at will, we shall discover a marked similarity between the conditions obtaining then and the conditions in Mexico during the middle of the last century.

The reader may well ask why the people endured this state of affairs — why they did not revolt? The answer lies in the fact that wherever the people have attained some stage of civilization and autonomy they would rather a thousand times suffer despotism than endanger their national integrity. The Church and Army were careful to keep the people in constant fear of war, for they well knew that in face of national danger effective domestic revolt was impossible.

The new President, General Joaquin Herrera, elected during

Santa Ana's last campaign, in spite of his clerical affiliations, proved to be a man of sane, patriotic, and humane ideas. Realizing that Mexico in her depleted condition was utterly incapable of contesting the United States' claim to Texas, and that the bogey of war so carefully fostered by the Clerical party was demoralizing the national life, he readily acceded to the proposals of the American Minister and officially recognized the annexation of Texas.

This was a vital blow at the cherished schemes of the Church. The menace of war gone, the people would turn with renewed energy to the prosecution of the domestic reforms so urgently demanded by the appalling conditions of the time. Not for a moment could this be permitted, and the Church immediately began to plot the overthrow of Herrera, as she had plotted the overthrow of Bustamante and Santa Ana. Again the cuartelazo was invoked under the leadership of the same Paredes Arrillaga who had headed the uprisings against Bustamante and Santa Ana.

On the 14th of September, 1845, this pliant tool of the Clerical party raised a rebellion at San Luis Potosi, where he had been stationed with six thousand men for the ostensible purpose of protecting the frontier against the United States. In his proclamation to his troops he charged Herrera with treachery to the fatherland in acceding peaceably to the annexation of Texas, and in endeavouring to supersede the army by the organization of bodies of civicos, significantly adding that the necessities of the country required a complete change of institutions, and for that reason an extraordinary Congress would be elected *for the purpose of putting an end to a system of government which had proved entirely inadequate*. The conspiracy of the Church to force a monarchy upon the country had by this time thoroughly matured, and this final announcement of Paredes Arrillaga was the first practical step toward its realization.

Instead of continuing his march against the United States, Paredes Arrillaga returned to Mexico City at the head of his

CLERICAL PRÆTORIANISM

troops. Herrera, too sane and too well versed in the political methods of the time to offer a futile resistance, peaceably resigned; and in a caucus of army generals and a few self-appointed delegates from the various states, under the chairmanship of Manuel Posada, Archbishop of Mexico, Paredes Arrillaga was appointed President of the Republic in his place. The caucus also proceeded to call for an election of representatives to an extraordinary Congress to be held within the next four months for the purpose of entirely changing the political institutions of the country.

The Liberal press, which had enjoyed a measure of liberty under the all too brief régime of Herrera, was now utterly suppressed by the new President; and it became evident to the Liberal leaders that the Church was preparing with the utmost energy to manacle the nation and deliver it up blindfold to the tender mercies of a despotic hereditary monarchy.

Meanwhile the war cloud, which had bid fair to dissipate under Herrera's peaceable administration, began to gather again in the north. Squadrons of United States battleships hovered off Mazatlan and Acapulco, while news began to arrive at the capital that Monterey and San Francisco in California were already occupied by United States troops.

The Church was not slow to take advantage of the agitation which this news caused throughout the country to push forward her plans for the establishment of a monarchy. On the 24th of January of the same year, 1845, there appeared the first issue of the Clerical official organ, *El Tiempo*, under the editorship of Lucas Alaman, and several other prominent ecclesiastics. In the third issue of this paper the caucus of self-appointed delegates and military chieftains, under the Archbishop of Mexico, Manuel Posada, published a call to the people for the election of an extraordinary Congress for the purpose of framing a monarchical constitution for Mexico.

In order to qualify as a representative to this Congress it was necessary for a candidate to be either a land-owner, a merchant, or a manufacturer, paying taxes of at least one hundred and fifty dollars a year. In addition to these regulations, aimed at the utter disfranchisement of the common people, the right to vote was denied to all salaried employees and wage-earners. To the soldiers, however, was given the right to vote without restriction of any kind.

Step by step with the Clerical conspiracy for the establishment of a monarchy in Mexico there had advanced another conspiracy germane to the first, the conspiracy for war with the United States. Only amid the carnage and confusion of a foreign invasion could the Church feel at all safe in the prosecution of plans so bitterly distasteful to the great mass of the people. The invocation of war had been in this instance an easy matter; for if the ruling class in Mexico desired war for their own salvation, no less did the slave-holding ruling class of the Southern States desire a war for the purpose of diverting the attention of the North from the now vexed question of abolition. This declaration, as we have seen, was published on the 19th of February, 1846, and in the next month, on the 6th of March, General Taylor received orders at Corpus Christi to march on Mexico, and on the 25th of April following, the first engagement of the war took place.

CHAPTER XI

THE WAR WITH THE UNITED STATES

THE war with the United States, like the war with Texas, was a preconcerted and predetermined affair on the part of the ruling classes of both of the nations involved. The popular furor aroused by these classes should not be allowed to obscure the real origin of the war. All that we have said in regard to the causes of the war with Texas remains equally true for the causes of the war with the United States.

Indeed the war with the United States can only be correctly regarded as a prolongation and enlargement of the war with Texas. It was but a mightier effort on the part of the planters of the South to gain fresh slave-holding territory in order to add to their representation in Congress, and to divert the attention of the North from abolition; it was only a mightier effort on the part of the Church in Mexico to divert the attention of the people from the question of domestic reform, and to hold in check the eternally impending insurgency by causing the wholesale massacre of the more devoted and patriotic spirits among the peons.

For many years, and more particularly since the Texan affair, the ruling classes of both nations had tried by every means to embitter, prejudice, and inflame the minds of their respective peoples against each other. While the Catholic priests and politicians of Mexico held up to their audiences the most appalling picture of the savage, rapacious, lustful, and heretical American, in the United States the politicians, Protestant clergy, and newspaper men hired by the Southern slavocracy held up to their audiences the no less appalling and ludicrous picture of the wild-eyed, treacherous, cruel, and idolatrous Mexican. It took years of this persistent psychological debauchery to stamp these pictures on the peaceable and right-minded people of both countries. But the work was well done, and to this day the ignorant American has just this view of the Mexican, and the ignorant Mexican has just this view of the American.

The causes of the war with the United States, as we have said, were essentially the same as the causes of the war with Texas, but since 1836 a new factor had arisen in the policies of the Church in Mexico which greatly added to her desire for war — her determination to establish a monarchy. She foresaw clearly that a war with the United States would be disastrous, bloody, devastating; not that, on level terms, the Mexican Roland was unequal to the American Oliver, but because the Mexican generals under her instructions *would see to it that the terms should not be level*. She foresaw that after the war the people, demoralized, exhausted, and humiliated, would be in no position to oppose her swift, determined action, and a monarchy could be established and intrenched — the lavish guardian of her policies and her interests — before concerted action on the part of the people became possible. It cannot be too clearly emphasized that in this war with the United States the Church was the confederate of the South. She not only did not wish to win, but desired to see the nation drained of its last drop of patriot blood. To that end her generals yielded up strategic points without a shot, led vast armies of gallant peons into waterless wildernesses and left them there to perish of thirst, removed arms and destroyed ammunition, and played into the enemy's hands in every conceivable way. The only effective resistance offered to the United States troops in Mexico was made by the volunteers and companies of guerillas operating independently of the military chiefs.

Subsequent to the Texan war the Democrats of the South, at that time in control of the national policies of the United States, immediately instituted a campaign of annoyance and insolence against Mexico in the hope of goading her into some act of open aggression. They realized that, in view of the enormous development of the North, the acquisition of Texas alone would be insufficient to secure their continued political dominance, and they were determined upon a war of aggression against Mexico for the seizure not merely of Texas, but of the whole territory of the Rio Grande del Norte, now known as Colorado, Utah, and New Mexico. At the same time they recognized that the great body of the American people were opposed to an armed invasion of the sister Republic without just and sufficient cause.

Such cause would soon have been forthcoming had the Clerical party constituted the majority of the Mexican nation. As a matter of fact, they were a small, if dominant, minority, and it was necessary to arouse the active aggression of the whole people before a war could be at all possible. In accordance with this policy General Gaines of the American army invaded Texas and occupied Nacogdoches. When the Mexican minister at Washington entered a protest against this infringement of international law he was not vouchsafed even the courtesy of a reply, and found himself forced to withdraw. This open affront proving insufficient to precipitate the desired *casus belli*, President Jackson proceeded to submit exaggerated and ridiculous claims to the Mexican Government for alleged offences against American citizens and property on the part of Mexican subjects. "The administration thought it necessary to raise a note of whining, concerning alleged offences against American citizens, coupled with the most exaggerated claims for compensation." (J. Williams, "Review of Causes," p. 24.) That these claims, some fifteen in number, were at least doubtful, is proved by the note accompanying them, addressed by Mr. Forsyth to Mr. Ellis, the United States Minister to Mexico at that time, which reads: "The State Department is not in possession of the proofs of all the circumstances of the injuries committed as alleged by the interested parties." The State

Department in pursuing this policy had, as we have said, a perfectly well-defined purpose. "It was only to a feeble nation, one whose hostility was courted for ulterior designs, that the administration would have hazarded such insolence." (J. Williams, "Review of Causes," p. 49.)

The claims mentioned were presented to the Mexican Government in the most offensive fashion with a scarcely veiled threat of armed invasion if they were not satisfied *within fourteen days!* The American Minister in Mexico City, Powhatan Ellis, to whom was assigned the task of goading Mexico into war, was admirably fitted for the purpose. His insulting behaviour added fresh point to the attitude of the United States Government and succeeded in arousing not only the anger of the official class but of the whole Mexican nation. "Mr. Forsyth of the State Department was a fit agent and Ellis was a fit instrument for the occasion; the latter was a Mississippian and a slave-holder. He wanted war, he wanted Texas, and he fulfilled his instructions to the letter." (Bancroft, "History of Mexico," Vol. 3, p. 309.)

And when Ellis notified President Jackson that only by the exercise of armed force could Mexico be compelled to honour the claims made against her by the United States, Jackson sent a message to Congress which ended with the following words: "I recommend that an act be passed authorizing reprisals, and the use of the naval force of the United States by the Executive against Mexico to enforce them, in the event of a refusal by the Mexican Government to come to an amicable adjustment of the matter in controversy upon another demand thereof made on board of one of our men-of-war in the Gulf of Mexico."

After the independence of Texas the planting interests of the South had decided, as we have said, upon the annexation not only of Texas but of as much additional territory as possible, in order to counterbalance the rising power of the North. According to a high authority, John Quincy Adams, "from the day

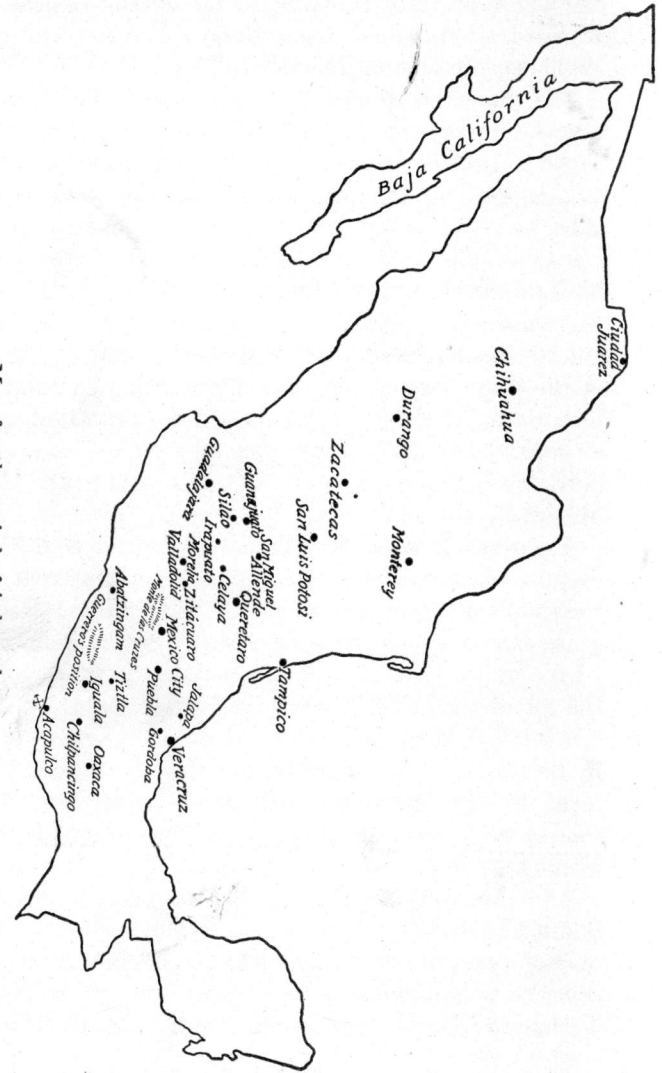

Map for the period of independence

THE WAR WITH THE UNITED STATES 143

of the battle of San Jacinto every movement of the administration of the Union would appear to have been made for the express purpose of breaking off the negotiations and precipitating a war with Mexico for the purpose of obtaining the concession of not only Texas but of the whole course of the Rio Grande del Norte. . . . Instructions on the 20th of July, 1836, from the Secretary of State to Mr. Ellis, almost immediately after the battle, were evidently premeditated to produce a rupture, and were but too faithfully carried into execution. . . . Ellis' letter of the 26th of October, 1836, to Mr. Monastario was the premonitory symptom, and no true-hearted citizen of this Union can read it, and the answer to it on the next day by Mr. Monastario, without blushing for his country."*

In view of the truculent attitude of the United States, and the eagerness of the Clerical party in Mexico for war, it might seem a matter of surprise that hostilities did not break out immediately. As a matter of fact it required eight years of persistent plotting and agitation on both sides to produce the war with Texas, and ten years more to produce the war with the United States. This alone would prove conclusively that these wars were not the spontaneous outcome of the antagonism of the two nations, but the product of the machinations of a numerically insignificant cabal. The truth is, history bears no record of a war instigated by the common people, or of a war fought by the ruling class. It is invariably the ruling class which instigates war in the furtherance of its own interests, and invariably the common people who do the fighting. To arouse an entire nation of peaceable and industrious folk to the point of bloodshed and slaughter is not the task of a moment. It is a task which often takes years of steady misrepresentation and calculated agitation. In spite of the bitter goadings of the United States and the wily intrigues of the Church in Mexico it required altogether eighteen years to produce the calamitous and disastrous war which came near to realizing the

*Quoted in Bancroft's History.

plans of the instigators, and near to hurling back the society of the larger half of North America into the slavery and despotism of the dark ages.

For the exercise of the United States policy of deliberate aggression against Mexico, the *post bellum* developments of the Texas affair provided innumerable opportunities. After the Texas colonists had acquired independence by the Treaty of 1836 they evinced no great eagerness to be admitted to the Union. That this indifference on their part caused considerable anxiety to the planting interests of the South was shown by a note of January 4, 1844, addressed by Mr. Upshur, President Tyler's Secretary of State, to the American agent in Texas, which reads: "Instead of being as we ought to be, the closest of friends, it is inevitable we shall become the bitterest foes. Without annexation Texas cannot maintain the institution of slavery ten years — probably not half that time."

The Texas colonists, however, presently found themselves compelled to change their minds and seek shelter within the Union when they discovered that the strong anti-slavery sentiments of the British Government were to be a constant menace to their liberty. "In August, 1843, Lord Brougham had made some remarks which were considered ominous to the slave interests, while as far back as 1829 Huskisson, in a speech before Parliament, denounced the manœuvres of Washington toward withdrawing Texas from the Mexican Union, and clearly stating that the British Government ought to maintain Mexico in possession of Texas." (*Revue des Deux Mondes*, March, 1840, p. 637.) The Texas colonists were, of course, well aware of the designs of the South upon them, and only consented to annexation when at last it seemed that no other course was feasible.

On the 23rd of August, 1843, the Mexican Government received the news that the United States was about to annex Texas, and notified the American envoy, for the information of his government, that such a step would be regarded as a *casus belli*. The next day the Secretary of State at Washington in his

THE WAR WITH THE UNITED STATES 145

reply warned the Mexican Government that the repetition of such a threat would be considered incompatible with the respect due to his government. When a little later Mr. Polk was nominated as candidate for President by the Democratic party to succeed President Tyler, it was solely on his open pledge to carry out the immediate annexation of Texas, and on his tacit pledge to invade Mexico. In the party convention the Democrats of the North had been out-generalled, and compelled to accept Polk's candidacy, and to submit to the demands of the Southern planting interests. In due time Polk was elected and took his stand at once as the champion of the South, not only in the matter of the annexation of Texas, but in the vigorous prosecution of the war with Mexico.

While these *post bellum* developments of the Texas affair had been providing the United States Government with an excellent lever for forcing the nation to accept an invasion of Mexico, the United States warships had been busily occupied in raiding Mexican ports, seizing Mexican war vessels, notably in the instance of the United States gunboat *La Natchez*, which confiscated the Mexican cutter *General Urrea* in the harbour of Matamoros. The claims entered by the Mexican Government against Washington for these acts of outrage were completely ignored, as also were its protests against the organization of filibustering expeditions in New Orleans for the invasion of Mexico. At the same time a United States warship landed troops at Monterey, California, before any declaration of war had been made.

"Texas secure, Mexico exasperated, and diplomatic relations at an end," says Bancroft, "everything was now favourable to secure the war determined upon, which would result in the acquisition of more valuable territory, including much-coveted California. Such a war, however, to be popular or even tolerated in the Northern States of the Union must be made to appear a deliberate act of Mexico. It would be a fine stroke to pretend to further negotiations and even feign a reconciliation, however hypocritical it might be. This failing, as care would be taken that it should fail, Mexico might easily be provoked to strike the first blow. It would then be, on the part of the United States, a war of defence, not of aggression, and the national conscience would be satisfied. This was the policy adopted by President Polk, and it met with the most infamous success." (Bancroft, "History of Mexico," Vol. 6, p. 340.)

At last the climax came, and the Clerical administration in Mexico was able to announce with scarcely concealed joy: "Mexicans! Mexican blood has been shed on Mexican soil by Yankee soldiers," while in the United States President Polk announced with no less satisfaction: "Americans! American blood has been shed upon American soil by Mexican soldiers." Both announcements were equally false, but they served their purpose, and war began.

The incident which led to the climax was the march of General Taylor from Corpus Christi to Point Isabel in Mexico with an army of thirty-five hundred men — a deliberate invasion of Mexican territory, although no war had been declared. When Taylor reached Arroyo, Colorado, he was notified by the citizens that his crossing the river could only be considered as a declaration of war. To this remonstrance he paid no heed, and, continuing his march to Point Isabel, he dispatched General Worth across the Rio Grande with a message to General Mejia, commander of the Mexican forces, expressing a desire for friendly relations.

In view of this unprovoked and unannounced invasion of Mexican territory on the part of General Taylor, such a message was an insult, and it was treated as such. By way of reply, on the 11th of April, 1846, General Ampudia, commanding officer of the Mexican forces on the frontier, ordered General Taylor to break camp within twenty-four hours and retire across the border to the left bank of the Nueces. The order was ignored, and thereupon hostilities began.

On the 25th of April the first blood of the campaign was shed

THE WAR WITH THE UNITED STATES 147

when a Mexican contingent ambuscaded a force of United States troops under Captain Thornton, killing several of them and taking the rest prisoners. As soon as the news of this affair reached Washington, President Polk sent a message to Congress affirming that American blood had been shed on American soil by Mexican soldiers, and requesting Congress to make the facts known, and to declare war on Mexico.

Completely blinded by the long campaign of misrepresentation, culminating in this last unscrupulous ruse, the people of the United States not only acquiesced in the war, but now were seized with a frenzy of blood-lust which must have appalled and terrified the men responsible for it, and yet, Mr. Bagby, Senator from Alabama, speaking on the floor of the Upper House, said: "The life of one citizen of the United States is of more value than the lives of a hundred thousand Mexican women and children." And his words may be taken as an accurate index of the spirit of the time.

The war began with the disastrous conflict of Matamoros, where over a thousand Mexican soldiers lost their lives. The survivors endeavoured to reach Monterey; the great majority of them, however, succumbed to thirst, starvation, and fatigue on the way. The United States Government took advantage of the victory to demand of Mexico the surrender of California and New Mexico, under pain of further armed castigation. The demand was indignantly refused, and the war proceeded.

On the 19th of September, 1846, at Monterey, after five days' battle, in which they exhausted all their ammunition, the Mexican forces again suffered defeat and the loss of a thousand men at the hands of the invading army. Meanwhile the savage Indians of the north renewed their raids into Mexico, carrying fire and slaughter into the very heart of the country.

Against the invading Indian as against the invading American the Mexican people had no protection other than they themselves could offer, for by this time the Clerical party was requisitioning all the troops of the country for another cuartelazo in order to rid itself of President Paredes. In spite of his bitter persecution of the Liberals, President Paredes had fallen into deep disfavour with the Church by requesting her to contribute a levy of two million pesos toward the necessary expenses of the war. Without considering that her own anarchy had impoverished the people beyond the possibility of taxation, and that by her exploitation and oppression she had absorbed almost the entire wealth of the country, the Church was greatly incensed by this request and immediately decreed the President's overthrow. The hero of no less than three antipresidential cuartelazos was now compelled to taste his own medicine.

On the 20th of May, 1846, the garrison of Guadalajara, headed by General Mariano Salas broke into revolt, and issued a proclamation in which it demanded that President Paredes be overthrown for conspiring to establish a monarchy, that Santa Ana be recalled, and, strange to tell, that the federal system be reëstablished. The hypocrisy of the charge against Paredes is obvious when we consider that this General Mariano Salas, who now waxed so indignant at the idea of a monarchy, was a few years later one of the most active conspirators in the plot which seated Maximilian on the throne of Mexico. The demand for the federal system was merely a lure thrown out to delude the populace and baffle the opposition of the Liberals.

The tortuous Clerical labyrinth of this period would defy analysis were it not for the clues of Greed and Fear. Armed with these clues we can soon penetrate the most secret recesses of involved Jesuitical chicanery. In this succession of political insanities, which appear to the casual observer inextricably involved and utterly unreasonable, we find at last only the determination of the Church never to relinquish her prey or face her foes.

A few days after the uprising in Guadalajara, the garrisons of Vera Cruz, Oaxaca, Mazatlan, and Mexico City followed suit. The unanimity of the revolt in such widely sundered

Copyright by Underwood & Underwood, N. Y.

THE FAMOUS FLOATING GARDENS NEAR MEXICO CITY

These tiny farms give eloquent evidence of the thrift and agricultural skill of the Mexican farmer on his own land

Copyright by Underwood & Underwood, N. Y.

FEDERALS

The splendidly equipped and well-trained Federals encamped outside the City of Mexico awaiting President Huerta's command

Copyright by The International News Service

CONSTITUTIONALISTS

A section of rebel cavalry advancing to the battle of Juarez of December, 1913

THE WAR WITH THE UNITED STATES 149

parts of the country shows that it had been well prepared and timed. In this cuartelazo, as in all the cuartelazos since the one which wrenched the fruits of the Independence from the old insurgency, the people took no part whatever. Since the noble constitution of Apatzingam had died still-born in the southern hills, the people of Mexico, except for a few brief months, had held no voice in the administration of the country. Paredes, when he recognized the strength of the cuartelazo, quietly submitted to his fate and resigned. The Church, acting through the instrumentality of Salas, imprisoned him for a while to demonstrate the possibilities that awaited her recalcitrant servants, and then dismissed him into exile in Europe.

Meanwhile, Santa Ana, having been summoned from Havana, arrived at the seaport of Vera Cruz, August 12, 1846. And here occurred an incident, small in itself, but affording proof, if further proof were needed, that the Clerical party and military chiefs in Mexico were coöperating in unison with President Polk and his cabinet in Washington. The ship which bore Santa Ana was seized and searched in the Bay of Vera Cruz by Commander David Connor of the United States fleet, but Santa Ana was released and permitted to land in compliance with the following note of instructions from the United States Navy Department: "May 13, 1846. Commodore: If Santa Ana tries to enter Mexican seaports, let him pass unchallenged. Respectfully yours, George Bancroft."

The cuartelazo had proved eminently successful. Paredes in exile, and Santa Ana in power, the Clerical party now proceeded to deflect and confound the opposition of the Liberals by inviting their coöperation in the support of the President in the establishment of the federal system, going so far indeed in their hypocritical overtures as to appoint Gomez Farias to the leadership of the new cabinet. In due time the elections were held, and Santa Ana was elected President, with Gomez Farias Vice-President, while Congress, in spite of the disfranchisement of the people, exhibited a strong Liberal minority.

Meanwhile, as we have seen, a division of the United States Army had already captured Monterey in the northwest. Other divisions were now invading Chihuahua in the north, and California in the west, while a United States squadron blockaded Mazatlan. In the absence of the regular army, deliberately withdrawn from the seat of war by the Clerical party, the Mexican volunteers, ill-equipped and unprovisioned, made heroic efforts to repulse the invaders, but with little success.

When Congress convened it authorized Santa Ana to take general command of the army, and appointed Gomez Farias interim President in his place. Santa Ana thereupon left Mexico City for San Luis Potosi, ostensibly to organize the country's defence and hurl back the invader. His first action, however, was to play directly into the hands of President Polk and the Mexican Clerical party, by withdrawing General Parrodi and his entire garrison from Tampico, thus abandoning the second seaport in Mexico to United States occupation without an effort at defence. A little later General Taylor arrived with his army before Cuidad Victoria, and again Santa Ana withdrew the garrison, giving up another strategic point to the invaders.

Gomez Farias, as President, was now compelled to face a problem which had caused the downfall of his predecessors, Bustamante, Santa Ana, Herrera, and Paredes — the problem of obtaining adequate financial support not only for administrative purposes but for the conduct of the war. He saw clearly there was but one method of procedure possible, and accordingly sent a message to Congress requesting the passage of the following measure:

"The Government is authorized to appropriate the sum of fifteen million dollars for the conduct of the war with the United States by mortgaging or selling in public auction the estates held in mortmain (Church property) . . . It is further authorized that all the funds collected under this law be used in the defence of the country, and that the Government give account to Congress of the use of these funds every six months."

THE WAR WITH THE UNITED STATES 151

This solution of the difficulty was, of course, viewed with wrath by the Church. To quote Baz: "This blow to the Church, whose selfishness had been the cause of more than one disgrace to the nation, caused tremendous consternation. As she then dominated the conscience of the nation through the medium of the confessional, and as her influence extended into the sacredness of the home, to the wives and children of her opponents, it was easy to create a powerful opposition to these laws, and all her efforts were bent with great energy against Gomez Farias." (Gustavo Baz, "Vida de Juarez," p. 45.)

Congress indeed passed the law in spite of the fierce opposition of the Church, but its effect was to a large extent nullified by the refusal of the Clerical governors of the states to carry its provisions into execution.

We now come to an incident which startlingly reveals the exact nature of this terrible mock-war. We refer to the deliberate destruction of a Mexican army of eighteen thousand men, the great majority of whom were volunteers, by all the horrors of starvation, thirst, and fatigue. This disaster was brought about by Santa Ana himself, in connivance with the Church and United States authorities.

When Santa Ana made San Luis Potosi his base of defence, his army was joined by thousands of Mexican patriots — peons, tenant farmers, and citizens — the brawn and muscle of the nation, who had willingly left wives and homes and children to offer their lives in defence of the fatherland. In this impetuous host, hardened by toil, filled with high courage, and eager to drive the invader out of the country, Santa Ana saw a grave menace to the cherished schemes of his co-conspirators, President Polk and the Church. He had seen too much of the old insurgent spirit and capacity not to know that these men properly officered would speedily put the control of the war out of his reach and bring it to a rapid conclusion — glorious for them, but disastrous for him and the schemes with whose execution he was entrusted. These men had to be put out of the way. Accordingly he organized them into an army which, with a few regular troops, totalled some 18,000 men, and led them out into the waterless desert, half armed, unequipped, and unprovisioned, on a march of three hundred miles, ostensibly to attack General Taylor at La Angostura, but in reality to die a thousand deaths, and to fall at last in battalions, crazed and exhausted, the prey of coyotes and vultures. For twenty-six days the rapidly dwindling host of doomed patriots struggled on, by day seared under a heaven of burnished brass, by night half paralyzed by the icy chill which only the desert knows, without tents or blankets, without food or water; while Santa Ana and his officers travelled ahead with a magnificent entourage, revelling in the choicest of foods and wines. The following picture by an eye-witness gives an intimate idea of the conditions of this terrible march: "The cold tormented us in a way difficult to describe, and the army was already broken-spirited. More by instinct in our desperation than from clear knowledge of our actions, we set fire in different places to the yucca plant grove in which we were. The flames ran up to the tops of the trees, and an ocean of fire swept from tree to tree in terrible waves of blasting flame. . . . The spectacle was sublime, and by its light we saw the hungry soldiers dying of starvation, shivering with cold, like an army of ambulant corpses." (Zamacois, "Historia de Méjico," Vol. 12, pp. 576 to 581.)

On the 23rd day of March, 1847, the spectre-army finally encountered the United States forces under General Taylor at a point on the Saltillo road called La Angostura. Santa Ana had undoubtedly calculated that those of his troops who survived the march would fall an easy prey in their exhausted condition to United States bullets. In this surmise he was only partially correct. For when the famished Mexican volunteers saw before them not only their hated enemy, to face whom they had endured such incredible hardships, but also substantial food supplies, they fought with such desperation that, mere ghosts that they were, they would have carried the day had not Santa

THE WAR WITH THE UNITED STATES 153

Ana in pursuance of his settled policy recalled them at the moment of victory, and ordered a general retreat. The battle that had begun without rest for the volunteers had raged for two days, and thirty-five hundred of them lay wounded and dead upon the field. During the preceding terrible twenty-six days' march, four thousand of them had perished. Now more exhausted than ever, and still without food, water, or shelter, they began the awful retreat. Of the 18,000 men, hale and full of courage, who had left San Luis Potosi but two months before, only 5,000 returned, and of these the majority were the regulars who had been better equipped and provided for than the heroic volunteers.

But Santa Ana had accomplished his purpose. The volunteer and largely Liberal army of defence had been wiped out.

It was necessary, it must be remembered, that the Mexican people should be disastrously and overwhelmingly defeated in order that the United States might enforce her sweeping territorial demands; it was necessary that the war should be protracted, and that the spirit of the people should be crushed and humiliated in order that all possible resistance on their part to the Clerical schemes for the establishment of a monarchy might be forestalled. To Santa Ana had been entrusted by both President Polk and the Clerical party in Mexico the task of achieving these ends, and no one can say he failed.

Meanwhile the Church had been plotting the overthrow of President Gomez Farias for his temerity in attempting to realize a war fund by the sale of her estates. Under the pretext of defending the country the idle aristocracy of Mexico City organized themselves into a militia, ironically nicknamed "Los Polkos" by the Liberal wits of the day, from the favourite society dance, the polka, then recently imported from France. In the absence of the regular army this aristocratic militia, reinforced by the friars themselves, raised a miniature cuartelazo against the President, and recalled Santa Ana to the capital. When the latter arrived he at once resumed his office as President, and a few days later Congress at the Clerical bidding abolished the office of Vice-President altogether. Following this, on the 2nd of April, 1847, Santa Ana was again given leave of absence to rejoin the army, and Pedro Maria Anaya was appointed his substitute.

While the ecclesiastics and polka dancers were rejoicing over the prosperous issue of their intrigues in Mexico City, the United States army, consisting of 12,000 men and 160 warships and transports, under General Winfield Scott, had already begun the bombardment of Vera Cruz. The garrison of the beleaguered city consisted of only 4,000 Mexican soldiers, and, according to Horace Greeley, "During four days and nights a torrent of burning iron fell upon the city, and so destructive was the fire that it reduced the place to ruins in a short time with a tremendous destruction of life. The Mexican garrison, numbering 3,000 men, another thousand defending the castle of San Juan de Ulua, displayed great courage, but they were lacking in artillery to oppose to ours, and a much larger force was necessary to serve the batteries in the city."

To quote from another historian: "Bombs were thrown upon hospitals, where men and women were killed, and while the volunteers of the national guard were fighting everywhere, scorning death, the women, the children, and the old men were running in despair and fear through the streets seeking a place of safety from the rain of missiles which the besiegers poured unceasingly into the city. . . . In view of the circumstances the foreign consuls tried to arrange a truce so that the defenceless people might leave the city. . . . Commodore Perry, however, refused." (Zamacois, "Historia de Méjico," Vol. 12, p. 653.)*

The action of Commodore Perry in this instance, sustained and endorsed by General Winfield Scott, was a practical application of Senator Bagby's speech in the Upper House to which

---

*Zamacois, whom we quote so frequently, let it be remembered, was a Catholic, a Spaniard, and an admirer of the United States.

THE WAR WITH THE UNITED STATES 155

we have referred. In this speech, it will be remembered, he advised the wholesale massacre of Mexicans, affirming that the life of one citizen of the United States was of more value than the lives of a hundred thousand Mexican women and children.

The irrefutable documents of this period prove that this policy of indiscriminate and wanton slaughter of Mexicans was not only openly advocated by President Polk and his cabinet, by the United States press, and even by the pulpit, but was zealously carried out on the field of action. "President Polk," says Bancroft, "waged a devastating war, and yet pretended to be sighing for peace. His supporters in the press advocated the bombardment of Mexican cities and inhuman destruction of Mexican life. These barbarous sentiments were aggravated by the false pretexts under which they were urged, namely: that Mexico had provoked the war." (Bancroft, "History of Mexico," Vol. 5, p. 547.) "Plunderings, massacres, cruelties, the killing of the wounded on the field of battle," says another, "even, in some cases, burning alive at the stake, have been recorded on the highest official authority as a part of the history of the Mexican War." (Livermore's "War with Mexico," p. 263.) "'Destroy the city of Mexico, level it with the earth on which it stands. Serve Puebla, Queretaro, Jalapa, Saltillo, Monterey in the same way, and then increase our demands,' says one. 'Unless we distress the Mexicans, carry destruction and loss of life to every fireside, and make them feel the rod of iron, they will not respect us,' says another. The *Union*, Polk's organ, says: 'Henceforward we must seek peace and compel it by inflicting on our enemies all the evils of war.' The foreign consuls wrote General Scott, March 24, 1847, of the frightful results. The New York *Herald* says that the bombardment placed the town in ruins, under which great numbers of non-combatants — men, women, and children — were buried." (Bancroft, "History of Mexico," Vol. 5, p. 546.)

This hideous slaughter continued for four days, and after 2,500 men and uncounted numbers of women and children had been destroyed, the city surrendered to the invaders. At the occupation of Vera Cruz, Gen. Winfield Scott issued the following ingenuous proclamation and caused it to be widely distributed among the people. It read: "Mexicans, at the head of a powerful army whose strength will be doubled shortly, which is about to advance upon the capital of the Republic, while at the same time another army under the command of Major General Taylor is on the march from Saltillo toward San Luis Potosi, I believe that it is my duty to announce to you that the Americans are not your enemies but your friends. But we are against those of your people who have compelled us to bring this unnatural war between two great Republics. We are friends of the peaceable people of this country; we are friends of your holy religion, of your prelates and ministers. In our own country we have the same Church and many devout Catholics who are well respected by our government, our laws, and our people. Since the beginning I have done everything in my power to put under the protection of martial law, and under my own protection, against lawless men, the Church of Mexico, and inoffensive people and their property."

The significance of the last paragraph becomes clear when we consider that Scott was acting with the knowledge of President Polk, in full connivance with the Clerical party in Mexico. After the United States occupation of Mexico City we shall witness him fêted and courted by the ecclesiastics, and entertained at picnics where all drank to the toast: "The annexation of Mexico to the United States."

After the fall of Vera Cruz, the peasants of the old revolutionary states of the coast adopted the method of guerilla warfare, and were thus enabled to make a much more effective resistance to the invader than the already betrayed troops of Mexican regulars. Meanwhile the emaciated remnant of the great volunteer army — 5,000 men who alone had returned from La Angostura to San Luis Potosi — had been hurried thence without rest to Mexico City and thence again to Cerro Gordo in the State of

THE WAR WITH THE UNITED STATES

Vera Cruz. Here they were joined by another body of 5,000 doomed patriots — mostly untrained peons, raw recruits — and the entire force commanded by Santa Ana in person, marched against the United States army under General Scott with the ostensible purpose of intercepting its advance on Mexico City. In view of the fact that the Angostura contingent was still suffering the effects of its recent ghastly experience, and that the local contingent was all untrained and unequipped, their chances of effective resistance, even under honest leadership, would have been small. But Santa Ana, true to his task, deliberately delivered them up — mere impotent cannon food — to the highly trained troops and powerful artillery of the United States army under General Scott, and scarcely a man of them survived. In this instance, as in the case of the La Angostura massacre, and all his connived defeats, Santa Ana sent a grandiloquent message to Mexico City announcing a glorious victory over the invader!

After the battle the English Minister to Mexico City proffered his services to the governments of the two contending nations in the interests of peace. When the fact became known, however, Congress was stormed with petitions from all parts of the country demanding the continuance of the war. The Mexican people, now thoroughly aroused, contemplated no cessation of hostilities short of the complete evacuation of the country by the invader; and the organization of new bodies of volunteers went on apace. Meanwhile the guerillas, supported and provisioned by the townspeople and peasantry, were causing the United States forces no little embarrassment. General Scott, therefore, issued a proclamation laying upon the alcaldes (judges) of the various districts in which these guerilla bands operated, the burden of suppressing them under pain of heavy fines and the confiscation of their property.

Following the defeat of Cerro Gordo, Santa Ana retired to Puebla ostensibly to intrench himself within its walls to again oppose the invader. When he entered the city, however, he found that the Clerical governor and bishop had already agreed to deliver it up to the United States army on condition that the persons and property of the ecclesiastics were properly respected, and he accordingly proceeded with the remnants of his army and a few pieces of artillery to San Martin Texmelucan. The inner history of this episode, as contained in documents placed at our disposal by Manuel Baranda, minister of foreign relations, is in small compass, the whole inner history of the war with the United States, and we make no apology for detailing it here at some length.

From these documents it transpires that as soon as General Winfield Scott had taken possession of Vera Cruz, he entered into communication with Monsgn. Pablo Vasquez, Bishop of Puebla, through the medium of the Curate of Jalapa, Father Campomanes, for the surrender of Puebla. In his reply the Bishop wrote: "If you warrant me that the persons and estates of the ecclesiastics are protected, I promise you that not one gun shall be fired from the city of Puebla." "Accepted," replied General Winfield Scott. The Bishop thereupon influenced the state legislature to appoint the brother of his private secretary, Rafael Inzunza, as governor of the state. The new governor, at the dictation of the Bishop, then dispatched a communication to the central government stating that the city of Puebla was lacking the elements for its defence, and that it could not be expected to offer resistance to the invading army. In addition to these measures, and to forestall any possible spontaneous defence on the part of the people, the Bishop induced Cosme Furlong, the local military commander, to remove to Izucar de Matamoros all the armament and war materials left in the city by the army which had recently passed through it on its way to the defence of Vera Cruz and Cerro Gordo. Thus, when Santa Ana entered the city with the relics of his army and a few pieces of useless artillery, he found no equipment for the organization of its defence, and was compelled to abandon it. It is not to be supposed, however, that this was a matter of either grief or surprise to the commander-in-chief. We have

THE WAR WITH THE UNITED STATES 159

no positive proof that Santa Ana was privy to this arrangement at Puebla, but his ready acquiescence in its results, coupled with the knowledge we have of his previous exploits at La Angostura and Cerro Gordo, makes it impossible to believe that he was not. In due time the invading army marched into Puebla with bands playing and flags flying, and peaceably bivouacked in the plaza. Thus fell the last outpost between the invaders and Mexico City.

On the 19th of August, 1847, the United States army, under General Winfield Scott, laid siege to Mexico City, and for two days the battle raged furiously, resulting in the loss of a thousand men on the American side, and of an unknown number on the Mexican side. A truce was then called for the purpose of peace negotiations. These having failed, on the 8th of September hostilities were renewed. In the ensuing battle, which with short intermissions continued for five days, the defenders — for the most part volunteers and citizen militia — stubbornly disputed every inch of the ground at a tremendous sacrifice of life on both sides. The fate of the city was still undecided, when on the night of the 13th of September the Mexican generals held a secret conclave in the national palace and decided that, having feigned a sufficient defence, it was now high time to withdraw the troops and betray the city into the hands of the enemy.

Accordingly, under cover of the darkness, the entire defending force was ordered out of the city to Guadalupe Hidalgo, a village some three miles distant; and on the morning of the 14th the citizens awoke to find the city abandoned and the United States troops already within its gates. The volunteers, helped by their wives, still kept up the now hopeless struggle fighting from barricade to barricade, and pouring a stream of fire from the house-tops upon the invaders. Again and again the defenders, mostly workingmen, sent to Santa Ana begging reinforcements or at least ammunition. Santa Ana refused to aid them in any way.

"The inhabitants of Mexico City" says Baz, "fought the invading army for three days in the streets and plazas, and from the roofs and balconies of the houses, without receiving any assistance from General Santa Ana, who was encamped with his army at Guadalupe Hidalgo, only three miles distant. An attack at this moment might have changed the entire aspect of the war." (Gustavo Baz, "Vida de Juarez," p. 51.)

At the end of the third day, the heroic volunteer defence was abandoned for lack of ammunition, and the city surrendered. On the same day, the 16th of September, 1847, Santa Ana, fearing the approaching storm of national indignation which his treacherous actions had evoked, resigned the presidency; and, according to the law, the office fell on the president of the Supreme Court, Manuel de la Peña y Peña. The remnants of the Mexican army now retired toward Puebla, many of them deserting en route, and many others forming themselves into guerilla bands.

The provisional President, Peña y Peña, although a prominent member of the Clerical party, was not personally involved in the conspiracy of the Church to devastate Mexico for the purpose of making her submit presently to a despotic monarchy; on the contrary, he was a man of good intentions, who endeavoured to handle the difficult situation which confronted him to the best of his ability. His defective education and fanatical devotion to the Church, however, blinded him to the real issues at stake, and prevented him from taking an effective stand against the intrigues and treachery which enmeshed him. His first act as President was to remove his seat of government from Mexico City to Queretaro. He then proceeded formally to discharge Santa Ana from his position as commander-in-chief of the army, ordering him at the same time to remain in Tehuacan pending a court-martial investigation into his conduct of the war.

At this time Mexico's wretched condition was being rendered still worse by the outbreak of a race war in Yucatan, by blood-

THE WAR WITH THE UNITED STATES 161

thirsty Indian raids in the states of Chihuahua and Zacatecas, and by the revolt of the military garrison of Mazatlan.

Again the American Minister, Nicholas P. Trist, addressed peace proposals to the Mexican Government. The President and his cabinet were willing enough to put an end to the disastrous war, but they were compelled to await the assembling of Congress at Queretaro before formally acceding to the proposals put forward.

Meanwhile Mexico City was enduring all the travail of a foreign occupation. The army, under General Scott, had been allowed to break loose from all restraints and had delivered itself up to an orgy of indescribable debauchery.* Murder, rape, and pillage went unchecked, while to add to the horror of the situation, hordes of raw recruits and volunteers — chiefly gunmen and the social offal of the underworld — poured into the city from the United States, ostensibly to join the army of occupation, but in reality to give full rein to their love of license.

"In the midst of this Saturnalia," says Zamacois, the Spanish historian who was in Mexico City at this time, "the most profound respect and consideration toward the Church was observed and enforced by the United States military authorities. The Catholic priests were respected and the churches were open all the time. No molestation was permitted to any of the religious ceremonies, processions, street parades, or public celebrations. General Scott, who had a very high idea of the wisdom and virtues of the Mexican clergy, publicly stated that he respected, and would make respected by everybody, the national religion; and thus owing to the tactics and talents of the illustrious Archbishop Juan Manuel Irisarri, the Church kept her rights and was fully respected. (Zamacois, "Historia de Méjico," Vol. 13, p. 49.) Proof enough of the perfect mutual understanding and good will which existed between the Church and the invaders! Indeed, when General Scott appointed council-

---
*Zamacois, "Historia de Méjico," Vol. 13, pp. 38–40.

men for the city of Mexico, he allowed the Church to advise him in their selection; and later when carousing with the same Clerical appointees at a picnic given by them in his honour he did not hesitate to respond to their infamous toast, "The annexation of Mexico to the United States!" One can imagine that banquet ringed by the menacing spectres of tens of thousands of slaughtered patriots whose bodies lay rotting on the battlefields of Mexico!

At last Congress convened; the representatives had been summoned again and again to Queretaro to transact the momentous business in hand, but owing partly to the disorganized condition of the country, and partly to the indifference of many of the Clerical members a sufficient quorum was not obtained until November 2, 1847. The governors of the states likewise had been summoned to attend the national council, but few of them obeyed. For the most part members of the Clerical party, they saw in the country's distress only the necessary preconditions for the establishment of a monarchy, and viewed the efforts of the administration to end the war with indifference or frank disfavour. A few there were, however, possessed of Liberal ideas, notably Governor Benito Juarez, of Oaxaca, and these promptly attended the President's summons.

On the 11th of November Congress elected Pedro Anaya as President *ad interim*, and on the 18th of the same month took up the consideration of the peace proposals put forward by the American Minister, Nicholas P. Trist. Their deliberations were, of course, greatly influenced by the utter bankruptcy into which the nation had fallen. The treasury was empty; taxation was impossible, and when some of the Liberal newspapers suggested that the administration enforce a loan from the Church, General Winfield Scott promptly checkmated with a circular published on the 23d of November, couched in the following terms: "The army of the United States having taken possession of the city of Mexico and its surroundings on the 14th of September, all the rights and authorities of the Mexican Government are invested in the United States; and it is declared that any transactions or agreements made in regard to the Church property in Mexico constitute an attack upon the United States authority, and that any act of this kind will be severely punished, and, further, that if the ecclesiastical interests are in any way endangered, those interests will be confiscated by the United States and kept under its control and protection."

Adequate financial resources are, of course, the prime necessity to the conduct of a war. This Scott well understood, and in order to render it still more impossible for the Mexican Government even partially to emerge from bankruptcy, he obtained authorization from President Polk to impose a levy of $2,500,000 on the revenues of the country for the maintenance of the United States army of occupation.

Meanwhile, however, both General Scott and Nicholas P. Trist were using every effort to conclude the negotiations for peace. Both men had seen enough of the temper of the common people of Mexico to fear a violent reaction from their present state of apathy and demoralization. Said Mr. Trist on this point: "Let the spirit of desperation be awakened and then things will have a very different aspect from what they now have. This country cannot resist ours with success, but the resistance of which it is yet capable, even if it is only partial and unsuccessful, must have a very different spirit. We ought to take into account that the best fights that have been put up yet on the part of the Mexicans in the Valley of Mexico have been by volunteers untrained and not belonging to the regular army."

In the matter of the peace negotiations Congress was much divided; for, although the Clericals having accomplished their object were now in favour of peace, some of them were aroused by the humiliating proposals advanced by Nicholas P. Trist, and voted against their own party in favour of a continuance of the war. The partisans of peace, however, were in control, and they were able to impose their will in the matter, albeit secretly, and against the wishes of the nation. Accordingly, on February 2,

1848, a peace treaty was signed by the representatives of the two governments.

Under its provisions Mexico agreed to cede to the United States Texas, New Mexico, and California, which included, likewise, all the territory known to-day as Arizona, Oklahoma, Colorado, and Utah, and to accept in compensation thereof the sum of fifteen million dollars. The treaty was drawn up, signed, and ratified by Congress with the utmost secrecy, for the Clerical party had good grounds to fear that if its humiliating provisions became prematurely known, the people would rise up, overthrow the government, and continue the war. Even the official announcement of the conclusion of peace dispatched by the President to the governors of the states was couched in hypocritical and misleading terms. When finally the news leaked abroad, the moment for action had already passed, and the people were compelled to accept the dismemberment of the country in addition to the horrors and miseries of the actual conflict.

One might well ask, in reviewing this war and the pact which terminated it, why the United States did not annex Mexico in entirety. The answer to this question lies in the fact that the United States was already strongly divided against itself. The war had been invoked wholly by the planting interests of the South. The North, largely opposed to it from the first on political, economic and humanitarian grounds, had viewed its bloody progress with rising wrath, and in face of an opposition now dangerously bitter, the planting interests dared not push their imperialistic schemes too far. Indeed, Nemesis was already approaching, and the South so far from extending the period of her supremacy had only hastened her inevitable conflict with the North. Furthermore, President Polk, General Scott, Minister Trist, and their associates foresaw clearly that even if the annexation of Mexico could be effected without invoking serious complications with the European powers — a matter much in doubt — the Mexican people themselves could never be subdued. To patrol indefinitely a territory, vast, arid, and

Copyright by The International News Service

A LITTLE REBEL PATRIOT

Guadalupe Candeleria, 15 years old, went into the thick of the fighting around Juarez, in November of 1913, and carried out the wounded

Copyright by The International News Service

GENERAL LUIS TERRAZAS CLAIMS UNITED STATES PROTECTION

One of the largest land-holders, Terrazas is here shown just after he had crossed the border to the United States after the revolutionists had taken possession of his vast estates in Chihuahua

A TROOP OF RURALES

The Mexican rural police, originally the roving bandits, were organized by General Diaz into one of the most efficient fighting machines in the country, and rendered yeoman service against the small land-owners

Copyright by The International News Service

A BATTERY OF MEXICAN FEDERAL ARTILLERY

The Federal artillery consists of about 250 pieces, more than half of which is of the most modern types — the Snider-Canet and the St. Chamaund-Mondragon

infested with guerilla bands, would entail an expense out of all proportion to the economic and political gains which would accrue from its possession. Moreover, the annexation of Mexico meant that the United States Government must support her ally, the Catholic Church, against the Liberals in their ceaseless struggles for democracy — a course of action which would be abhorrent to the Northern traditions and policies. And, finally, the South knew well that Mexico, if annexed, would join with the North against her own cherished scheme of disrupting the Union and establishing an independent republic based on chattel slavery. Indeed, scarcely was the peace treaty signed before the strong anti-slavery sentiments of the annexed territories, Colorado and New Mexico, became clearly evident, and the South had to recognize that for all her bloodshed she had gained only Texas. These territories at the time of the Civil War, far from helping the South, contributed larger and better equipped contingents to the cause of the North, in proportion to their population, than any other two states in the Union.

The war was ended. A war made by slave-holders and priests in which slave-holders and priests lost neither life nor property — a war made to strengthen the grip of the oppressor upon the people, and to destroy that noble element to be found in every nation, whose glory it is, in peace, to labour for the emancipation of the enslaved, and in war, to fight for their fatherland. The men who died in this struggle were, on the one side, the deluded American regulars, youths from the farm and the homestead, raw, ignorant, hot-headed, and hypnotized to their death and their manhood's disgrace by the false shibboleths of their country's ruling class; on the Mexican side, the volunteers, for the most part workingmen, who, knowing nought of the base conspiracy to betray and murder them, freely sacrificed their lives to preserve their hearths and homes from the invader. These alone paid the penalty.

The official military classes on either side were but slightly damaged. Twenty-five thousand men of the United States working class had lost their lives, and $165,500,000 of money contributed by the United States working class had been spent. The loss in life and money on the Mexican side is unknown; at a conservative estimate it must have been at least double the loss of the United States. The war was ended; to what good? It had made of Mexico a shambles, and of her capital a brothel; it had left a legacy of ungovernable race hatred between the two nations which persists to this day. It failed to achieve even the miserable object of its instigators, for the new territories opposed slavery, and never permitted a slave-holder within their borders. Indeed, in its reaction twenty years later it destroyed its instigators, broke the power of the South and abolished chattel slavery from America. And in that single glorious achievement, may be, all the bloodshed and travail found historical compensation. It seems a tortuous and bloody path to so elementary a goal, but while class rule persists it must be even so.

NOTE — (See Page 159, line 8). After the occupation of Puebla Santa Ana and Scott gave the final touch to the agreement, which it was generally understood had been made between the Mexican clericals and the Polk administration. The two generals agreed that Santa Ana should receive $10,000 in cash as an advance payment of $1,000,000 to be given him from the United States secret funds, as soon as the peace treaty was signed. (See Bancroft's "History of Mexico," Vol. V, Page 466.)

CHAPTER XII

CLERICAL INTRIGUES FOR THE ESTABLISHMENT OF A MONARCHY IN MEXICO

PRESIDENT ANAYA'S term of office had now expired, and Congress elected General José Joaquin de Herrera in his place. On the 31st of May, 1848, the new President assumed office, and on the 12th of June the American army, having withdrawn, he reëstablished his seat of government at Mexico City.

The demoralized and exhausted condition of the country proved, as had been anticipated, the best possible milieu for the Clerical agitation for a monarchy. Under the sinister and capable leadership of Lucas Alaman the conspiracy throve apace. The ably conducted Clerical journal, *La Patria*, was already in the field, and now another journal, *El Universal*, was established to educate the masses into a proper appreciation of the benefits to be derived from a monarchical form of government.

Bustamante, an old royalist and a willing monarchist, had already returned to the country from his exile, and was now commander-in-chief of the army; there was even some movement made toward recalling Santa Ana. The peons were once more tilling the fields, peacefully yielding up the products of their toil to the Church and the big land-owners. The danger of domestic revolt was now far removed, and had it not been for the numerous bands of guerillas still at large, who, no longer required by their country, preferred to become bandits rather than again yield to the yoke, the country would have been in an ideal condition *from the ruling class point of view.*

Meanwhile the arrears of pay due to the generals and officers of the army were settled in full. So numerous were the latter, however, that this effort on the part of the government to forestall the military discontent, and at the same time to meet the usual administration expenses, almost bankrupted the exchequer. The people were crippled, the army contented, the Church triumphant, and a monarchy at last in plain view.

The intensely reactionary and jealous temper of the Church at this time was revealed when a Liberal paper in the city of Vera Cruz suggested to Congress the enactment of a measure establishing religious freedom in Mexico. The suggestion, of course, evoked a storm of indignation from the Church, and President Herrera, in an exaggerated and theatrical rebuke, sent an appeal to the Pope of Rome, copies of which were published broadcast, beseeching him to come and establish his earthly reign in Mexico. "But if in the decrees of Providence the Roman Pontificate were to come to the New World, you, Father, would find in Mexico seven millions of your children filled with love and veneration toward your holy person." These were Herrera's words. It is indeed highly probable that the success of her intrigues toward establishing monarchy had caused the Church to indulge the hope of going still further and instituting a Theocratic power in Mexico.

Soon after the above appeal had been made to the Pope, the Council of Mexico City, ecclesiastical appointees, under the chairmanship of Lucas Alaman made the first open move in the conspiracy by officially declaring the city to be in favour of a monarchy. The declaration caused an unexpected reaction on the part of the Liberals; vigorous protests appeared in their papers, and street parades were held which ended in riots. The affair, however, soon subsided, for the Liberals still suffered from the after-effects of the war, and from the loss of a great number of their keenest and ablest leaders. The Clericals, on the contrary, were in the full tide of their power, a tide they were to enjoy unmolested for many years.

CLERICAL INTRIGUES

Meanwhile, the race war in Yucatan between the Mayas* and the Spaniards, to which we have previously referred, had assumed terrible proportions; while in the north the savage Indian tribes were still ravaging the country unchecked. The Clerical government, however, was unable to conceive the necessity of taking any action not directly concerned with the interests of the Church and big land-owners, and made no effort to restore order or to defend the people.

The government was now, as usual, in severe financial straits. In order to meet the expenses of the administration and the upkeep of the army, a crushing poll-tax and interurban tariff were levied upon the people, in spite of the fact that they were already mulcted in tithings and rents by the Church. Under these conditions the people sank into a poverty unequalled in the history of civilization.

With the close of President Herrera's term, General Mariano Arista was elected in his place on the 15th of January, 1851. The increase of poverty, the vigorous development of the agitation for a monarchy, and the suppression of the Liberal press, were the characteristics of the new régime. The Liberal opposition was slow in gathering way after the war with the United States.

During Arista's term, however, some advances were made in the provinces where the Clerical vigilance was not so strictly maintained as in Mexico City. This was notably the case in the State of Oaxaca, where the governor, Benito Juarez, himself a Liberal, quietly filled all the positions in his gift with men of his own ideas. In the State of Michoacan, the Liberal governor,

---

*The Maya race, like all the native races of Mexico, are not Indians or Mongols, or black men. On the contrary, they belong to the Aryan or Caucasian division of the human family, and are ethnologically fully entitled to the popular caption of "White Men." It will probably interest many readers who have not enjoyed the privilege of travelling in Mexico to know that, if there are whole territories where the people are as dark-eyed, dark-skinned, and dark-haired as are, for instance, the Welsh, or the Spaniards, or the Basques, there are also large territories where the people are as fair-skinned, blue-eyed, and fair-haired as are the English, Norse, or the Andalusians.

Melchor Ocampo, not only succeeded in creating a Liberal administration, but by its aid succeeded in eliminating Clerical interference in education and even in taxing the Church for the support of the public schools. The states of Nuevo Leon and Tamaulipas also began to make similar advances. Arista possessed neither the courage nor audacity to curb this unostentatious but menacing activity, and accordingly the Church decreed his overthrow.

Again the cuartelazo was invoked. In July, 1852, Colonel Climaco Rebolledo headed the uprising of the garrison at Córdova, in the State of Vera Cruz. A few days later Colonel Jose' Maria Blancarte joined the movement at the head of the garrison at Guadalajara, and compelled the Liberal governor to remove to Zapatlanejo. In both of these uprisings proclamations were made demanding the discharge of Arista from the presidency, while at Michoacan the uprising which took place under Colonel Bahamonde demanded not only the discharge of Arista but also of Melchor Ocampo, the governor of the state.

Similar scheduled uprisings followed in all parts of the country. Guadalajara was the storm-centre, however. Here a joint convention of the chief officers of the army, and high dignitaries of the Church announced that President Arista was discharged, and that Santa Ana would be immediately recalled from his exile in Colombia to become again the President of the Republic. Arista needed no second warning but peaceably resigned, January 6, 1853, and a few days later left the country for the usual exile in Europe.

By virtue of the law the President of the Supreme Court, Juan Bautista Cevallos now became President. Cevallos' first action was to issue a decree abolishing Congress. It was an entirely unreasonable and unjustifiable step even from the Clerical point of view; for Congress, since the war with the United States, had consisted almost entirely of meek and faithful servants of the Church. The institution *per se*, however, was a relic of democratic government, and as such its continued existence had become incompatible with the monarchial schemes of the Church. In this abolition the last vestige of the Constitution of 1824 disappeared.

A few days later the President *pro tem.* resigned, and a caucus of military chieftains and prelates, who now posed as the lawful representatives of the nation, appointed Juan Manuel Maria Lombardini his successor. The same caucus likewise declared all previous systems of government and constitutions ineffective, and summoned delegates from the various states to a special convention to decide upon a new constitution and system of government. To the legislatures of the states, however, the caucus left the right to elect the President on a basis of one vote to each legislature. Accordingly on the 17th of March, 1853, the state legislatures, dominated completely by the Church, elected Santa Ana, still absent, to his third term as President.

The methods, the purposes, and ambitions of the Mexican ruling class — the Church, Army, and Aristocracy — at this period are vividly revealed in the letter of instructions written by Lucas Alaman, the "man of the black brains," to the President-elect, Santa Ana. In this letter, a portion of which we append below, the master mind of the Church speaks to the tool in words around whose dignity and sombre force there plays the irony of an illimitable contempt:

"It is our will to sustain the ecclesiastical welfare with splendour and to arrange with the Pope everything relative to the ecclesiastical administration. We do not care, as some papers have said, in order to discredit us, to establish the Inquisition nor religious persecution, but it is understood that the duty of the public authority is to prevent the circulation of impious books. . . . We are absolutely opposed to the federal system; to the representative system in the matter of elections which has obtained hitherto; and the elective city council (municipal home rule), and to everything which bears any relation to popular election. . . . We believe in the necessity of a new territorial division that will entirely extinguish and obliterate the present form of federal states. In order to facilitate good administration we believe it necessary that the most drastic measures be taken to prevent the resprouting of the federal system. There will be an army of numbers competent for the needs of the country. . . . And we are persuaded that any and all of these things can be satisfactorily carried out without Congress. We desire, however, that you proceed under the counsel of a few advisers *who will outline your executive action.* Those are the essential points of our political faith. These we reveal to you frankly and loyally. We do not wish to conceal our opinions. Indeed in the propagation of these ideas we are supported by the general opinion, and by the newspapers in the capital and in the states which are all ours. We have the moral strength of the united clergy, and likewise of the land-owners . . . . For the rest we do not care, no matter what your personal convictions may be, to see you surrounded by flatterers who will influence you. . . . We are against your going to live in Tacubaya, because this will be a source of inconvenience to us in the transaction of the governmental business; and we are against your usual leave of absence to go to your estate, Manga de Clavo, leaving the government in hands that will make the authority to be regarded with ridicule, and ending in your downfall, as has happened before. You are already possessed of our desires, of the strength and support which is ours, and we presume you have the same ideas. *If it should happen not to prove so, it will be bad for the nation — and you.* . . . Señor Haro will give you more detail in regard to these points, and, *advising you to destroy this letter*, and wishing you happiness, etc., I affirm myself to be your faithful and obedient servant, LUCAS ALAMAN."

No very elaborate study of this document is necessary to discover in it the whole program of the Clerical party in Mexico, and in miniature the whole program of the master class of the

CLERICAL INTRIGUES

world. This dark figure which stirs, silent and stealthy as a shadow, behind all the events of the period, this Lucas Alaman, was the very genuis of the Clerical party. We have seen him directing the policies of the Church, from the conspiracy which ended in the overthrow and murder of Guerrero, through the Texas question, the abolition of the federal system, the war with the United States, and down to this moment when he places Santa Ana once more in power, instructing him in the desires of the Church as to his personal behaviour, with the cool, ironic insolence of the superior mind for its tool. To Alaman, more than any other man, is due the power which the Church attained in this period, and the impetus of his master mind sustained her in power years after his death. It may seem surprising that such a man should choose Santa Ana for the execution of the Clerical policies. There was, however, a reason for the choice. Santa Ana possessed the trick of popularity, of effective stage acting. He was the only man who knew how to satisfy the army's love of lax discipline without permitting it to degenerate into a mob. He was, moreover, a man without a mind or soul of his own — an obedient lackey who took the lash or the bribe with equally facile servility. Such a man in the hands of an Alaman was an exquisite tool for the schemes of the Church.

On the 20th of April, 1853, the new President took the oath of office, together with the cabinet selected for him by the Church; Lucas Alaman, Secretary of State and President of the Cabinet; José Maria Tornel, Secretary of War; Antonio Haro y Tamaris, Treasurer; and Teodosio Lares, Secretary of Justice.

In accordance with the policy outlined by Lucas Alaman, the first act of the new administration was the promulgation of a measure dictated by Minister Lares, the Secretary of Justice, and hence called "Lares Law," by which every publisher of newspapers, books, or pamphlets was compelled to place with the government a bond of not less than three thousand dollars to be confiscated by the government at discretion for offences against the ecclesiastical and civil authority. The law proceeded to define such offences as: Attacks upon the dogmas of the Church, or expressions of doubt in regard to her creed; and criticisms, however slight, directed against the government, or of its officers. It likewise established a secret tribunal similar to the star-chamber of the Stuart régime in England to deal with violations of its provisions. The operation of this measure immediately suppressed the Liberal newspapers *El Monitor*, *El Instructor del Pueblo*, *El Telegrafo*, and *Biblioteca Popular Mexicana*, as well as a number of smaller publications. *El Universal*, the Catholic monarchist organ, on the contrary, greatly increased its size and circulation.

To overawe the Liberals and impress the masses, the administration proceeded to increase the army to the enormous number of ninety thousand men. For the support of this idle host, in addition to the now vastly increased numbers of friars and nuns who battened upon the people, a direct taxation was imposed and enforced with the most brutally coercive measures. By fines and imprisonment and seizure of goods, the last centavo was wrenched from the hunger-wasted poor in order to sustain a ruling class that was indifferent to the needs of the people.

El Siglo, one of the few newspapers that survived the Lares Law, in its issue of the 20th of January, 1852, said: "In the capital, according to official information, many corpses have been left to be buried by the police, because the families have no money wherewith to pay the funeral expenses. This horrible fact needs no comment. It is a blot upon the morals of any Christian civilized country, and energetic preventive measures ought to be taken at once by the authorities." Human misery such as this mattered little to the Clerical administration. For a large standing army and a well-filled exchequer were necessary not only for the repression of a possible revolt but as a reserve weapon for enforcing upon the people, after long years of conspiracy, the now rapidly approaching establishment of a monarchy. To quote the Catholic historian, Zamacois, in this respect: "Don Lucas Alaman, in spite of the change of

CLERICAL INTRIGUES

government, believed in good faith that the only way of obtaining permanent peace, prosperity, and power for Mexico was the establishment of a monarchy with a Spanish prince at its head. In this firm conviction he suggested the scheme to Santa Ana; the latter assented to the reasons that the minister laid before him. . . . From that moment both began to work for this end, but with the greatest secrecy . . . and in order to carry out their purpose they agreed to seek the intervention of England, France, and Spain." (Zamacois, "Historia de Méjico," Vol. 13, p. 672.) Thus the armed forces of England, France, and Spain were to be invoked to support the Church and the enormous Mexican army in the task of imposing a foreign monarch on the people — this in the name of peace and prosperity!

In close pursuit of his object, Alaman dispatched official instructions to Don José Maria Gutierrez Estrada, and private ones to Don José Manuel Hidalgo, Secretary of the Mexican legation at Madrid, to press forward the negotiations with the Count de San Luis, president of the Spanish cabinet, for the accession of a Spanish prince to the throne of Mexico, and at the same time to engage the interest and coöperation of England and France in the matter. In order further to facilitate the negotiations, the conspirators even endeavoured to bring Mexico under a Spanish protectorate.

The people in Mexico were in complete ignorance of the conspiracy, for all of the negotiations had been carried out in the darkest secrecy; while the rigid censorship of the Lares Law effectually suppressed any news that might have leaked out. In the month of July, 1854, however, *El Clamor Publico*, a Spanish Liberal newspaper, published in Spain and widely read among Mexican Liberals, proclaimed and denounced the whole conspiracy in an editorial, concluding with these words: "For Mexico to look for the end of the wrongs with which she is afflicted in the protectorate of Spain, whose strength is exhausted, or in a monarchy, a name which only awakens there the remembrance of infinite disasters, is an erroneous adventure, if not a punishable project."

The revelation aroused keen surprise and fierce indignation not only among the Liberals in Mexico, but among the Liberals in Spain also. This incident, coupled with the sudden death of Count de San Luis, caused the collapse of this particular phase of the monarchical intrigue, not, however, of the intrigue itself. During the negotiations, it is interesting to note, the astute Spanish premier had succeeded in extorting from the Mexican administration the recognition of several claims lodged by Spain against Mexico. One of these was, absurdly enough, an indemnification for the funds expended by Spain in fighting the insurgency at the time of the Revolution for Independence; another, equally absurd, was lodged in the name of a Spanish priest, José Moran, for reimbursement for estates occupied by the Mexican Government which had been set aside by Spain for the support of missions in the Philippines and California.

In the first claim Mexico, now independent, was asked to pay the expenses of an army against her independence; in the second she was asked to reimburse the Church in Spain for lands necessarily sequestrated by the Independence which, moreover, were intended for the support of the missions in California, now annexed to the United States, and in the Philippines, which were merely another Spanish possession having no relation whatever to Mexico. The two claims amounted to over eight million dollars, and notwithstanding the financial exhaustion of the country, and the enormous army appropriations, they were both duly recognized by Alaman, Santa Ana, and their confederates in the hope of hastening the arrival of a Spanish prince at Mexico City. These claims, together with a number of others equally disreputable, constitute to this day a part of the enormous Mexican national debt.

In the midst of these infamies Lucas Alaman died on the 29th of May, 1853. The "man of the black brains," the only intellect in the Church capable of dealing with the situation, was

CLERICAL INTRIGUES

gone, but the impulse he had given to the Clerical policies still continued to be felt. The suppression of the city councils, the imposition of an interurban tariff on the transfer of produce from one locality to another — a measure of bitter cruelty in a starving country — and the iniquitous Lares Law had been the outstanding features of his home policy. What his foreign policy had been we have already seen.

Subsequent to his death his influence still appeared in the terrible *Ley de conspiradores* (Law of conspirators), a measure promulgated by the Clerical administration, which decreed that any one convicted or suspected of uttering opinions adverse to the Church or government should be arrested and tried without jury or civil procedure before the local military commander or nearest army officer; and, after a summary investigation of the facts, punished with death or imprisonment at the discretion of the military court. Under this law, which exaggerated the worst effects of the Inquisition, thousands of innocent victims were done to death for merely holding Liberal opinions. Not only men, but women and even children as well.

In contrast to this starvation, slavery, and strangulation of the people, the ecclesiastics, government officials, military, and aristocracy openly flaunted their luxury and license. Cholera had come to scourge the land from end to end, rendering conditions still more appalling; while in the national palace Santa Ana smilingly cast up his latest receipts — like a Porfirio Diaz after him — from the sale of thousands of Maya natives to the planters of Cuba!

It will be remembered that in Alaman's letter of instructions to Santa Ana he made express mention of a "few advisers" who would direct the President's executive action. This Supreme Council of State, organized and led by Alaman, consisted of twenty-one high prelates, aristocrats, and generals, who were directly responsible for all the acts of the government. Those men, encouraged by the success of their past efforts, now entered upon the penultimate step in the monarchical conspiracy, by promulgating a law which gave President Santa Ana the official title of President Dictator. This law also extended his term of office indefinitely, placed in his hands the right to appoint a successor, and endowed him with authority to assume the address of "Most Serene Highness!"

The next step, of course, would have been the last — the armed intervention of the European powers in favour of a monarchy, the abdication of Santa Ana, and the enthronement of a foreign prince with despotic powers. For this consummation the Church had laboured long and assiduously. It was a climax, however, destined to be fulfilled only after years of bloodshed. Scarcely had she promulgated this edict so fraught with sinister significance than she was startled from her dream of unlimited, unbroken power by the distant rumblings of a revolution. Nemesis was at hand.

CHAPTER XIII

THE AYUTLA REVOLUTION

THE premonitory symptoms of a new revolution in Mexico appeared in 1854 in the form of a series of local uprisings as sporadic and spontaneous as they were indefinite in character. Blended with them in confusing fashion were several purely military uprisings headed by disgruntled army officers — mere accidents in the general process. It was in Guerrero that the Revolution first arose in a nebulous condition and later assumed full shape, mass, and momentum. Here it was moulded and guided by Juan Alvarez, that same Juan Alvarez who had fought shoulder to shoulder with Guerrero in his last stand against the forces of oppression. The insurgent masses of the south instinctively turned for leadership to this gray-bearded patriot who had fought for them, lived for them, and was prepared to die for them— Tio (uncle) Juan Alvarez as they called him.

Together with Ignacio Comonfort, a customs inspector in Acapulco, Tomas Moreno, an old insurgent comrade of Morelos, Diego Alvarez, Eligio Romero, and others, Juan Alvarez drew up and published a platform outlining the purpose and policy of the Revolution. This platform, famous in history as the Plan de Ayutla, was proclaimed March 1, 1854, in the town of Ayutla, in the State of Guerrero. Its main provisions read as follows:

I. The President Dictator, Santa Ana, is hereby discharged from power, together with all the officers of the government who are undeserving the confidence of the people.

II. In the adoption of this plan by the majority of the

nation, the commander-in-chief of the revolutionary forces will call a delegate from each state and territory to meet in a certain place on a certain day to be chosen at a later time, to elect an interim President of the Republic, and to work as his advisers.

III. In each of the states the chief commander of the revolutionary forces will choose seven persons to frame the provisionary statutes, to rule the said state or territory upon the basis that the nation is, and will be, one, indivisible, and independent.

IV. Fifteen days after the taking of power by the interim President he will call for the election of an extraordinary Congress, said election to be held according to the law given to that effect in the year 1841. The said Congress will work exclusively to constitute the nation under the form of a representative popular Republic, and to revise the acts of the provisional President.

V. The laws in regard to the organization of the army and individual taxation and the interurban tariff are hereby declared null and void.

Terrified and spurred to swift action by the promulgation of this platform, the Clerical administration dispatched punitive expeditions to Guerrero, to Oaxaca, and later to Acapulco, where Ignacio Comonfort was in command of a strong force of revolutionists. In every encounter, however, these expeditions were defeated. Thereupon Santa Ana, with characteristic egoism, undertook "to scatter the sacrilegious enemies of the Lord," and left Mexico City for the south at the head of five thousand men amid the utmost pomp and splendour. The revolutionists intercepted his march at El Puerto de Coquillo, delivering a sharp attack, and then retired in skirmishing order on Acapulco, where Comonfort, with a handful of six hundred men, was well entrenched—tactics which proved trying enough to the government forces already exhausted with much marching and suffering from the effects of heat and thirst.

After three or four ill-managed and disastrous assaults on

THE AYUTLA REVOLUTION

the city, Santa Ana abandoned the attempt to carry it by storm, and resorted to strategy, offering a bribe of a hundred thousand dollars and a highly desirable appointment in the European diplomatic corps to Comonfort, together with good positions in the army for the rest of the revolutionists. Needless to say these overtures were repulsed with scorn. Santa Ana thereupon raised the siege and countermarched to the capital, venting his rage and spleen by shooting every peon he could lay hands upon, and burning and sacking the towns and villages through which he passed on the pretext of destroying the support of the revolutionists.

Meanwhile, true to his usual practices, he dispatched grandiloquent messages to Mexico City and all parts of the country, proclaiming that he had utterly crushed the revolution and won another glorious victory over the enemies of God. The revolutionists, by reason of their small numbers and lack of ammunition, were compelled to refrain from pursuit, and Comonfort, in view of this, left Acapulco for the United States to obtain the war equipment necessary for the further conduct of the campaign.

When Santa Ana arrived in Mexico City the Clerical party, realizing the seriousness of the occasion, and determined to dupe the populace to the last, welcomed him with grandiose festivities on a scale never before witnessed. To further confuse the people and add an appearance of popularity to their régime they ordered a national plebiscite to be made on the following questions:

First: Shall the President continue to possess the dictatorial powers which he is exercising to-day? Second: If he be not authorized to continue the exercise of said powers to whom shall he delegate them?

The transparent absurdity of these questions could have deceived no one, but thousands of ecclesiastical, military, and official retainers throughout the country worked assiduously to obtain favourable signatures to them. In view of the fact that more than 80 per cent. of the population were unable either to read or write, and must make their signatures through government proxies, and that all those refusing to give unconditional and immediate assent to the first question were summarily imprisoned, exiled, and bereft of their property or executed, it is easy to see the exact value of the plebiscite. In this respect the following document from the minister of war is illuminating:

"Excellent Sir: With surprise and indignation His Most Serene Highness has seen that some individuals, boasting anarchistic ideas, and insulting with bold impudence the Supreme Authority of the nation, have dared to vote for President of the Republic in the elections of the 1st and 3d instant in favour of that leader of marauders, Juan Alvarez. In consequence, His Most Serene Highness has ordered that those who have voted in this way be arrested and adjudged according to the Ley de Conspiradores, for by this fact they have shown that they are in sympathy with the rebellion. God and Liberty. Mexico, December 11, 1854. Blanco, Minister of War, to His Excellency, the General Commander of the Army in San Luis Potosi."

Closely following this plebiscite the terror of the Church in face of the avenger found expression in a decree promulgated by the Supreme Council of State amplifying the horrors of the Ley de Conspiradores. According to its terms, "not only were individuals to be punished for expressing an opinion against the Government, *but the towns in which these rebels were living were to be destroyed by fire and their inhabitants to be shot in groups.*" ("México, á través de los Siglos," Vol. 4, p. 850.)

Meanwhile the Revolution, so far from succumbing to the oppressive measures of the Clerical party, burst forth with renewed energy in all parts of the country — in Huanustitlan, Marcial Caamano; in the State of Jalisco, Santos Degollado and Epitacio Huerta took the field at the head of large bodies of peons in favour of the Plan de Ayutla; while the states of Morelos, Mexico, Michoacan, Tamaulipas, and Nuevo Leon witnessed great spontaneous uprisings, almost leaderless, and in many cases devoid of definite program.

According to one authority, "The Revolution of Ayutla, like all other revolutions in Mexico, was a really popular revolt, and as such there was a lack of leaders and direction to organize it in the different places where it broke out. The oppressed, tyrannized by the long dominion of the privileged class and conservatives, were eager to shake off the yoke that they had borne for so many years, and when the extreme measures of repression adopted by the government caused the south to burst forth in revolt, all these oppressed and downtrodden seconded the movement spontaneously by an irresistible impulse toward liberty. Indeed so spontaneous was the revolt of the people that the majority of these men joined the uprising without knowing the principles of the Plan de Ayutla, and only because they were told that they were to fight for Liberal principles." ("México á través de los Siglos," Vol. 4, p. 856.)

We have seen one of the twin dominant characteristics of the Church — Fear — impelling her to fan the flames of revolution by repressive measures of hysterical cruelty and absurdity; we have now to see the companion characteristic — Greed — impelling her to refuse financial support to the only bulwark which lay between her and destruction — Santa Ana and his army. With the larger part of the country in revolt, the usual sources of revenue — the poll-tax and the interurban tariffs — destroyed, Santa Ana was obliged to turn to the Church and great landowners for the funds necessary to the maintenance of the army and the conduct of the campaign. In the matter of taxation, the unchanging theory of the Church, as of every ruling caste or class, is: that since the common people cannot be trusted to submit peaceably to exploitation, save under the pressure of government and an army, the common people themselves must support that government and army. Hence any deviation in practice from this principle sorely disturbs the oppressor.

Accordingly when Santa Ana began to ply the Church with

requests for money she turned upon him with the most scathing censures and denunciations for his lack of ability in failing to crush the popular revolt without funds. Meanwhile some minor successes of the army encouraged her to promulgate through the medium of the Supreme Council of State further decrees against the revolutionists, ordering the indiscriminate destruction of the life and property of all those even suspected of opposition to the government. One of these ordered "all rebel towns to be destroyed, and all who are in any way hostile to the national army to be shot at once." Another, amplifying the above, ordered "all rebels or suspected rebels to be shot, and to be hanged from the branches of the trees by the roadside, and the villages and rancherias (dwellings of the peons), and their food, cattle, and other means of subsistence to be utterly destroyed." ("Historia de la Revolucion en México en contra de la dictadura de Santa Ana, 1853 to 1855.")

As might be expected, the more exasperated and hysterical the repression the stronger and fiercer the revolt. The least vigorous and courageous peon seeing before him certain death as a suspect, if he submitted, chose rather to fight for possible life and freedom. By the month of May, 1855, the states of Nuevo Leon, Tamaulipas and Coahuila were in full control of the revolutionists, and the revolutionary government provided for by the Plan de Ayutla was well established. Santa Ana seemed by no means eager to achieve another of his "glorious victories," and it was not until the prelates of the powerful Clerical State of Michoacan urgently summoned him to their aid that he consented to leave the safety of Mexico City for the hazards of the field. As usual, his military operations consisted only of a showy parade. After recommending the officers in charge of the garrisons in Michoacan to exercise the utmost severity against the rebels he returned to the capital without striking a blow.

It was the first time that Santa Ana had been called upon to engage in a real struggle and to face a situation not already "arranged" for him. His rank cowardice and incompetency now revealed itself to the fullest extent, and the Church, disgusted with his failures and enraged at his financial exactions, pronounced his overthrow. Santa Ana sensed the coming storm and fled, leaving behind him a communication to be opened on a given date, which reads:

"I. The President of the Republic having been given ample faculties by the nation to appoint a successor to his office in the event of his resignation, hereby appoints as executive power the President of the Supreme Court and the Generals Mariano Salas and Martin Carrera. If some of these generals die their places may be filled by General Romulo Diaz de la Vega and Ignacio Mora y Villamil.

"II. These men will come into power if the actual President dies, or if he makes declaration signed by himself of his inability to continue the exercise of the supreme power for any cause that he may deem sufficient. As soon as this executive power assumes the functions of office, its main activity must be the keeping of order, and the calling of the nation to frame a constitution."

Before leaving he bid his personal followers to pay no heed to the rumours already current that he was about to leave the country, announcing to them that the activities of the revolutionists in Puebla and in the State of Vera Cruz necessitated his personal supervision of the defence in those parts. On the 18th of August, 1855, Santa Ana left Mexico City forever, to die an exile and a forgotten man.

We now come to a very decisive turning point in the history of Mexico's struggle for democracy. Hitherto, in the ruling class trinity — Church, Army, and Aristocracy — the Church has been all-powerful, using the Army and Aristocracy purely for the furtherance of her own interests. Hitherto there has been but one policy, the Clerical policy, to which all others have been compelled to accommodate themselves. Henceforward we are to witness the diversion of the Army and Aristocratic policy from the Clerical policy, accompanied by the decline and fall of the power of the Church, and the rise and consolidation of the power of the Army and Aristocracy of big land-owners. In short, we have come to the point which divides old Mexico from modern Mexico.

For this change there were a number of reasons, chief among which were: The complete loss of prestige sustained by the Church among the more intelligent section of the nation, the disproportionate numerical strength and, therefore, political power of the Army, and more important than this, the first faint beginnings of the industrial era in Mexico. The organizer of industry and the industrial wage-slave alike, trained unconsciously to a scientific mode of thought by the necessities of their respective tasks, are prone to carry the reason and logic of the counting house and the workshop into other departments of life with disastrous results to their faith in the dogmas of the Church; or, indeed, in the tenets of any organized religious sect or ethical cult. From its very inception, the era of industry, with its well-marked materialism, has not only immensely improved the power of man over his material environment, but has gone far to destroy the suffocating emanations of the past; it has not only prepared the way for a collectivist organization of society, but it has made straight the path for a new spirituality in society. This great change which had already begun to sweep over all the civilized world could not long escape Mexico, and it is in this year of 1855 that the first faint indications of its influence are to be detected.

The immediate impulse, however, which led to the severance of the Clerical and military policies was the effort of the Army to shelter from the coming storm. The Church begrudged it the necessary support; the national character of the Revolution had already abolished its customary revenues; it, therefore, had but one safe course to pursue — to execute a nimble volte-face and compromise with the Revolution in the secret intention of perverting it to the furtherance of its own interests at the first opportunity. Accordingly General Diaz de la Vega, *acting independently of the Church*, called a convention of the leading citizens of the capital and the states to elect a President. This self-appointed assembly, without consulting the revolutionists on the one hand, or the Church on the other, elected General Martin Carrera to the presidency, *and declared for the Plan de Ayutla*. In addition to this main movement of the Army and Aristocracy there were two smaller counter-movements, one representing the recalcitrant element in the Army, who clung to all the old traditions and refused to compromise, and the other inspired solely by the personal ambition of Antonio Haro y Tamariz, the confidant of the late Lucas Alaman. Conciliatory measures are invariably disastrous in a revolutionary state of society. But President Carrera, true to the new policy, established his régime with a number of measures intended to appease and reconcile the revolutionists. The most important of these was a measure creating a national guard on the same principle and footing as the old bodies of civicos. As opposed to the regular army, the chief weapon of class oppression, the civicos, as we have seen, were a free citizen militia, the very bulwark of the Liberal party and the rights of the people. This organization of the national guard, therefore, was a subject well calculated to make an inroad into the ranks of the revolutionists. Other seductive measures followed. On the 20th of August, 1855, a nation-wide summons was issued by President Carrera, under the provisions of the already adopted Plan de Ayutla, for the election of representatives to Congress for the purpose of framing a new constitution.

Thus, almost miraculously it seemed, the aspirations of the people were to be realized — aspirations cherished with growing ardour since the clerico-military cuartelazo which overthrew the Constitution of 1824. At the same time all political prisoners were liberated, and those in exile were permitted to return to the country. These measures were, of course, purely diplomatic, dictated not by principle but by motives of fear and self-interest. The revolutionary host was advancing on Mexico City, and the Army, having made these dispositions, awaited the turn of events before deciding whether to realign with the Church, or oppose her; to rend the Revolution, or to embrace it, work with it, and ultimately capture and betray it.

"It was clearly seen when the triumph of the Revolution was proclaimed in the capital of the Republic that those who proclaimed this triumph were trying to impress upon its course a direction utterly at variance with its spirit. The Conservative reaction during the Santa Ana dictatorship had displayed a superabundance of despotism and arbitrariness which incited the people, embittered by recent experience, to demand such radical measures as would destroy root and branch the old wrongs, in which, as by a band of iron, Mexico had been bound for years. All hope for conciliation between the Conservatives and the Liberal party was entirely out of the question; a chasm of hatred separated them, and there could be no other outcome but that of a fight to the death between these two political parties which, holding opposite principles, must needs come to contradictory results. . . . No matter what may have been the qualities and personal credit of General Diaz de la Vega and President Carrera, the truth is that both were leading members of the last dictatorship, and that they were appointed by Santa Ana to take the executive power. This alone was enough for the people to refuse all confidence in them. The Plan de Ayutla proclaimed by the garrison in Mexico City had been changed by them in an essential point in making General Diaz de la Vega chief of the Revolution instead of Tio (uncle) Juan Alvarez as declared in the original plan. In other words, by some dexterous conjuring the same man who the day before had been strenuously combating the revolutionary movement which had overthrown the dictatorship, was now chief and leader of this very movement; while its authors and supporters, those who had gone to the fight defying the wrath of the government, were dropped to a second place." ("México, á través de los Siglos," Vol. 5, p. 59.)

Meanwhile the states of Jalisco, San Luis Potosi, Zacatecas, Tamaulipas, Nuevo Leon, Coahuila, together with the states of the northwest had fallen completely under the control of the revolutionists. Already provisional decrees had been promulgated by the revolutionary juntas in the various states, branding all the members of the Santa Ana government as enemies of the nation, suppressing the Army, abolishing individual taxation, and forbidding all exaggerated titles, as, for instance, "His Excellency," "His Most Serene Highness," etc. It was under these circumstances that, *according to the original purpose of the Plan de Ayutla*, the revolutionists convened at Cuernavaca, and after the representatives of the different states had been appointed, proceeded to elect Tio Juan Alvarez, President, with Melchor Ocampo, that recalcitrant Liberal Governor of Michoacan, Secretary of State; Benito Juarez, Secretary of Justice and Ecclesiastical Affairs; Guillermo Prieto, Treasurer; Ponciano Arriaga, Secretary of Interior, and Ignacio Comonfort, Secretary of War. At the same time President Carrera, unable longer to sustain his false position, resigned, and General Diaz de la Vega took military command of Mexico City pending the arrival of the revolutionary leaders. A little later Juan Alvarez at the head of his army entered the capital unopposed.

The first act of the revolutionary government was to suppress the poll-tax which had been levied upon the people by the late administration for the support of the army; the next, to stop further payment of the unjustifiable claims allowed by Lucas Alaman in favour of the Spanish Government and Father Moran. These preliminary acts were followed by a decree authorizing the organization of the national guard or bodies of civicos, and by a comprehensive measure abolishing the Clerical and military fueros, drawn up by Benito Juarez, the Secretary of Justice and Ecclesiastical Affairs, and known as the Ley de Juarez.

The fueros not only exempted members of the Church and

Army from the jurisdiction of the civil courts but also compelled a citizen having a claim against a member of the Church or Army, or a citizen accused by a member of the Church or Army, to submit to the jurisdiction of the ecclesiastical or military special courts — a state of affairs which made an utter mockery of the civil law. The fueros, indeed, constituted a positive expression of that brutal and cynical despotism to which the Mexican people had been so long subjected, and the Ley de Juarez in abolishing them struck at the very heart of the old system of oppression and injustice. It showed clearly to the forces of privilege the spirit of the Ayutla Revolution. The abolition of the military fueros, coupled with the organization of the civicos, pointed inevitably to the final suppression of the Army; and undoubtedly this was intended. "The Conservative party," says Baz, "and the moderate faction were immensely scandalized by this law; and the belief that the Army was to be suppressed was the cause of violent opposition against the government." (Gustavo Baz, "Vida de Juarez," p. 96.)

In addition to these measures the complete freedom of speech and press was established, and the Liberal papers, long forced into silence, made vigorous use of their opportunity, attacking the forces of Privilege with the pent-up wrath of years, and holding up before the people the great principles upon which the new order was founded. These attacks seemed to the Church and Army the very death-knell of their power. They now saw clearly that nothing short of extermination awaited them at the hands of the people. Once more, therefore, if only for a brief period, they determined to join hands and make a united effort to overthrow the new order and reëstablish the old.

President Alvarez was an old man, worn out by his long life-battle for liberty, and when once he had witnessed the firm establishment of the revolutionary government he resigned, leaving to stronger hands and younger minds the completion of the task he had so well begun. In his speech of resignation he said: "A poor man, I was made President, and I resign this high posi-

THE AYUTLA REVOLUTION 191

tion with the satisfaction of having done something for the people. Trained to hard labour since my childhood, I go back to handle the plough for the support of my family. I have not received one penny from my public position, and I trust that none who occupy it hereafter will use it to gain the riches that are an outrage to the misery of the people."

At this moment there came into prominence as the choice of the people for President one of the most tragic characters in Mexican history, Ignacio Comonfort. A member of the official class, as we have seen, Comonfort had forsaken a lucrative government position to embrace the cause of the people, and had played a part in the Revolution second only to that of Juan Alvarez himself. But from the moment he became President he began to exhibit a tendency toward the use of conciliatory methods in dealing with the enemies of the popular government — a policy at once dangerous and unjustifiable. There is no possible reconciliation between the wolf and the sheep, between the master and the slave, between autocracy and democracy. Between them there can exist only a war to the death. In that struggle between the two classes which had faced each other through three hundred years of the most bitter hostility, there was no room for conciliation or concession. The very heart of the people was at stake. The hour needed not a Comonfort, but a Cromwell, a Spartacus. On the one side, the Church, Army, and Aristocracy stubbornly refused to relinquish the least of their privileges and plunder; on the other side, the people all flushed with victory, exulting in their new liberty, were in no mood to temporize with the destroyers of their families, their homes, and their freedom. Such leaders as Comonfort, loving the new, yet still clinging to the old, doing much good work, and yet spoiling with doubtful tactics and compromising attitudes the final issues of the fighting masses, are spawned by all popular revolutions and constitute the gravest, because the most subtle, menace to their success.

Under this uncertain leadership the national situation became highly critical, providing, indeed, a favourable milieu for the natural and inevitable reaction of the Conservative forces. Throughout the country the Clergy were assiduously plotting and endeavouring to terrorize the superstitious masses into relinquishing their gains. The revolutionary cabinet against Comonfort's wish answered these pernicious activities with a law disfranchising the clergy altogether.

"By the clamour that was raised everywhere," says the Catholic historian, "in disapprobation of these measures it was easy to see that a revolt was brewing amongst the clerical, military, and official classes of society, and that the enemies of the government were taking full advantage of the discontent that was produced in order to work actively in secret for its overthrow. The laws attacking the ecclesiastical fueros met with the disapproval of the great part of society * and with the protest of the bishops. The Catholics saw in these laws the beginning of sweeping legislation against their religion. Their foundation for believing this was the knowledge they had of the advanced ideas of the members of the cabinet." (Zamacois, "Historia de Méjico," Vol. 14, p. 128.)

The conspiracy of the Church and Army against the government now arising in all parts of the country was headed by the bishops of San Luis Potosi, Guadalajara, and Puebla. Its most prominent and mischievous exponent, however, was Father Francisco Xavier Miranda, a man of remarkable activity and intelligence, and the confessor of Comonfort's mother.

In this last fact lies in great part the secret of the President's disastrously vacillating policy. Comonfort's mother — a fanatically devout Catholic — was continually subjected by the wily Jesuit to the extreme of spiritual anguish by reason of her son's antagonism to the Church. To Comonfort, a man of

---

*"The great part of society"— this statement is an error into which a Catholic historian might easily fall. The Revolution of Ayutla expressed the will of not less than 80 per cent. of the entire population of Mexico, at that time a population almost entirely Catholic. The ecclesiastical fueros indeed found bitter opposition in the ranks of Catholic citizens and extreme Jacobins alike.

Liberal principles, warm-hearted and sensitive, called upon by his country and his own judgment to use the utmost severity against the Church, and who at the same time loved his mother with a devotion almost idolatrous, this insiduous attack proved utterly demoralizing. Too late he summoned courage to have Father Miranda and some of his co-conspirators arrested. The evil had been done. His action only provoked the open revolt of the Church, and the President, endeavouring to palliate his action and appease the suffering of his mother, appointed the bitterly anti-clerical Juarez as governor of Oaxaca to keep him out of the cabinet.

Throughout the country the reaction raged furiously. Everywhere the clergy denounced the Liberal government as the enemy of God, and openly called upon the people to disobey its laws. "The pulpits were converted into political platforms whence were hurled the most furious invectives against the Liberal party, misrepresenting its policies and denouncing it as the most ferocious enemy of the Church and her ministers. The Conservative papers also repeated in various ways the same accusations, writing long articles to prove the divinity of the Catholic religion, and placing in circulation all kinds of rumours, no matter how absurd they might be, in order to overthrow the authorities, and to stop the current of reform initiated in the laws." ("México, á través de los Siglos," Vol. 5, p. 88.)

On the other hand, according to Baz, "The policy of Comonfort was not only an obstacle to the reforms advocated by the Liberal party which the time had come to sanction, but failed to satisfy either soldiery or Clergy. The first accustomed to absolute immunity, and the second accustomed to unlimited dominion, were not long in discovering that the Ley de Juarez was depriving them of the desirable privileges they had hitherto enjoyed; and to retain them they were prepared to plunge the country in civil strife. . . . If for the Liberal party this struggle was a question of principles it was not so for the retrograde faction. The bishops, the curates, and the friars were opposed to these reforms because they were opposed to the loss of their influence upon the masses, and of their omnipotent power upon the conscience of the people. The soldiery were opposed to these reforms because they recognized that the law of the sword, brutal force, and the tinsel of military glory are absurdities in a Republic where the civil rights are the foundation of the law." (Gustavo Baz, "Vida de Juarez," p. 97.)

During the month of January, 1856, the revolt broke out in full force. The garrisons of Morelia, Michoacan, Queretaro, San Luis Potosi, Guadalajara, and San Juan de Ulua started cuartelazos with the war-cry: "Religion and Fueros," while in Oaxaca, the curates, Carlos Parro, José Gabriel Castellanos, and José Maria Garcia, together with Capt. Bonifacio Blanco, headed a military uprising proclaiming the full reëstablishment of the ecclesiastical and military fueros, and the upholding of the Catholic religion to the exclusion of all others. In Jalisco the friars of the monastery of El Carmen joined with the soldiery in a military revolt; at the same time government troops which had been dispatched against the cuartelazo at San Juan de Ulua mutinied, joined the rebels, and marched with them to Puebla which they besieged and finally captured after a six days' battle with the national guard.

Leaving the governors of the states to deal with the more distant and less important cuartelazos, President Comonfort gathered an army consisting of twelve thousand civicos and a loyal remnant of the regular army and marched on Puebla. In the fourteen days of continuous and desperate fighting which ensued, both sides suffered severely; finally, however, the government forces carried the town, and the mutineers surrendered.

In the midst of this national turmoil, on the 18th of February, 1856, the Plan de Ayutla reached its triumphant climax in the convening of the constitutional Congress. At the same time

Comonfort issued a decree mildly punishing the Clerical leaders in the recent revolt, couched in the following terms:

"Article I. The governors of the states of Puebla and Vera Cruz and of the territories of Tlaxcala will seize in the name of the national government the ecclesiastical property of the diocese of Puebla.

"Article II. With a part of said property, and without interfering with religious worship, and necessary expenses, the Republic will be indemnified for the funds expended in the suppression of the reaction which ended in said city; an indemnity will be paid also to the inhabitants of the said city for the damages that they have suffered during the conflict, and pensions will be assigned to the widows, orphans, and those disabled as the result of this conflict.

"Article III. The seizure of the above-mentioned property will continue until peace and order has been established in the Republic."

The soldiers who deserted the government to join the cuartelazo received a short term of imprisonment in place of the death sentence which they had incurred under the law. In these gentle measures Comonfort undoubtedly was influenced not only by his mother's wishes but by the hope that a policy of liberality and mercy would appeal to the better nature of his opponents and bring to weary, blood-stained Mexico a period of peace and good will.

Like the idealists of all ages, notably of to-day, he refused to recognize the impassable, unbridgeable gulf which yawns between the two contending classes in society, the exploiting and the exploited. He fell short of the fundamental good sense of the French Revolutionists, of Cromwell and Spartacus, and like another Hamlet he dallied with a distasteful duty, until the sin of omission became a bloody, monstrous crime of commission, and he fell, dragging with him the high hopes of a nation. This policy of reconciliation, although it was effective in arousing the bitter discontent of the Liberals, utterly failed to placate the enemy. The Church, indeed, boldly redoubled her efforts to arouse the people against the government, and every pulpit in the land became a centre of sedition and treason. The Bishop of Puebla, unperturbed by the castigation his diocese had recently received for its support of the cuartelazo of Miranda, openly continued to preach revolt in the cathedral and to bid his priests and curates to do likewise.

Meanwhile Congress was engaged in framing the most brilliant constitution that democracy has yet achieved — the Constitution of 1857 — and in passing measures embodying the deepest aspirations of the people. Amid storms of protest from the opposition, and oftentimes amid the howling mobs gathered by the clergy and marshalled to the House for the purpose of obstructing the work of the Liberals, principle upon principle was enunciated and established abolishing the bulwarks of privilege, and upholding the social, political, and economic equality of men.

Among the first of these were the abolition of the ecclesiastical and military fueros, the cancelling of all military appointments made by Santa Ana, and the suppression of the Jesuits. Against this bold enunciation of Mexico's future laws President Comonfort struggled with but little effect, save to anger the Liberals, disgrace himself in the eyes of the people, and weaken his prestige with the opposition. He succeeded indeed in modifying several measures for the establishment of religious freedom, but in spite of these misguided efforts at obstruction Congress continued to pursue with vigour its great task of realizing the hopes of the nation.

The one outstanding achievement of President Comonfort's policy of reconciliation, however, was a measure initiated, fostered, and finally forced through Congress under his influence, which effectually forestalled the efforts of the people to confiscate the estates of the Church, by providing that these estates

THE NATIONAL PALACE

The National Capitol of Mexico and the centre of the stage in the great drama of human rights that has been going on in that country for so many years

CONSTITUTIONALISTS AND THEIR FAMILIES

"Never for a moment since Diaz came into power in 1876 had the spirit of revolt ceased to fire the hearts of the people" (See page 341)

Photograph by R. J. Carmichael

CHAPULTEPEC CASTLE

The official White House of Mexico on the outskirts of Mexico City where Diaz reigned so many years

Copyright by Underwood & Underwood N. Y.

MEXICO CITY AFTER THE BOMBARDMENT OF FEBRUARY, 1913

be subdivided, appraised, placed on the market, and sold to private individuals on a mortgage held by the Church bearing interest at the rate of 6 per cent. per annum. Thus the Church would not only realize the full cash value of her holdings with an interest on her mortgages higher than she had received from the cultivation of the land, but all her immense holdings of rental residential property in such cities as Mexico, Puebla, Queretaro, Guadalajara, Guanajuato, Durango, Zacatecas, and others, remained untouched. To make this measure more effective and impressive, particularly in the eyes of the Catholic population, and at the same time to gain the good will of the clergy, Comonfort appointed Pedro Escudero y Echanove special delegate to the Vatican with instructions to explain this measure to the Pope, and obtain his consent and authorization thereto.

Such an action would seem inexplicable, even in the compromising Comonfort, did we not consider that the Church was carrying on a violent and unprincipled propaganda throughout Europe with the purpose of arousing intervention in Mexico on the part of the powers to prevent a further curtailment of her privileges. Comonfort realized the imminent danger of such intervention and foresaw the disastrous consequences it would bring upon the nation, and undoubtedly hoped by this measure to ward off the greater evil with a less.

"Certainly it was an unhappy event for the Comonfort government," says one historian, "that Escudero y Echanove was not dispatched immediately on his way to Rome; and perhaps this was a great error committed by that government. Everywhere it was considered as a government of the most unbridled demagogy whose purpose was to ransack the temples and demolish the altars. The Catholics all over the world pitied the Mexican Church, which was presented as weeping under the persecution of a mob of impious men. . . . The Mexican delegate would have enlightened the Vatican as to the real state of affairs and would have prevented the Supreme Pontiff from saying at a later date *words that gave at once the death sentence to the Liberal cause and a new lease of life to its enemies.*" (Anselmo de la Portilla-Gobierno del Gen. Comonfort.) Later we shall witness the Pope of Rome in complicity with the European powers curbing the power of the popular legislation against the Church in Mexico, and finally drowning the new-born Mexican democracy in seas of blood.

In all this vacillation and compromise the Liberals took no part whatever. They knew exactly what to expect of Europe, and particularly of Rome, and so far from exposing their weakness to the enemy in the manner of Comonfort, they made every effort to strengthen the nation to the point where it could successfully contend with its foes both within and without. It was the President alone who by his fatuity lost prestige with the Church and people alike, and spoiled with his half measures the glorious achievements of the revolutionary Congress. His indeed was a wretched plight, suspended between Liberal and Cleric and spurned by both. When a widespread conspiracy against the government was discovered in the convents of San Francisco, San Augustine and Santo Domingo and in Mexico City, he was compelled by the pressure of public opinion to punish the offenders. But ever fearful of severe measures he confined his retribution to the convent of San Francisco, imprisoning the friars and razing the building for the opening of Independencia Street, permitting, however, all the others to go unharmed. Even Father Miranda, whose pernicious activities had caused the President so much distress, was released after a short confinement to become at once the head and forefront of a powerful nation-wide conspiracy against his liberator. Comonfort was perfectly cognizant of the Jesuit's plans and purposes but took no steps against him, in deference, we must suppose, to the wishes of his mother.

The situation at this time was further aggravated by the arrival of a Spanish squadron at Vera Cruz, accompanied by the Spanish Minister, Don Miguel de los Santos Alvarez, with instructions to enforce under threat of armed invasion the pay-

THE AYUTLA REVOLUTION

ment of the two claims recently dishonoured by the Mexican Government. Fortunately, however, Don Miguel de los Santos Alvarez was a man of honour and intelligence, and when the real nature and history of these disreputable claims were explained to him by the Mexican Minister of Foreign Relations he refused to press their payment and withdrew — an act of honesty which highly displeased his master, the King of Spain, and cost him his office.

The time had now arrived for Congress to take up the consideration of the land question — that great question wherein is found the fundamental cause of all Mexico's popular revolutions from the Independence to our own day. Already in many parts of the country the peasantry had begun to appropriate the lands formerly owned by the Church to their own use, and in order to protect them in their holdings, a large minority in Congress went on record as favouring a law which in a few simple words defines the most advanced property right the world has yet seen:

"Article I. The right of property consists in the occupation or possession of land, *and these legal requisites cannot be conferred unless the land be worked and made productive*. The accumulation in the hands of a few people of large territorial possessions which are not cultivated, or made productive, is against the common welfare and contrary to the principles of democratic and republican government." ("México á través de los Siglos," Vol. V., p. 176.)

The violence of the Church against the Liberal government was increasing daily; everywhere throughout the land the priests openly preached disobedience and sedition as a duty to God. In a circular letter to his parishioners the interim Bishop of Puebla, Don Antonio Reyero y Lugo, commanded them, "not to obey the government but to work against it by all possible means, for such a government represented the enemies of religion who were attacking the independence and sovereignty of the Church, trying to subdue her temporal power, dispossessing her of her property, and compelling her, with imprisonment and exile, to bow before an idol raised up by impiety. . . . That they should follow the divine example of the first Christian martyrs who refused obedience to temporal power, and that they — the true children of the Church — must remain firm against the enemies of faith and become the revengers of the injuries against God." ("México, á través de los Siglos," Vol. 5, p. 199.) In Puebla, in San Luis Potosi, in Queretaro, and in many other cities cuartelazos and Clerical riots were of daily occurrence. In the midst of this storm on the 5th of February, 1857, the constitution was proclaimed by Congress in Mexico City, and Valentin Gomez Farias, the Speaker of the House, walked on crutches in the last breath of his life to take the oath of obedience to the supreme law of the land. The oath was then taken by the representatives and by the President of the Republic. The constitution was to take effect on the 16th of September following.

CHAPTER XIV

THE CONSTITUTION OF 1857

THE Constitution of 1857 is the exact expression of the aspirations of the Mexican people as distinguished from the Church, Army, and Aristocracy. Forty-seven years was this constitution in the making — forty-seven years of such national travail as no modern people has endured; and for fifty-seven years thereafter the Mexican people fought against foes within, and the power of the civilized world without, to make it a reality in the land — and they are fighting yet. It is no Magna Charta framed by medieval barons, no French Civil Code framed by bourgeois property-worshippers, no United States Constitution framed by land speculators and capitalists for their own immediate profit;* it has no parallel in history, no kindred human document with which it may be compared, *because it is the first Constitution of the People, the first expression of a pure democracy — as opposed to a bogus democracy, the first national enunciation of the principle that the foundation of all social institutions is the Rights of Man — as directly and unalterably opposed to the Rights of Property.*

If you shall ask of the Mexican man of the people, be he peaceable peon tilling the fields, or skilled mechanic in the shop,

---

*The exhaustive researches into the official records of the period conducted by Prof. Charles Beard of Columbia University and embodied by him in his recent work "An Economic Interpretation of the United States Constitution" (Macmillan Company), incontrovertibly proves that the United States Constitution was framed in complete disregard of the common people, by a small coterie of men belonging exclusively to the former colonial master class whose chief interest in the matter was the immediate enhancement of capitalistic as opposed to small agrarian interests.

or student in the schools, or miner toiling in noisome depths, or fighter with rifle at back for the fatherland and liberty — what is the deepest desire of his heart his answer will be "The Constitution of 1857." And even if he, being untutored in his own history, cannot name you so precisely his desires, he will give you in his own simple words the very essence of that constitution. It is for the fundamental principles of this constitution that the Mexican people have fought for a hundred years; it is for the constitution itself that they have fought for the past fifty-seven years.

Article I. *The Mexican people recognize that the rights of men are the foundation and the purpose of social institutions. In consequence they proclaim that all the laws and authorities of the country must respect and sustain the warranties stipulated by this Constitution.*

Here is the keystone of the New House of the People, and the keystone for all social structures for the future in Mexico and throughout the world. The age-long struggle of humanity for freedom might well be defined as the struggle of the Man Right against the Property Right. In all ages, in all places, the Property Right has triumphed, and to-day it dominates the entire political, economic, social, intellectual, and domestic life of the world. Only in Mexico has the Man Right found an exponent. The Mexican people had been familiar with chattel slavery and serfdom; they had seen the abolition of slavery and the breaking down of serfdom succeeded by another form of slavery more dangerous because more entrenched, more insidious because more flexible and less patent to the eye — wage slavery. They saw that all three systems were equally vicious and equally founded on the assumption of the superiority of the Property Right over the Man Right. Therefore in the first article of the constitution they abolished them utterly, upholding for the first time in constitutional history the complete supremacy of the

THE CONSTITUTION OF 1857

Man Right. From the day that this article of the constitution becomes effective, all economic, political, and religious institutions in Mexico must be based upon, and conform to, the principle of the rights of men.

Article II. *In the Republic every one is born free. The slaves who step into the national territory recover their liberty by this mere fact, and have the right of the protection of the law.*

In Mexico at this time the serfs were still to a large extent considered as attached to the land. If an estate changed hands the serfs went with it as part of the equipment. This is a system common to all agrarian autocracies. It was prevalent under the Roman Empire, and later spread throughout Europe as an integral part of the feudal system. The Spanish Conquest imposed it on Mexico, supplanting thereby the milder and more liberal feudal system of the Aztecs.

"In the Republic every one is born free." This declaration was intended to destroy forever any restraint upon the freedom of men. In later articles of the constitution we shall witness the extension and elaboration of this basic principle to encompass the most complete freedom of the human family. The second part of the article recalls to us the fact that this constitution was framed at a time when the institution of slavery was still in power in the United States. The fugitive slave was a common figure in Mexico, and the constitution not only granted to him the full right of asylum, but declared that from the moment his foot touched Mexican soil he "*recovered his freedom,*" thereby recognizing that he was born a free man. This provision is profoundly significant of the passion for human liberty in its fulness which inspired the Mexican people at this time — a passion, indeed, breathing in every line of the constitution.

Article III. *All education is free. The law will determine which profession needs a diploma for its exercise, and what requisites are to be fulfilled.*

This fundamental principle was later amplified to make education universal, free, non-sectarian and compulsory. The

Catholic schools of Mexico were sorry institutions, and even such rudimentary education as they gave was restricted to the rich. For the poor there was nothing but the most complete illiteracy. Since the presidency of Gomez Farias in 1833, however, the Liberals had maintained a courageous struggle to establish non-sectarian schools where Mexican children of all classes could obtain a clean, adequate education based on scientific principles.

The thirst for knowledge, accompanied by a natural vigour and brilliancy of intellect, is a characteristic of the Mexican common people. It is a characteristic directly inherited from the original allied races of Mexico — the Aztecs, Toltecs, Mistecs, Mayas, and others. Before the Conquest, in Tenoxtitlan (Mexico City), Michoacan, Oaxaca, and Tlaxcla, there were schools, colleges, and universities where the national trades, science, art, history, and literature were taught, and the great national library was filled with precious and valuable manuscripts, the records of the intellectual progress of ages. The stupidity of the Spanish Conquistadores, supported by the bigotry and superstition of the Spanish clergy destroyed all trace of this glowing intellectual life, and effectually crushed all possibility of its renaissance. For three hundred years the people subjected to the heel of Spain remained passive and mute in the darkness of ignorance and despair. Then came the trumpet call of Hidalgo, and the living spirit of the race which had so long smouldered in secret burst forth in the Independence, and sank amid blood and tears in the war with the United States, to rise again, magnificent and victorious in Article III of the Constitution of 1857.

Article IV. *Every man is free to adopt the profession, trade, or work that suits him, it being useful and honest; and to enjoy the product thereof.* . . .

We have revealed the conditions to which the common people of Mexico were subjected. To toil in peonage on the land of the Church or the Aristocracy was their only destiny. This article,

THE CONSTITUTION OF 1857

which gave them the right to choose their employment without restraint, *ipso facto* broke the bonds of peonage, and it did more: it recognized the right of the people to the enjoyment of the *full product of their labour*. No other constitution in political history has ever enunciated this simple, obvious, and fundamental right of Man. No constitution based on Property Right could do so without violating its own foundation. The framers of this constitution were students of economics; they understood perfectly well that it would be useless and criminal to abolish chattel slavery and peonage merely to pave the way for wage slavery; they knew the world of plunder and exploitation that lies between "wages or salary" and "full product of labour;" and they struck at the very root of the evil, abolishing economic exploitation in its entirety, chattel slavery, peonage, wage slavery.

Article V. *No man shall be compelled to work without his plain consent and without just compensation. The state will not permit to become effective any contract, pact or agreement with the purpose of the curtailment, the loss, or the irrevocable sacrifice of the liberty of any man, may the cause be for personal labour, education, or religious vows. The law in consequence does not recognize monastic orders, and will not permit their establishment, no matter what may be the denomination or purpose for which they pretend to be established. Neither will be permitted a contract or agreement by which a man makes a pact for his proscription or exile.*

Chattel slavery, peonage, serfdom, contract labour, are all of them institutions created for the express purpose of exploiting and enslaving the people. Utterly opposed to freedom, civilization and humanity as they are, they must be destroyed root and branch before further progress becomes possible. The workers constitute the only useful portions of society. They are the makers of nations and the builders of civilization. The constitution recognizes this and proceeds to safeguard their freedom, not only by recognizing their right to choice of labour, and the right to the full product of that labour, but by declaring null and void any relinquishment of these rights that by force or fraud they may be induced to make. Compulsory work is the essence of slavery, and the constitution is the embodiment of the most complete civil liberty the mind of man can conceive. Here again we have the Man Right clearly placed high above the Property Right; the right of a man to disown any pact into which he has entered to the curtailment of his freedom is recognized as sacred and inviolable, and incomparably more worthy of safeguard than the sanctity of the most righteous property pact.

No man can be compelled to work without his plain consent *and just compensation*. The framers of this constitution were men of the people. They knew perfectly well, as we have said, the vast gulf of exploitation and plunder which lies between *salary* or *wages* on the one hand, and the *full product of labour* or *just compensation* on the other, and they proposed to make that knowledge effective. Mexico in this article has the honour of being the first nation to lay down the great economic principle which some day must govern the earth: that society, not the individual, is the arbiter of the social equivalent for labour.

The monastic orders were suppressed because bitter experience had proved them to be an unmitigated evil, the breeding grounds of sedition, oppression, exploitation, and social depravity. The basic immorality of a parasitic life further undermined their common integrity and it was a normal consequence that the parasite and sexual pervert should become the traitor and the intriguer. Out of the cloisters sprang all the cuartelazos which had flayed the common people; out of the cloisters sprang all the misery and poverty of the common people, their degradation and national disgrace. To maintain the monasteries would have been the prolongation of a social crime; to suppress them was the first step toward the salvation and redemption of the nation.

"Neither will be permitted a contract or agreement by which a man makes a pact for his proscription or exile." The constitution thus makes the rights of men the absolute condition of life.

THE CONSTITUTION OF 1857

The Life Right and the Man Right are one in the new social order, and proscriptions by which the individual resigns his Man Right are deemed absurd and of no effect. No man without rights had a place in Mexico.

Article VI. *The expression of ideas shall not be subjected to any judicial or governmental prosecution except in cases of attack upon the public morality, the rights of a third party, or the prevention of a crime or a disturbance of public order.*

Article VII. *The liberty of writing and publishing writings upon any matter is inviolable. No previous censorship nor imposition of bonds upon the writers nor the publishers for the purpose of curtailing the freedom of the press can be established by any law or authority, such freedom being restricted to respect of private life, morals, and public business.*

In these articles is firmly established the right of free speech and the right of free press. These constitute the very foundations and bulwark of a pure democracy, and therefore are continually assailed and beset by the forces of reaction.

Article VIII. *This deals with the right of petition to the government.*

Article IX. *This gives the right of assembly.*

Article X. *This establishes the right of every man to possess and carry arms for his safety and legitimate defence.*

Article XI. *This deals with immigration to the country and other travelling both from the country and into the same.*

Article XII. *This establishes the invalidity of all titles of nobility, prerogatives, and hereditary honours.*

Article XIII. *In the Mexican Republic no one shall be subjected to private laws nor special courts. No man or corporation shall enjoy fueros nor receive emoluments unless they be a compensation for public services and already fixed by law.*

Thus end the forty-seven years of bloody battle against the ecclesiastical and military fueros which have played so prominent a part in the history of Mexico. So long as a large privileged class existed immune from the civil law no social organization, much less a democracy, was possible. Article XIII, therefore, destroys clerical and military privilege as the fundamental prerequisite of a healthy social life.

"No emoluments unless they be a compensation for public services and already fixed by law." Thus was abolished not only the rents, tributes, tithings, and taxes which the Church had been accustomed to extort from the poor by the aid of the executive force, but also the universal practice of the clergy of extorting the last centavo from the dying peon and his superstitious relatives under threat of the law, and the still more terrifying threat of refusing the last unction. Henceforth neither the priest as an individual nor the Church as an organization could prostitute the political institutions of the country to the purposes of fraud, plunder, and oppression.

Article XIV. *This establishes the principle that no one shall be tried by retroactive laws.*

Article XV. *No treaties can be made for the extradition of political offenders; neither for those criminals whose crime was committed in a country where they had been slaves; neither can a treaty or agreement be made by which the warranties or rights that this constitution gives to man or citizen be altered.*

From the establishment of the full freedom of person, of labour, of speech, and of press in Mexico the constitution logically proceeds to the recognition of similar rights in the individuals of all nations, and refuses to permit the complicity of Mexico with the acts of foreign powers in violation of these rights. Thus was the full right of asylum established not only for political and religious refugees but even for criminals whose crime was committed in slavery. It must be remembered that at this time slavery was the dominant issue in the United States; runaway slaves, some of them perhaps with blood on their hands, continually fled to Mexico, and it behooved the framers of the constitution to see to it that their policy in regard to these men be clearly defined, lest Mexico be drawn into complicity with the most dangerous enemy of her liberty.

Article XVI. *This article establishes the principle that the family and domicile are inviolable, except for the purposes of arrest under a warrant from a proper court expressing the charge.*

Article XVII. *No one shall be arrested or imprisoned for debts of a purely civil character. No one shall exercise violence to claim his rights. The courts will always be ready for the administration of justice. This will be free, the costs being abolished.*

A characteristic of the old barbaric legislation of Mexico, as of all Europe and the United States in former times, was the right of the creditor to imprison his debtor for default. This was a curse which fell principally upon the labouring class, for the exploiting class, having absorbed the wealth of the country, were alone in the position to become creditors. The framers of this constitution were men of the people, and as such they naturally abolished a usage which had oppressed the people for centuries.

Article XXVII. *Private property shall not be taken without the consent of the owner, except in case of public utility, and by just payment therefor. Religious corporations or institutions, no matter of what domination, character, durability, or purpose, and civil corporations when under the patronage, direction, or superintendency of religious institutions, or ministers of any cult, shall not have the legal capacity to acquire or manage any real estate except the buildings which are used immediately and directly for the services of the said institutions; neither will the law recognize any mortgage on any property held by these institutions.*

All the principles for the establishment of the most complete human freedom and for the upbuilding of a civilization of surpassing splendour had been laid down in this constitution. But these of themselves could be of no avail unless every individual in Mexico from the least to the greatest was placed in immediate possession of the full means of subsistence adequate for the present and capable of indefinite expansion in the future. Agriculture is the economic base of man: cultivable land and equality of access thereto is the foundation of democracy and all potent civilization. We have seen that, pending the proclamation of the constitution, a bill had been introduced in Congress entitling every man to as much land as he could make productive. Article XXVII of the constitution now at a blow places the vast illicit holdings of the Church at the disposal of the people. Thus were established the foundations for an agrarian democracy. Articles IV and V, recognizing the right of the workman to the full product of his labour, or just compensation for his task, would have been impotent if there had not been given to the workman at the same time free access to the land, thereby making of him an independent man, sovereign over himself, his land, and its products, and in that very fact endowing him with the economic power which alone could make these provisions living realities in society. It is needless to point out that an independent farmer will not work for another unless it be at a higher rate of remuneration than he can achieve by the cultivation of his own land. Automatically, therefore, the vexed question of what constitutes the full product of labour is decided and enforced. In Mexico to-day the big land-owners have seized and appropriated thousands of the small land holdings established under the Constitution of 1857, not because they need more land — they could not possibly cultivate a tenth of what they already possess — *but because they need slaves.*

Article XXVIII. *State and Church are independent. Congress cannot make any law establishing or forbidding any religion.* . .

The foregoing constitute the fundamental principles of the constitution. Other articles followed, establishing the form of government as republican, federal, representative, democratic, and popular; adopting the Montesquieu system of the division of the functions of government into executive, legislative, and judicial; defining the rights and duties of citizenship, and formulating the methods of election in accordance with methods generally adopted in other federal republics.

From the moment when this constitution was proclaimed the

THE CONSTITUTION OF 1857

peons began to take full advantage of it. If at first the majority of them, overawed by the threats of the Church, homesteaded on the ecclesiastical estates in fear and trembling, little by little they began to gain confidence, and in two or three years some million of them at least had become sturdy, independent farmers.

But the constitution which had brought such blessing to the peon brought naught but destruction to the strongest and best-organized institutions in Mexico. Accustomed only to the exercise of tyranny, and utterly unused and untrained to obedience to the civil law, the Church and Army struggled fiercely against the impending destruction of their privilege to plunder and oppress. When the Secretary of the Interior issued orders that all government employees should take the oath of obedience to the constitution, the Church deliberately advised and commanded disobedience to the order. According to Zamacois, "The Archbishop of Mexico, Don Lázaro de la Garza, announced in circulars sent to the bishops a few days after the order for the taking of the oath had been given, that since the articles of this constitution were inimical to the institution, doctrine, and rites of the Catholic Church neither the clergymen nor laymen could take this oath under any pretext whatever. In view of this communication the bishops of all the dioceses sent circulars to their respective country vicars and the parish curates, and to the other ecclesiastics informing them, First: That it was not lawful to swear allegiance to the constitution because its articles were contrary to the institution, doctrine, and rites of the Catholic Church. Second: That this communication must be made public, and copies of it distributed as widely as possible. Third: That those who had made this oath must retract it at the confessional and make this retraction as public as possible, and that they must notify the government of their action." (Zamacois, "Historia de Méjico," Vol. 14, p. 525.)

To a devoutedly Catholic population these orders were disturbing enough. Torn between their opposing political and religious beliefs, they hesitated and fell into the utmost confusion. Even so, political good sense undoubtedly would have won the day in the teeth of the Church had not a tremendous mandate come to them from the Pope of Rome, the vicar of Christ on earth, to disobey utterly and completely all the commands of the impious Liberal government. This mandate of Pope Pius IX not only unified and reinforced the Catholic opposition in Mexico, but the Catholic opposition throughout the world against the Liberal government, thus paving the way for the internecine strife and the armed European intervention which followed hard upon it.

The last paragraph of this significant document in which Pope Pius IX deliberately preaches treason, sedition, and rebellion to a free people enjoying the benefits of an enlightened democratic government, is here given as being well worth careful consideration. After detailing at great length and with much complaint the various and numerous curtailments of the ecclesiastical privilege and prerogative sustained by the Church in Mexico at the hands of the Liberal government, the document concludes:

"Thus we make known to the faith in Mexico, and to the Catholic universe, that we energetically condemn every decree that the Mexican Government has enacted against the Catholic religion, against the Church, and her sacred ministers and pastors, against her laws, rights, and property, and also against the authority of this Holy See. We raise Our Pontifical Voice with apostolic freedom before you to condemn, reprove, and declare null, void, and without any value, the said decrees, and all others which have been enacted by the civil authorities in such contempt of the ecclesiastical authority of this Holy See, and with such injury to the religion, to the sacred pastors, and illustrious men. For this we command that those who have contributed to the fulfilment of the said decrees by action, advice, or command shall seriously meditate upon the penalties and censures imposed by the apostolic constitutions, and by the canons of the councils against the violators of sacred persons

Copyright by American Press Association

GENERAL CARRANZA ON CAMPAIGN

Guard of Yaqui Indians escorting General Carranza to the mines at Cannanea, Sonora, during his campaign for election in October, 1913

Copyright by Underwood & Underwood, N. Y.

YAQUI SOLDIERS

Strong of will, of almost superhuman endurance, of indomitable courage, of superior intelligence, the Yaquis make excellent workmen or soldiers

Copyright by Underwood & Underwood, N. Y.

GENERAL ZAPATA, CALLED "THE ATILLA OF THE SOUTH"

The revolt in southern Mexico has centred about the "Zapatistas" for three years. In spite of his sanguinary reputation, Zapata has restored thousands of acres of land to small native farmers. He recognizes Carranza as the head of the 1912–1914 revolt

Copyright by Underwood & Underwood, N. Y.

ZAPATA AND HIS MEN

"In the latter state (Morelos) the far-sighted Zapata had never for a moment relinquished the fight, directing his forces as vigorously against Madero as against his predecessor" (See page 350)

and things, against the violators of the ecclesiastical liberty and power, and against the usurpers of the rights of this Holy See."

The entire document may be verified in "México á través de los Siglos," Vol. 5, p. 226.

This papal mandate fell like a bomb upon the people of Mexico. In any society there are always two main conflicting factions, the exploiting and the exploited, the rulers and the ruled, the parasites and the workers. The issue between them, however, has never been clearly discerned by the common people as a whole, for the parasitic class always make it their prime business to use the avenues of education and publicity which lie solely in their hands utterly to confuse the minds of the common people, and to prevent them from discovering the existence, purpose, and history of this great division in society. Thus the common people are forever divided against themselves, the more astute, refusing to be hypnotized by the master class, follow the party of revolution (not reform); the less astute, following the dictates of the school, the press, the pulpit, and the cheap politician, become in the hands of their masters the very weapons, by ballot or bullet against their own emancipation and the emancipation of their fellows. The division is not clearly made nor seen until some social climax is reached — some national crisis. Then the great mass rends apart, and the emancipated mind beholds the greatest tragedy known to man — the people divided among themselves, shedding each other's blood, while the masters direct the fight, gather the spoils, and retire to the banquet of victory, there to toast amid loud laughter those who have prostituted their vote or mutilated their bodies in the destruction of that which alone could bring them freedom and development.

In the period which we are now observing the same cleavage was latent; but not until the great crisis produced by the papal mandate had occurred did it become apparent. Then it was seen that the Mexican people, magnificent as had been their Revolution of Ayutla, all emancipating as had been their Constitution of 1857, superbly sane and bold as had been the work of their great popularly elected Congress, were still, to a large extent, in the thrall of Rome, that the word of the Pope was still more powerful in their ears than the approaching heavy tread of tyranny, of hunger and of death, and more to be obeyed than the trumpet-call of freedom. They had sent their representatives to the metropolis pledged to work for their liberty and rights against the material interests of the privileged class. They had found in the proclamation of the constitution the fulfilment of their long-expected redemption. They now saw before them an upward march of such freedom, dignity, and wealth as had scarcely entered their boldest dreams; but when they heard the mandate of the Pope, listened to the dread commands of this Super-man, the vicar of Christ, inspired by the Holy Ghost with the wisdom of the Most High, they fell back, startled, dumfounded, and afraid. The power fell from their strong arms, the light went out of their newly awakened intelligences, and the psychological debauchery of centuries at the hands of the Church triumphed in them over the united force of all the highest instincts of humanity.

The Pope's mandate, as we have seen, was no half-hearted affair. On the contrary, it condemned to destruction the whole glorious edifice of human liberty reared at the cost of such tremendous sacrifice in the Constitution of 1857. It not only denounced, as a sacrilegious crime against God and the Holy See, the confiscation of the ecclesiastical estates, and the abolition of fueros, the prohibition of labour contracts and religious vows, the freedom of conscience, speech, and published opinion, but it counselled and upheld sedition, treason, and rebellion against the constitutional law of Mexico as worthy of the praise and honour of men and the reward of heaven. Thus there was no possible middle course, no conceivable compromise left to the Mexican people as a body. The Pope deliberately rent them asunder, father against son, brother against brother, to their own destruction and the glory of God!

THE CONSTITUTION OF 1857

The real significance of this papal mandate, as likewise the real significance of the Constitution of 1857, which it was intended to overthrow, would seem to have escaped all historians, and to have left no impress upon public opinion. The fundamental importance of the one can only be measured by the fundamental importance of the other. No document in history is profounder or of more far-reaching consequence than this Mexican Constitution of 1857. It may yet become — and that shortly — the engrossing subject of international diplomacy, the *casus belli* between international reaction and international revolution, and ultimately the Magna Charta of a new civilization.

In like manner the papal mandate aimed at its destruction is a document of equally profound and far-reaching consequence. *The fact that within the last sixty years the papal power has been directly exerted to overthrow the lawfully constituted authorities of a free Republic should strike the discerning mind as a fact of more than passing significance.*

These two documents, therefore, are of immense importance. If the constitution is the challenge of the impending world-wide social revolution, the papal mandate of Pius IX is the answer of world-wide reaction; and the struggle which began then is in full force to-day and must go on till the world be ruled by one or the other.

At first only a few sporadic uprisings in different parts of the country occurred to attest the fact that reaction, now unified and supported by the vicar of Christ, was preparing to overthrow all the hard-won triumphs of the people represented by the Liberal government and the Constitution of 1857.

It will be remembered that a decree authorizing the organization of civicos, and the suppression of the regular army had been enacted by Congress and supported by the constitution. In spite of this, however, and in spite of the patent untrustworthiness of the regular soldiery as evinced in the outbreak of several cuartelazos against the government, Comonfort on one pretext or another had managed to retain the larger part of Santa Ana's army. This fatal mistake again gave into the hands of the Church the very weapon she had used for fifty years against the liberties of the people and the supremacy of the civil authority — the very weapon she needed and whose destruction would have left her impotent.

In the rapid succession of events the time had now arrived for the election of the first President, Congress, and Supreme Court under the new constitution. Comonfort's actions as pre-constitutional President, although they had angered the Liberals in Congress, had not alarmed the people at large to any extent, and they now elected him to office by a vast majority. Undoubtedly his prestige as the heroic leader of the Ayutla Revolution outweighed in their minds the weakness of his indeterminate policy. At the same time Benito Juarez was elected President of the Supreme Court, and on the 1st of September both officers, together with a strong Liberal Congress, were duly inaugurated. In his inaugural address Comonfort astounded the vast concourse of people who had gathered to partake of a ceremony monumental in their history by declaring, "One of the greatest remedies for the salvation of our country will be, it is my belief, the adoption of certain healthy and useful amendments to the constitution. To this end the Government will draw up as speedily as possible the alterations that are deemed necessary, and confidently expects you to adopt them without delay. . . ." This declaration, a clear and unmistakable betrayal of the constitution, and the popular conquests of the Revolution of Ayutla, filled the people with dismay, and further added to the moral confusion wrought in them by the recent papal mandate.

Meanwhile the Church, although publicly defying the government's authority, had shrouded her practical plans for its overthrow in the utmost secrecy. Well guarded as these plans were, however, their general tenor and purpose could not be entirely suppressed, and the air was vibrant with the vague apprehension that heralds a storm. "The moment was impending when the

THE CONSTITUTION OF 1857

veil would be torn asunder, and the nation would be compelled to face in all its nudity the intrigues that for a long time had been hatching, thus clearing a situation that scarcely could be further prolonged." ("México á través de los Siglos," Vol. 5, p. 365.)

According to arrangements previously made, the constitution took effect on the 16th of September, 1857. The next day — only fifteen days after the inaugural ceremonies mentioned above — Felix Zuloaga, the commander-in-chief of the army, headed a powerful cuartelazo against the government, proclaiming that the constitution was not acceptable to the nation, and that it was therefore abrogated; that Comonfort would remain President as the choice of the people, and that a Congress would be elected forthwith for the purpose of framing a new constitution more adapted to the needs of the country, and that in the meantime the President would appoint representatives from each state to act as his provisional council.

The prominence of Comonfort's name in this proclamation, coupled with the fact that Zuloaga was his own appointee, and that the cuartelazo was started and the proclamation made at Tacubaya, his summer residence, shows that the vacillating President had at last fallen so utterly into the hands of the reactionaries that he had conspired with them to betray the Constitution of 1857, and to destroy the very triumphs of the people for which he had fought so hard and so well. Scarcely, however, had the news of the *coup d'état* shocked the nation than Comonfort, deserted by his cabinet, his personal friends, and the entire Liberal party, realized the terrible mistake he had made. "I have changed my legal title of President for that of a miserable brigand," he cried, "but everything is done and there is no remedy. I resign myself to the course of events, and God will show me my path."

He now discovered that the ecclesiastics, whom he had befriended by his treason, scorned him as fiercely as the Liberals, while from all parts of the country came the news that the people and the state governments utterly repudiated him. Half frenzied with chagrin and remorse he endeavoured to right the wrong he had committed by proclaiming the full reëstablishment of the constitution.

Too late! Felix Zuloaga had already entered Mexico City at the head of his army and had attacked the government forces from the arsenal. For two days the fight raged, Comonfort opposing his own cuartelazo with the scanty remnant of the national guard who remained loyal to him. "Then, as in the revolt of 1847," says Baz, "the friars patrolled the trenches of the revolting soldiery, exciting them to the fight; then, as in that other epoch, the clergy paid the wages of the troops, and their agents were bribing the officers of the government that swelled the ranks of the enemy. The city was deserted; at night time the only light was the blaze of the artillery fire and the sinister flashing of the bombs; in every street there were breastworks, and from every door came forth the groans of the dying and the moans of the wounded." (Gustavo Baz, "Vida de Juarez.")

Before the close of the second day Comonfort found himself alone in the fight, defeated, deserted, despised. Filled with bitter remorse, he wrote out his resignation and left Mexico City forever, to die in voluntary exile. The epitaph of his career is aptly expressed in his own words: "I have been a good son but a bad patriot."

To quote Baz again, "The reaction was victorious in the capital, and the wickedness of one man and the ambitions of others had provoked a civil war that was destined to last until the extermination of one of the contending factions. The joyous clamouring of the bells, the majestic music of the Te Deum, the rejoicing of the Clericals everywhere, and the drunkenness of the soldiery, welcomed that victory of fraud, ambition, and reaction. . . ." (Gustavo Baz, "Vida de Juarez," p. 133.)

Felix Zuloaga was now proclaimed Provisional President by the soldiery and clergy. His first activity was to abolish the constitution, reëstablish the clergy in the full possession of their property, fueros and privileges, and to suppress the freedom of

THE CONSTITUTION OF 1857

speech, of press, and of religious creed. He then hastened to dispatch a message to the Pope announcing in joyful terms the overthrow of the constitutional government and the complete triumph of the Clerical party; and in due time received the papal congratulations in the following form:

"Pope Pius IX, to our beloved son, the illustrious and respectable man, Felix Zuloaga, President *ad interim* of the Mexican Republic.

"Beloved Son, Illustrious and Respectable Man, Greetings and Apostolic Blessings. We have had great pleasure in receiving in the last days your letter of the 1st of January, dictated by deep sentiments of piety and veneration toward us and toward this Apostolic See. The relation therein of the change of circumstances which has recently occurred in your Republic gives us to understand that, having been elected President *ad interim,* your ardent wishes are to nullify and abolish without delay the laws and decrees that were instituted during the late unhappy condition of the nation against the Church and her sacred ministers. Certainly we have received great consolation from the purport of your letter which shows how earnestly you and your government desire to reëstablish relations with this Holy See, and to work assiduously that our Holy Religion may flourish in its height of power in Mexico according to the deep aspirations of all good Mexicans. . . . Bestowing upon you the blessings of God, and in testimony of our paternal affection and good-will, we give with great love our Apostolic blessings to you, Beloved Son, Illustrious and Respectable Man, and to all the clergymen, and to the faithful men of that Republic. Given in St. Pedro de Rome, March 18, 1858. Pius Nono."*

These documents, considered in connection with the events which evolved them, vividly portray the success of the reaction achieved by the clergy and soldiery under the counsel and patronage of the Pope.

---

*These documents can be verified in "México á través de los Siglos," pp. 281, 282.

CHAPTER XV

THE UPHOLDING OF THE CONSTITUTION

BY THE mere fact of complicity in the *coup d'état* which had abolished the constitution, Comonfort had impeached himself as President of the Republic. To Congress alone belonged the right to amend, reform, or abrogate the constitution, and Comonfort by his attempt to appropriate the congressional prerogative had become an outlaw. According to the constitution, the President of the Supreme Court, who was likewise Vice-President of the Republic, succeeded to the presidency of the Republic *ad interim* whenever that office became vacant before the expiration of the full presidential term, owing to the absence, incapacity, resignation, impeachment, or death of its incumbent. Benito Juarez now, therefore, became constitutional President of the Republic.

In view of its impossible position Congress agreed to dissolve by its own act, not, however, until it had proclaimed the impeachment of Comonfort, recognized Benito Juarez as lawful President, and recommended the governors of all the various states to uphold the constitutional authority and defend the government.

Immediately after his recognition by Congress Juarez left Mexico City for Guanajuato and proceeded to organize a cabinet of staunch Liberal veterans, Guillermo Prieto, Melchor Ocampo, Manuel Ruiz, and Leon Guzman. Again the struggle of fifty years was renewed between the oppressor and the oppressed; between the Clergy, Army, and Aristocracy on the one hand, and the common people on the other. But now for the first time in their history the common people fought for a clear-cut constitution, the full expression of their aspirations, embodying their principles of liberty, and adopted by the majority of the nation as the supreme law of the land.

"On one side," says Baz, "were the revolutionists armed with the buckler of legal power and ready to shed their blood for freedom of thought and speech, for the suppression of the monasteries, the confiscation of the ecclesiastical estates, the support of the civil power as the only recognized authority in society, and for the upholding of the complete equality of men and the liberty and civilization of the Republic. On the other side were the Clergy and the Army banded together to reëstablish a government born of treason and mutiny, to reënforce all the abuses that were left as a legacy to Mexico by the colonial régime, and to proclaim as invulnerable and divine rights the rule of the clergy, the army fueros, and the inviolability of the Church estates, and damning as heresy the freedom of conscience and the equality of men.

"The revolution was a genuine social revolution; it was a struggle to overthrow many years of deeply entrenched interests, three centuries of prejudice, and ideas as old as the world, as old as fanaticism and liberty. The programme of the one element was to destroy in order to create; the programme of the other to conserve in order to destroy." (Gustavo Baz, "Vida de Juarez," p. 136.)

The strength of the reactionaries lay in the army, powerful, disciplined, well entrenched in all parts of the country; the strength of the people lay in the national guard or bodies of civicos rapidly organized by the governors of the states.

The first considerable encounter of a civil war destined to deluge the country in blood for three long years took place at Salamanca, State of Guanajuato, and resulted in the defeat of the Constitutionalists at the hands of a superior force of reactionaries. This reverse forced Juarez to remove his seat of government from Guanajuato to Guadalajara, whence he was again compelled to remove to Vera Cruz. The Liberals, however, once organized, rapidly gained full control in the north, sweeping the states of Zacatecas, San Luis Potosi, Aguas Calientes, and later extending their control to all the states of the south, thus confining the power of the reactionaries to Mexico City and the adjacent states of the centre. But the fight was destined to be bitter and prolonged, for against the limited resources of the Constitutionalists were pitted the millions of the Church, and against the calm statements of the constitution were pitted the inflammatory, seditious harangues of every priest in the country.

The Church, indeed, leaning strongly upon her fundamental policy of psychological debauchery, exploited every device known to the science of class rule in order to counterbalance the simple, mighty appeal to the people of the great Constitution of 1857. Her priests throughout the land proclaimed a "holy war," characterizing the struggle as one against the enemies of God. The soldiers marched to battle bedizened with scapularies and crosses, bearing aloft flags and banners inscribed with the sacred images and symbols of religion. Those who fell were extolled as martyrs in the holy cause — the peers of the first Christian martyrs under the Roman Empire. To the commander-in-chief of the Constitutional forces, Santos Degollado, the clergy gave the nickname "Antiochus Epiphanes," after the conqueror of Jerusalem who endeavoured to uproot the Jewish religion, 170 B. C., and to Miguel Miramon, the commander-in-chief of the reactionary army, the name of "Judas, the Maccabee," or "Young Maccabee," after the great defender of the Jewish faith; and to complete the farce, they gave to the Constitutionalists the name of "Philistines," and to the reactionaries the name of "Israel, the appointed of the Lord." All this elaborate misrepresentation to obscure the real issue and blind the peon to his economic birthright, and *in spite of the fact that the Constitutionalists were as fervent devotees of the Catholic faith as the most ardent reactionary!*

UPHOLDING OF THE CONSTITUTION

Meanwhile the conspiracy for the establishment of a monarchy was developing with great rapidity. It was no longer a matter of secret sessions in the cloister but of public pronouncement. If any doubt had existed in the minds of the people in regard to the purpose of the ruling class, that doubt was definitely set at rest by an editorial published in *La Sociedad*, the Catholic official organ in its issue of December 14, 1858, an excerpt from which is given below:

"It is necessary for our national Conservative party to be united with a foreign power from Europe in order to safeguard forever our own existence. The Conservative party ought to interest, for the sake of its own life, one or two European nations, generous enough and sufficiently strong and united to protect the great principles of national equilibrium *in what concerns us in particular*. It is necessary to make a strong alliance with those European nations that we may be protected in our religion and nationality from the Protestant power north of us (the United States). Our happiness and the safety of our Catholic religion depend upon our close union and obedience to the Vatican, and on our alliance with the Catholic nations of Europe. To the Catholic European world it will be by no means convenient that the Catholic world of America degenerate into Protestantism; to the political European world, and its general interests, it will be by no means convenient that America become democratic or fall under the influence of the Washington Capitol."

Zuloaga, of course, was the very heart of the conspiracy. "In following that policy, Zuloaga, in his character of President, officially sought the intervention of Spain, England, and France, and particularly of the last." (Francisco Arrangoiz, Mexico, desde 1808, hasta 1865.) To obtain the Spanish good-will and coöperation he recognized again the fraudulent Spanish credit which had been repudiated by Juarez with the consent of the

Spanish minister himself, the high-minded Don Miguel de los Santos Alvarez. And as if this were not burden enough to lay on the backs of an impoverished and exhausted people he dared to recognize as a national debt a loan of $15,000,000 drawn by the "Young Maccabee" on a French-Jewish banking firm, Jecker, Torre & Co.

Meanwhile Juarez, from his seat of government at Vera Cruz, not only roundly denounced and repudiated those flagrant acts of treason and embezzlement, but he immediately enacted the celebrated *Leyes de Reforma* for the drastic enforcement of the constitution within the range of its power. These *Leyes de Reforma* (reform laws) decreed:

I. The immediate suppression of all monasteries and convents, and the immediate and complete confiscation of all Church property to the use of the nation.

II. The adoption of the jury system, and the thorough enforcement of the abolition of fueros.

III. The entire freedom of public instruction and the establishment of free primary schools, high schools, universities, professional, and trade schools.

IV. The adoption of a policy by which school teachers and professors were to become the most highly remunerated and responsible officers of the government.

V. The establishment of civil recording authorities for births, marriages, and deaths, thus abolishing the much abused privilege of the Church in the matter of establishing the civil status of persons.

VI. The establishment of friendly relations with foreign powers.

VII. The recognition of the national guard as the sole military support of public liberty and of the constitution.

VIII. The national construction, ownership, and operation of all railroads and telegraph lines, to the subordination (not exclusion) of the right of private individuals and corporations

UPHOLDING OF THE CONSTITUTION

to build railroads and operate industries subject to certain conditions.

IX. The subdivision of the great estates into small farms to be assigned to the tillers of the soil upon the payment of a small sum to cover the expenses of subdivision and assignment. And the encouragement of foreign immigrants to settle in Mexico upon the same footing as the Mexicans.

Articles VIII and IX are well worthy of emphasis. Juarez undoubtedly aimed at an ultimate, fully-developed collectivist administration of the means of wealth production, and in these two articles he paves a royal road to that consummation. The means of transportation and communication absolutely control industry and commerce. Therefore, *so long as the political power lay in the hands of the people* it meant their full political and economic control of the exploiting class, pending its ultimate expropriation. Again, a nation of small land-holders, owning their own means of transportation and communication, is the only real foundation of any economic or political freedom. On such a basis the development of a full system of coöperative industry to the annihilation of capitalist production is but a matter of time and logical growth.

When this remarkable document, which reaffirmed the issues of the Constitutional party in the civil war, was promulgated in Vera Cruz on the 7th of July, 1859, Europe was still reverberating to the thunders of the Communist manifesto of Marx and Engels; the first volume of "The Analysis of Capitalist Production" had already diagnosed the stupendous ills of society and pointed the path to emancipation; the Spectre of Democracy had already arisen to strike terror into every court and cabinet in Europe, and to arouse in them a frenzy of repression. *It is no matter for wonder, therefore, that the Constitution of 1856, the complete political expression of the revolutionary demands not only of the Mexican proletariat but of the world proletariat, should have been regarded with bitter fear and hatred by the capitalist powers of*

Europe: no matter for wonder that at the moment of its victory they combined without so much as a protest from the United States, to destroy it utterly, and lay waste the land which had given it birth.

From the moment of its inception the civil war had developed in intensity and bitterness. Scarcely a day passed without a bloody encounter between the contending factions. As in the present revolution (1910–1914), the reactionaries endeavoured to strike terror into the Constitutionalists by the summary execution of all prisoners of war, and, as in the present revolution, the Constitutionalists retaliated. The seriousness of the economic issue admitted no dalliance, no mercy.

Religious issue there was none — in spite of the persistent efforts of the Church to create the illusion of a "holy war." Constitutionalists and reactionary alike professed the Catholic faith. Human liberty and economic emancipation alone was the question. On the field of battle the dying revolutionist begged for a priest to perform the last rites and speed his soul heavenward equally with the dying reactionary; and when the priests, acting under the orders of the high prelates and the Pope, began to refuse the last unction to their enemies on the field of battle the Liberal leaders retorted with stringent orders for the summary execution of any priest who failed to perform this duty.

In spite of the largess of the Church and the harangues of the priest the struggle must soon have ended in the triumph of the Constitutionalists had not the reactionaries possessed in the person of Miramon, the "Young Maccabee," a leader of remarkable energy, ability, and courage. Aided by Leonardo Marquez, a leader of hardly less ability, he was the scourge of the Constitutionalists in numerous encounters. His crowning achievement, however, was the capture of Guadalajara, the storm-centre of the south, and in the early stages of the war the seat of government of President Juarez. The assault was one of the most bloody, as well as one of the most important in its results, in the history of the war.

When the victor entered the town at the head of his troops

UPHOLDING OF THE CONSTITUTION

he was welcomed in a frenzy of joy by the clergy and aristocracy, and escorted to the cathedral, where with all the pomp of celebration and the singing of "God Save the President" he was proclaimed President of the Republic.

At the same time the garrison of Mexico City had risen in revolt against the self-appointed President Zuloaga, and had proclaimed its allegiance to the "Young Maccabee." The new President, however, seemed to have little taste for the civil office. War was his trade. Arriving in Mexico City after a rapid march from Guadalajara, he formally refused the presidency, sought out Zuloaga, who was hiding from the soldiery, restored him to power, and then, organizing a picked body of troops, marched on Vera Cruz, the seat of the Juarez government. He was not destined, however, to repeat his triumph of Guadalajara. Juarez inflicted upon him a crushing defeat, and he returned to Mexico City with his army broken and demoralized. Again he organized a picked force and went against Vera Cruz and again was defeated.

In the meantime the Constitutionalists had been steadily gaining ground throughout the country. Already the states of Tamaulipas, Nuevo Leon, Coahuila, Chihuahua, Sonora, Michoacan, Baja California, Durango, Sinaloa, Tlascala, Oaxaca, Chiapas, Tabasco, Campeche, Yucatan, Zacatecas, Aguas Calientes, and Vera Cruz were under their control, and only the states of San Luis Potosi, Puebla, Queretaro, Guanajuato, Jalisco, and Mexico remained in the hands of the reactionaries, and even these were already invaded. Closing in from all sides upon Mexico City, the Constitutionalists finally made a fierce attack upon Tacubaya, one of its suburbs. Here, however, they were repulsed by Leonardo Marquez. The encounter was made notorious by the order of the "Young Maccabee," delivered to Leonardo Marquez, to kill all the prisoners of war, including a number of doctors and medical students from the School of Medicine at Mexico City who had gone to the fight to care for the wounded on both sides.

In spite of an occasional victory such as this of Tacubaya the reactionary army was rapidly losing ground; and the strong, steady advance of the Constitutionalists, north, south, east, and west, showed that the end was near. So sure of speedy and complete victory was President Juarez that on November 6, 1860, he issued a call to the country for a congressional and presidential election to take place within the following two months.

On the 20th of the same month occurred the final and decisive conflict of the war. The Constitutionalist army of sixteen thousand men, under Gonzalez Ortega, utterly routed the reactionary army of eight thousand men and thirty pieces of artillery, under Miramon, in the hills of San Miguel Calpulalpan close to Mexico City. The shattered remnants of the defeated army fled in disorder to the city, thence to the hills, not before, however, the alert Miramon had seized by force from the English legation some sixty thousand dollars which had been deposited there for the payment of the interest on the English credit. Five days later the Constitutionalist army entered the capital, and on the 11th of January, 1861, President Juarez and his cabinet reëstablished constitutional rule in Mexico.

. . . .

The first act of the constitutional government was to expel from the country the high prelates and foreign representatives directly responsible for the recent civil war.

Having cleansed the country of its more potent adversaries, the government bowed itself to the tremendous task of rebuilding the ruined and desolated country. The reactionary army, headed by Felix Zuloaga who still assumed the title of President of the Republic, was shattered and broken but not altogether vanquished. In various parts of the country its operations continued to be a source of trouble, and the government had to begin its painful and laborious work of reconstruction in a yet incompletely pacified state of society.

Fifty-two years of alternate master-class anarchy and working-

UPHOLDING OF THE CONSTITUTION

class revolution, coupled with a foreign war and three armed invasions, culminating in the recent three years of bloody internecine strife, had left Mexico in a state of ruin, poverty, and paralysis difficult to conceive and impossible to describe. It is probable that no civil administration ever faced a more stupendous or more important task than the government of Juarez now faced; it is certain that no administration ever faced its task in a spirit more sane, more strong, more illumined with genius. Agriculture had almost ceased to exist; industry was annihilated; famine ravaged the land. Thousands of strong men lay dead; thousands of women wept in bitterness; thousands of children cried for bread.

The tremendous vitality of the Mexican people, however, stood them in good stead. Under the leadership of Juarez they gathered themselves for the great task of reconstruction. With a united will, government and people turned from mourning and disaster to the inauguration of what — but for the infamous foreign hand — would have been the brightest, most promising era in the history of humanity.

On the 1st of May, 1861, the constitutional Congress opened its session for the first time since the *coup d'état* of the unhappy Comonfort; and President Juarez, in delivering the greatest message ever listened to by a constitutional body, reaffirmed the government's policy of the past, outlining its endeavours for the future, and voiced, as no man has voiced, the full aspirations of a united and determined people. In the course of this message he said: "From that moment [the outbreak of the Clerical rebellion] began for the government and the country a new epoch filled with difficulties and conflicts. But now the war is ended, and it is necessary to again begin our task of reparation and reorganization. War and oppression have disorganized all things. We have to face complications and difficulties in every branch of public administration, from the rural municipality to the department of foreign affairs. The habit of observance to law having been broken, and the jurisdiction of the different officers having been disarranged, this state of affairs might seem fraught with menace to our national unity. But, thanks to the good sense of the federal states and the conscientiousness and the good-will of the people throughout the country, this menace has not arisen, or has been of very little account. The federation is now compact, firm, and united by constitutional ties and ready to sustain our national institutions, and to enforce and obey the laws enacted by this sovereign assembly. . . .

"To the different states and territories has been given the fullest authority to deal with their particular problems; and all the concessions they have required for the benefit of public education, health, and general welfare have been granted them. . .

"The institutions of public education, the greatest glory of our country, from whose well-planted seed will spring the amelioration of our evils and the uplifting of the Republic, were all but destroyed in some places and completely so in others. This government believes that one of its first duties is the restoration of these institutions. And they have laboured earnestly to the end that they be reopened without delay. . . .

"It is necessary that society procure free development of material wealth, and in view of this necessity, well understood by the Executive, *adequate measures have been taken for the construction by the government of a railroad between Vera Cruz and Mexico City and between Chalco and Mexico City.* . . .

"The spirit of enterprise and coöperation has been awakened, and for its further development we hold in reserve another undertaking for whose execution this government seeks with assurance the sanction and support of Congress. . . .

"The public treasury is in a very depleted condition, but strict economy and honest watchfulness in the distribution of public money will no doubt replenish it in the future. . . .

"*Great care has been given to the important task of nationalizing the former clerical lands, a task from which it has been impossible to reap all the results that would accrue under normal conditions,*

UPHOLDING OF THE CONSTITUTION

owing to the embarrassed position of the government and the turmoil of the civil war. . . .

"Great economies have been effected by the reduction of the army by this government's orders. The soldiers who were the supporters of oppression and tyranny have been discharged from service as unworthy to carry arms for the Republic. . . .

"Those who have fought for liberty, and who, with great courage, defended our democratic principles on the battlefield, are returning to their homes, but holding themselves ever ready to fight for our institutions. . . . "

In these simple, masterly words was expressed the purpose of the government — the making and moulding of a new nation in the light of a vast understanding. The people saw their own collective good sense and political genius reflected back upon them by their government, and they entered into the spirit and purpose of its plans with all the ardour of a full accord. A remnant there was — as there must be in all societies born and reared in the pathological conditions of the class struggle — who were too depressed to rise, too debased to respond to the high energies of their fellows, too maimed in mind to appreciate the new order, too crippled in spirit to take advantage of their liberty. These still clung to their servitude and delivered themselves up an apathetic prey to the old superstitions.

The strong, however, and they were in the vast majority, entered with a will upon the exercise of their new-found freedom and economic independence. The land was there — the land for which they had fought for fifty years — and they laid hold of it in a spirit of energy and promise. Their title was full and unimpeachable, a title whose terms aroused their manhood, and gave them the fullest self-respect — "To every man as much land as he can make productive." It was not to be expected that these things should come to instant perfection. But the whole institution of society in Mexico had been lifted bodily from the vicious vortex of chaos and contradiction, and placed on the open road to an unending progressive development.

Society had been started right; as it gathered way, its onward course was bound by all dynamic law to become more direct, more purposeful and powerful, and to draw all halting, contradictory elements into its wake. In the brief space of the Juarez régime before the foreign hand laid foul hold upon this splendid infant democracy, at least a million peons became independent farmers upon their own land. Had they been given time to firmly establish, foster, and mature their nascent institutions, they would have swept the remnants of reaction from the land, and have founded an unique agrarian democracy, upon whose foundations must have arisen the first great industrial democracy of the world. But this triumph of the social man, which found expression in the Constitution of 1857, was a menace to the exploiting capitalist class of Europe and the United States, a menace more bitter than was the French Revolution to the old feudality. Had it survived and flourished it would have vindicated the power of the people to govern themselves. It would have illustrated the splendour of human happiness and progress that can be achieved, and must be achieved, by a community whose political institutions are based upon Man Right, and whose social institutions are based upon economic equality. So fair a thing could not be permitted to live by the capitalist powers that governed and still govern our complex barbarism — misnamed civilization. It was a moral rebuke to their squalor of soul, a summons to heights beyond their reach, a denunciation of their cherished system of exploitation, a rising menace to their power, an atheism to their Moloch of Property, and — most important of all — a tocsin to their own hardly suppressed proletarian revolutions. *It had to be destroyed.*

On the 11th of June, 1861, Juarez was proclaimed constitutional President of Mexico, and on the 31st of October of the same year, France, England, and Spain signed a compact in London pledging themselves to a joint invasion of Mexico for the purpose of overthrowing the constitutional government, and establishing in its place a monarchy, supported by bayonets.

CHAPTER XVI

THE FRENCH INTERVENTION OF 1861–1865

THE one preponderant cause which led to the intervention of Europe in Mexico, in connivance with the United States, has been already defined in the preceding chapter. A second fundamental cause of intervention is to be found in the struggle for commercial supremacy in the Latin-American market which had sprung up between Europe and the United States, after Mexico and the Spanish colonies of Central and South America had conquered their independence from Spain, and opened their ports to the trade of the world. By the year 1861 the struggle had already become acute; and the European manufacturers and shippers, alarmed by the tremendous industrial advance of the United States, were eager to support any policy which would checkmate the influence of so formidable a rival in the Latin-American republics.

The spokesman of this powerful element in Europe was the petty bourgeois Napoleon III. Possessed of a mania for imperial expansion, the Emperor was already revelling in visions of a monarchist Latin America — the abject commercial slave of France. His Gargantuan ambition not only contemplated the establishment of a monarchy in Mexico subservient to France, not only contemplated the subsequent establishment of a chain of similar monarchies throughout Central and South America, but even contemplated the permanent seizure of the State of Sonora and the State of Baja (lower) California for the sake of their gold mines, and as a base of operations for the future conquest of the United States! It is no wonder then that international capitalism, the Clerical party in Mexico, the Papal See, and the disgruntled European manufacturers and shippers, saw in the "Little Napoleon" the *deus ex machina* who would serve all their allied ambitions in serving his own, who would crush the dangerous Mexican democracy, restore the power of the Church, and checkmate the commercial encroachments of the United States.

To Napoleon III and the French army, therefore, was entrusted the sacred mission of Europe to destroy the new-born Mexican democracy. The United States, not sufficiently astute to recognize the ultimate import of such an intervention to herself, played into the hands of Europe.

In spite of the gross misconception of Mexican affairs which existed in Europe and the United States in 1861 — a misconception which has persisted to recent times — it required all the glamour of papal bulls, the proclamations of the false President, the calumnies of the Mexican monarchist agents, and all the outcries of a foreign prostituted press and pulpit, to trap the common people of England, France, and Spain into acquiescence in the policy of intervention. To the Catholics of France and Spain the expedition of the allies against Mexico was made to appear a "holy war," a crusade against the sacrilegious enemies of God; to the British Protestants it was made to appear an act of mercy undertaken solely for the purpose of saving the Latin-American races from absorption by the United States.

As far back as 1855 Lord Palmerston, the English Secretary of Foreign Affairs, had agreed with Napoleon to offer the crown of Mexico to the Duc d'Aumale. That plan, however, failed, and the powers were compelled to fall back upon the second choice, Maximilian of Hapsburg, brother of Franz Joseph, Emperor of Austria.

After much vacillation Maximilian finally consented to be enthroned Emperor of Mexico by the allied armies of intervention, on condition that France pledge herself to support him with her army, and continue to do so until such time as he could

FRENCH INTERVENTION

firmly entrench himself in power. By the year 1861 the plan was fully rounded out, and all preparations had been made for its execution. It now only remained for the powers to find or invent some popular pretext for intervention, one at least sufficiently plausible to appease the conscience of the nations.

For the reasons previously stated the United States had maintained an attitude of non-committal connivance toward the European policy of intervention in Mexico, partly influenced, no doubt, by her feeling of impotence pending the inevitable convulsion of her own approaching civil war. The outbreak of hostilities between the North and the South now convinced Europe that it would be beyond the power of the United States to change her policy even if she would. Thus the road was clear to intervention and the establishment of a monarchy in Mexico. The "Little Napoleon" indeed saw in events the most favourable portents for the accomplishment of his dream of subjugating even the United States.

Quick action was necessary. Still no adequate pretext could be found. At this moment, however, Juarez addressed a note to the English, French, and Spanish ministers in Mexico City informing them that in view of the recent civil war in Mexico, and the consequent disorganization of the national finances, his government deemed it necessary and unavoidable to withhold the payment of the interest on the foreign credits for a period of two years. There was no attempt at repudiation; merely a request for forbearance on the part of the powers in view of Mexico's stricken condition. It seems incredible to the unprejudiced mind that this act of common business procedure, well within the generally accepted rules of international finance, should have been made the pretext for intervention. The fact remains that it was. Europe was eager to act; some pretext must be found; and why might not this serve as well as another?

Accordingly, with a grave parade of outraged dignity, the English, French, and Spanish ministers, acting under orders from their home governments, broke off all communication with the Mexican Government and left the country. This was immediately followed, as we have said, on the 31st of October, 1861, by the signing of the convention for intervention by the representatives of England, France, and Spain assembled in London. The principal articles of this convention, which, it must be remembered, was but a thin covering to the real purpose of international capitalism, were as follows:

Article I. Her Majesty the Queen of Spain, his Majesty the Emperor of the French, and her Majesty the Queen of the United Kingdom of Great Britain and Ireland, bind themselves, upon the signing of this convention, immediately to give the necessary orders for sending to Mexico naval and military forces combined in sufficient numbers to take and occupy all the fortresses and military posts of Mexico. . . .

Article II. The high contracting parties are not endeavouring to impose any form of government in Mexico. . . .

Article III. A committee of three, representing each high contracting party, shall decide all questions in regard to the distribution of the money collected in Mexico for the payment of the claims due to each high contracting party. . . .

Article IV. . . . It being known that the United States also has claims against Mexico, she will be invited to take part in this intervention. . . . London, October 31, 1861.

(Signed) ZAVIER ISTURIZ. (Seal.)
(Signed) FLAHAUT. (Seal.)
(Signed) RUSSELL. (Seal.)

THE ATTITUDE OF THE UNITED STATES

The invitation to the United States to participate in this intervention and the refusal of that country to join with the powers in invading Mexico deserve the most careful consideration in view of the commonly accepted opinions now entertained in the United States with regard to the whole affair. History

FRENCH INTERVENTION

has created a tradition to the effect that the United States Government looked with profound disfavour upon intervention by the European powers, and would have defended the sister Republic to the south had it not been for the civil war at home. This tradition further represents the departure of the French from Mexico in 1865 as the result of the policy of the United States, then freed from the domestic conflict and ready to render that aid to Mexico which would have been given in 1861 if necessity had not prevented. The leading facts cited in support of this tradition are President Lincoln's offer to assume Mexico's financial obligations to Europe for six years, and his unwavering recognition of Juarez as the constitutional executive of the Mexican Republic.

This tradition deserves the most rigid examination. It is true that the United States did recognize Juarez as the constitutional President, but it must be remembered that Juarez had promptly complied with a request from Secretary Seward asking him to refrain from recognizing the new Confederate slave republic. To have thrown the Mexican Republic into the arms of the Confederacy would have been poor diplomacy in view of the geographical relations of the two countries. Recognizing Juarez was making a virtue out of a practical necessity.

As to the second fact brought forward in support of the tradition — namely, that the Government of the United States generously offered to assume Mexico's European obligations in order to spare her from the ordeal of invasion — it is necessary to consider the nature of that offer and the circumstances connected with it. In response to pleading representations made by the Mexican Republic to the government at Washington, the latter communicated with its Minister in Mexico City as follows: "The President ardently wishes that the political status of Mexico as an independent nation will be maintained. The events you communicate have alarmed him upon this subject, and he believes that the people of the United States will not consider him just if an effort is not made to impede such a calam-

238   THE MEXICAN PEOPLE

ity in this continent as will be the extinction of a republic. He has decided to authorize you to negotiate a treaty with the Republic of Mexico by which the Government of the United States will assume the payment of the interest of the 3 per cent. consolidated debt which that country owes to the owners of the Mexican bonds, which debt is figured out to be nearly sixty-two million pesos, for the term of five years from the date of the decree given by the Mexican Government suspending that payment, on the condition that that government undertakes to pay to the United States for the reimbursement of the money loaned an interest of 6 per cent., warranting such payment with specific retention upon all public lands, and upon the mines in the different Mexican states of Lower California, Chihuahua, Sonora, and Sinaloa, these mortgaged properties to fall under the absolute domain of the United States at the end of the term of six years counted since the signing of this treaty, if the said reimbursement has not taken place during that term.* The circumstances, which are as new as extraordinary, make necessary this determination because the Mexican crisis does not permit any delay."†*

In order to understand the Mexican's point of view on this transaction, it is necessary to examine a few additional facts which lie on the surface of things. The exhausted financial condition of the Mexican people after fifty years of struggle for democracy and independence was well known in the United States. It must have been known that if Mexico could not pay 3 per cent., which was the rate fixed on her European loans, for the next two years, much less could she afford to pay 6 per cent. on the entire amount to the United States and fulfil the contract within the allotted six years. Must not the capitalist advisers who swarmed around the Government of the United States after the triumph of the Republican party — the party of protective

---

*Translated from "México á través de los Siglos."

†The public lands referred to consisted of vast areas widely distributed throughout the various states, while the immense mineral deposits of Chihuahua, Sonora, Sinaloa, and Lower California constituted Mexico's greatest national asset.

interests, railway interests, and high finance* — must they not have known that Mexico could not meet those Shylockian terms and that the cession of the precious lands and mines to the United States would be the inevitable outcome of the contract if once signed? Whatever may have been the personal views of Lincoln, the Great Liberator, those high in authority with him must have looked upon the contract as an ultimate triumph for American capitalism in Mexico. At all events, the patriotic Mexican, contemplating the long history of American aggression in Mexico, will hardly be persuaded that this was anything more than a new conspiracy to seize more territory and natural resources in Mexico. The impartial student will admit that it partook of the nature of a usurer's proposition to a poverty-stricken applicant.

So much for the "facts" commonly brought to support the tradition of the "friendly" interest of the United States in Mexico in the great trials of 1861–1865. Now we may inquire whether the diplomatic notes sent out by Mr. Seward indicate deep solicitude on the part of the United States to prevent European interference. To the United States Minister at Vienna Mr. Seward wrote: "The United States is not indifferent to the events that are occurring in Mexico. They are regarded, however, as incidents of the war between France and Mexico." To the United States Minister at Paris Mr. Seward wrote: "The United States has neither the right nor the disposition to intervene by force in the internal affairs of Mexico, whether to establish or retain a republic, or even a democratic government there, or to overthrow an imperial or foreign one, if Mexico chooses to establish or accept it." In the presence of the Minister of Spain in the United States, Señor Tesara, Mr. Seward officially recognized "that Spain had the right to make war on Mexico in order to protect her rights and to obtain reparation for her grievances."†

---

*W. A. Dunning, "Reconstruction: Political and Economic."
†Zamacois, "Historia de Méjico," Vol. 15, p. 809.

Finally we may examine the other element of the tradition — namely, that the friendly interposition of the United States forced the withdrawal of the French troops. It is true that Mr. Seward sent some rather mild mandatory notes to Napoleon III in reference to the withdrawal of his army, but this was eighteen months after the latter had made arrangements for that withdrawal in view of the serious losses and the menacing attitude of Germany. To deal with this latter point somewhat more precisely: *On the 10th of April, 1864,* Napoleon signed the treaty of Miramar in which he signified his intention of withdrawing his army from Mexico by instalments, beginning in the year 1865. *On the 11th of September, 1865,* Messrs. John Corliss & Co., bankers of New York, furnished the Mexican Government with the first instalment of a loan of $30,000,000 at 6 per cent. *On October, 1865,* Napoleon III sent a note to his Minister in Washington undertaking to withdraw from Mexico if Maximilian were recognized by the United States Government — a childish attempt to "play politics," in view of the fact that he had already determined to withdraw his army, and indeed had withdrawn a considerable portion of it. *On December 6, 1865,* Mr. Seward replied to this note in the following mild terms: ". . . I believe the cause of the discontent produced in the United States by the occupation of Mexico has not been well understood by the government of the Emperor. The main reason for this discontent *is not for the presence of a foreign army in Mexico,* and much less that it is the French army; *we recognize the right of the nations to make war among themselves as long as our rights and our just influence are not attacked.* The real reason of the discontent of the United States consists in the fact that the French army in invading Mexico is attacking a republican government. . . ." *In January, 1866,* Napoleon officially announced in the French Chamber that the army would be withdrawn from Mexico. The sequence of dates tell their own tale. Mr. Seward's apologetic note could hardly be supposed to be responsible for "driving the French out of Mexico." *The fact is that the United States throughout the war of intervention acted in complete diplomatic subservience to the policy of Napoleon III, only mildly changing her tone when the French army was already retiring from Mexico, and Wall Street had become financially interested in the support of the Juarez government.*

THE WAR OF INTERVENTION

On the 2nd of January, 1862, the fleets of the three allies entered the harbour of Vera Cruz. Spain was represented by six thousand soldiers and twenty-six warships and transports; France by three thousand soldiers and eleven warships, and England by a thousand men and seven warships. The relative insignificance of the English contingent showed that England proposed merely a formal participation in the intervention. Europe indeed had agreed to give France and Spain a free hand in Mexico, and England's support was simply moral and diplomatic.

The invasion, of course, meant the suspension of all social reconstruction for the Mexican people. They had conquered for themselves liberty and a democratic constitution in the teeth of the Clerical party; they had now to defend their entire programme of reform against all Europe. The recent civil war had left them exhausted and famine stricken. With scarcely a pause they had now to enter upon a still more desperate and prolonged conflict; and the fact that the Constitutionalists in this war held at bay the vastly superior combined army of the French and Mexican reactionaries for more than three years, and then proceeded slowly but surely to drive them out of the country, is a remarkable proof of Mexican valour and vitality.

It was an effort and an achievement to which no modern nation can bring a parallel, but it left Mexico in a state of paralysis and degeneracy from which she has not recovered to this day. The most energetic and valiant spirits of a nation cannot be persistently destroyed through fifty years of struggle, culminating in three devastating wars, without leaving a terrible mark on succeeding generations. The breed of Juarez is all but destroyed from Mexico; in that lies her acutest problem; in that lies the crime of the Church, of the United States, and of Europe against her.

With rare wisdom Juarez met the invading host, courteously withdrew the Mexican garrison from Vera Cruz, and placed the city at their disposal. "Under the adverse circumstances in which the Republic found itself, all the efforts of the government were turned toward the dissolution of the compact between the three nations whose combined action was a death-threat to her national existence. To this end it was necessary to prevent an armed conflict which, no matter what might be its results, undoubtedly would only arouse the obstinacy of the belligerents and precipitate a struggle whose end no man could foresee. This policy was highly diplomatic and gave a very beneficial result." ("México, á través de los Siglos," Vol. 5, p. 489.)

The first act of the allies was to send a deputation to President Juarez to obtain satisfaction for the claims made by them — a highly significant procedure, in that it amounted to a practical recognition of the constitutional government. Juarez replied to the deputation with firmness and honesty in the same words he had used in previous negotiations with the European powers, expressing his willingness to recognize all justifiable claims against his government, and to meet the interest upon those claims as soon as the financial condition of the country warranted.

In the meantime the forces of the allies were beginning to suffer severely from the unhealthful climate of Vera Cruz, and Juarez with characteristic magnanimity and hospitality placed the hill towns of Tehuacan, Orizaba, and Cordoba at their disposal, on condition that they withdrew to Vera Cruz in the event of the outbreak of hostilities. The commissioners from Spain, France, and England — General Prim, Dubois de Saligny, and C. Lennox Wyke — now made formal demands for the recognition of their claims by the Mexican Government,

FRENCH INTERVENTION

and President Juarez accordingly officially recognized in favour of England a debt of $69,311,657; in favour of Spain a debt of $9,460,086, and in favour of France a debt of $200,000. The English and Spanish commissioners expressed themselves fully satisfied with this arrangement, and shortly afterward withdrew their forces from Mexico and returned to their respective countries.

The matter requires some little explanation. So far as England was concerned her parade of intervention had been a mere formality. Lord Palmerston, the most astute Foreign Secretary Great Britain ever possessed, saw in the egomania of Napoleon and the bourgeois imperialism of the Third Empire a suitable and adequate tool for the destruction of the Mexican democracy. He foresaw the affair was liable to be odious in the extreme to the already seething proletariat of Great Britain and the Continent, and he wisely refrained from identifying his government with it.

Spain, on the other hand, was saved from sharing the disgrace of active intervention solely by the personal valour and integrity of her commissioner, General Prim. This remarkable man had risen by sheer ability from the position of a Catalan peasant to the supreme command of the Spanish army. By the prompt repression of several home insurrections, as well as by a brilliantly successful campaign against the Moors, he had earned the favour of the tottering Spanish monarchy, while his Liberal ideas and striking personality made him equally popular with people. To such a man the conspiracy of Europe to strangle the Mexican democracy was utterly repellent; and as soon as he had made himself thoroughly acquainted with the real position of affairs in Mexico, and had received President Juarez's recognition of the Spanish debt, he withdrew his forces and returned to Spain — to face disgrace and discharge for his loyalty to his own convictions and the cause of the people.

But if England and Spain withdrew from the intervention, Napoleon III was the more eager to exercise his now unrestricted power, and accomplish his purpose of establishing a monarchy in Mexico. To that end the French Commissioner, Dubois de

Saligny, proceeded to make himself as obnoxious as possible to the Mexican Government. He scoffed in the most insolent manner at the claim of $200,000, recognized by Juarez as the lawful indebtedness of Mexico to France, protesting that the amount of that indebtedness was $12,000,000, basing his protest on the fact that Miramon had contracted a loan of $75,000, from Jecker, Torre & Co., French-Jewish bankers, signing in return a note for $12,000,000! In plain view of the fact that Miramon was a rebel, and as such no constitutional government could hold itself responsible for his actions or his debts, the reiteration of this claim could only be taken by the Juarez government as a declaration of war.

During the course of these negotiations those birds of ill omen, the Clerical leaders, Miramon, Almonte, Haro y Tamariz, Father Miranda, and others, began to return from Europe and to congregate in Vera Cruz under the protection of the French flag. Almonte indeed brought with him authorization from Maximilian to organize the reactionary forces, and from the safety of Vera Cruz proceeded to send out commissions to all parts of the country for the appointment of officers in the army of the *soi-disant* emperor.

Under these circumstances President Juarez requested Dubois de Saligny to withdraw the French troops from the hill towns to Vera Cruz, according to the treaty of Soledad. Saligny, in a manner worthy of his master, Napoleon III, refused. From that moment the war began in earnest. After a series of skirmishes and minor encounters between the French and Mexican armies, General Laurencez, the commander-in-chief of the French army, with six thousand men and seven parks of artillery, advanced upon Puebla. Here, on the outskirts of the city, he was met by a small force of some thirty-seven hundred Mexicans and severely repulsed.

While the blood of French mercenaries and Mexican patriots mingled on the ground, three thousand miles away Napoleon III, reclining at ease, was explaining the whole matter to his confidant, General Foray: "There will be people who will ask

FRENCH INTERVENTION

us why we are going to waste lives and money in order to place an Austrian prince upon the throne of Mexico. In the actual conditions of the world's civilization the prosperity of the United States market is by no means a matter of indifference to Europe, because it feeds our industry and gives life to our trade. We may be interested in the prosperity of the Republic of the United States, but we have no intention of allowing them to overpower the Gulf of Mexico, thence to extend their control to the Antilles and South America, and to become the sole master of the markets of the New World. Owner of Mexico, and in consequence of Central America and of the pass between the two seas, there will be only one power in America, and that will be the United States. If, on the contrary, Mexico, having made the conquest of her independence, can retain the integrity of her territory; if by the aid of the French arms she can maintain a stable government, then we shall have built up an impassable barrier against the invasion of the United States; we shall have maintained the independence of our colonies in the Antilles, and also those of ungrateful Spain; we shall have extended our beneficent influence to Central America, and this influence will extend gradually to the north and to the south, opening immense markets for our productions, and give to us the raw material for our industries. In regard to the prince who will be placed upon the throne of Mexico, he will be compelled to act always for the benefit of the interests of France, not only by reason of gratitude, but because the citizens of his new country are with us, and he will be maintained there only through our influence. In this way our military honour, the interests of our policy, the interests of our industry and our trade, all impose upon us the duty of marching upon the capital of Mexico, there to raise up our flag audaciously and to establish a monarchy that may suit the national sentiment of the country, or for that matter any other form of government that may prove beneficial to our interests. . . ."*

---

*"México á través de los Siglos," Vol. 5, p. 548.

The disaster of Puebla taught Napoleon III that the task before him was not so simple as he had anticipated. He now found himself compelled to send reinforcements to the number of 20,000 men, and to mulct the French nation in the sum of $15,000,000 for the expenses of the campaign. On the other hand, the Liberal government continued to hold its own against not only the French forces, but against the considerable army of Mexican reactionaries, by this time fully organized and equipped. With the arrival of reinforcements the French army advanced once more upon Puebla, the 22d day of March, 1862, exactly one year after their first repulse. Before the opening of the siege the American and Prussian vice-consuls requested General Foray, the commander-in-chief of the French forces, to permit the women and children and non-combatants to leave the city. The request was refused. For fifty-six days the heroic defenders kept the invaders at bay. Finally, the town in ruins, food supplies and ammunition exhausted, they surrendered, and, refusing parole, were sent as prisoners of war to France.

The fall of Puebla — the gateway to the capital — was a serious blow to the constitutional government. Mexico City was in no position to withstand a long siege, nor was it good policy for the patriot army to risk a second serious reverse at this stage of the war. Juarez, therefore, very wisely withdrew his forces, and removed his seat of government to San Luis Potosi. Accordingly, on the 10th of June, 1862, the French army entered Mexico City without striking a blow.

Ten days later General Foray appointed a "Junta de Gobierno," or "governing junta," to act as the provisional national authority, composed of the leading monarchist conspirators — Juan Almonte, Pelagio Antonio de Labastido, Archbishop of Mexico, and General Mariano Salas. The first activity of the junta was to issue a manifesto to the people which concluded with the following words: "At last the freedom of the Catholic religion is reëstablished. The Church will exercise her authority without having an enemy in the government, and the State in

Photograph by Brown Bros.
MEXICAN PLANTER AND PEON
The peon is quick to learn and has considerable mechanical ability whenever given a chance to develop along his own lines

CULTIVATION OF HENNEQUIN, YUCATAN
"Their (the government's) method was to round them (the Yaquis) up with . . . cavalry, ship them like cattle — men, women, and children — to Yucatan, and there to sell them to the hennequin planters, admittedly the most brutal class of men in the world" (See page 323)

THE TOILERS

"In the fields toiled the peons, still tilling the land from dawn till dark, under the lash of the master, still enduring the pangs of hunger and the darkness of ignorance" (See page 60)

alliance with the Church will solve the serious questions which are pending." A few days later they appointed some two hundred leading ecclesiastics, military chieftains, and landed aristocrats as a national council, or "junta de Notables," as it was called, "to express the national aspirations in the matter of choosing a new form of government." The "junta de Notables" immediately set about their task of voicing "the national aspirations" and issued almost immediately a proclamation worded as follows:

"1. The Mexican nation adopts as a form of government hereditary monarchy of a Catholic prince.

"2. The sovereign will take the title of Emperor of Mexico.

"3. The imperial crown of Mexico is offered to his Highness the Prince Fernando Maximiliano, Archduke of Austria, for himself and his descendants.

"4. In the event that through unforeseen circumstances the Archduke Fernando Maximiliano be unable to take possession of the throne offered to him, the Mexican nation will submit itself to the benevolence of his majesty Napoleon III, Emperor of the French, for the appointment of another Catholic prince."

In pursuance of this policy, a committee, consisting of José Maria Gutierrez Estrada, José Hidalgo, Tomas Murphy, and Father Francisco Miranda, the veterans of the monarchist conspiracy, was thereupon dispatched to Austria to offer the throne to Maximilian.

By this time the forces of intervention had reached the considerable numerical strength of fifty thousand men, of whom thirty-five thousand were French regulars and fifteen thousand Mexican reactionaries. But by no means can they be said to have established themselves in Mexico; they controlled only the immediate vicinity of the cities which they occupied, Vera Cruz, Puebla, and Mexico City, and a few inconsiderable places in the surrounding territory. Even here they were daily beset and harassed beyond measure by the Liberal patriots. They moved, an army of embarrassed aliens, among a nation of enemies; for the whole Mexican people, as distinguished from the ecclesiastics and military and hired mercenaries, remained devotedly loyal to the constitutional government. The imperialists, indeed, clearly foresaw that so long as the organized power of the national Liberal government remained, their efforts would be futile, and they accordingly concentrated all their attention on the capture of the President and his cabinet. Juarez, however, was fully alive to the danger, and by continuously changing his seat of government, successfully eluded the forces sent against him.

Maximilian meanwhile had consented "to sacrifice himself for the happiness of Mexico, and reluctantly to accept the emperorship," and on the 12th of December, 1864, he entered Mexico City accompanied by his wife, "the Empress." At last the long-cherished dream of the Church was realized — at what cost in blood and tears, in anguish and bitterness, these pages have endeavoured to attest.

The Church was intoxicated with joy. She saw before her an eternally unfolding supremacy, uninterrupted golden ages of plunder. With a foreign army and a monarch-puppet at her command, she stood at last on the pinnacle of her ambition. But the long expected fulfilment was destined to be of short duration. The Church knew it not, but the reign of the Priest had passed from Mexico forever.

The character of the two leading figures in this notorious rape of democracy — the folly of the one, the brutality and avarice of the other, may be fittingly judged in the following treaty drawn up and signed by them as a compact of partnership. That Maximilian was no match for his master, Napoleon III, in the matter of driving a bargain, and that both of them regarded Mexico simply as a field for unlimited brigandage, is clearly attested in every line of the document quoted below:

FRENCH INTERVENTION

"I. The French troops which are already in Mexico shall be reduced as soon as possible to twenty-five thousand men, including the foreign legion.

"II. The French troops shall leave Mexico as soon as his Majesty the Emperor Maximilian shall be able to organize the necessary forces to replace them.

"III. The foreign legion at the command of France, consisting of eight thousand men, shall remain in Mexico for six years after the withdrawal of the French army, *remaining in the pay of the Mexican Emperor*. . . .

"VII. For the necessary transportation of the French troops army transports will make the voyage between France and Vera Cruz every two months, *and these shall be paid for by Mexico at the rate of four hundred thousand francs for each trip of each transport*.

"VIII. From the French naval station in the Antilles and in the Pacific Ocean warships will frequently be sent to Mexican seaports to display the French flag.

"IX. *The expenses of the French expedition to Mexico shall be paid by Mexico at once, and these are fixed at the amount of two hundred and seventy million francs for the whole period ending in July, 1864. This indemnity shall bear an interest of 3 per cent. per annum. From the first of July, 1864, the expenses of the army shall be met by Mexico.*

"X. The indemnity which it is agreed *shall be paid to France by Mexico* for salary, food, and maintenance of the French troops after the first of July, 1864, is fixed at the amount of a thousand francs annually per man.

"XI. *Mexico will pay immediately to the French Government the amount of sixty-six million francs in bonds, which will include fifty-four million francs of the debt mentioned in Article IX. together with twelve million francs in instalments due to French citizens.*

"XII. *As extra pay for war expenses Mexico shall pay annually to France the amount of twenty-five million francs.*

"XIII. *The Imperial Government of Mexico shall pay at the*

end of each month to the general paymaster of the army the total amount due to be paid to the army according to Article X.

"XIV. The army shall be reduced annually as follows: 28,000 men in 1865; 25,000 men in 1866; 20,000 men in 1867.

Given in the Palace of Miramar on the 10th of April, 1864.

Signed in the name of Napoleon III, Emperor of the French. — Herbert.

In the name of Maximilian, Emperor of Mexico.— Joaquin Velasquez de Leon."

The full significance of this treaty will become more apparent if we glance for a moment at the sequence of events whence it was evolved. The allied armies landed at Vera Cruz on the 2d of January, 1862. It was not until the following 22d of March, 1862, that the French forces made their first assault on Puebla, and not until one year and fifty-six days later, the 18th of May, 1863, that the city finally fell into their hands, opening their way to the unresisted occupation of Mexico City on the following 10th of June, 1863. From this last date, the 10th of June, 1863, to the 10th of April, 1864, the date of the signing of the treaty of Miramar, ten months had passed, and the imperialistic forces had done little more than hold their own. Napoleon, therefore, by this time had realized the task he had before him was no child's play. While still talking loudly of success he undoubtedly recognized imminent possibilities of failure. His aim, therefore, in this treaty was to wring from Mexico the largest possible loot in the shortest space of time, and to relieve himself of any responsibility for the further conduct of the war, when it should become indubitably profitless and unsuccessful, by arranging for the entire withdrawal of the French army in three yearly instalments, to begin in the year 1865, only ten months after the signing of this treaty, and, as it proved, only a month or two after Maximilian and his wife entered Mexico City as Emperor and Empress of Mexico, December 12, 1864. The following year (1865) Napoleon found it necessary to induce the French Government to disburse another vast sum for the further

FRENCH INTERVENTION

conduct of the campaign. The amount accredited to Maximilian on this occasion was 250,000,000 francs. Very little of this, however, reached Mexico, the greater part of it remaining in the imperial pocket. Mexico's indebtedness to France of 270,000,000 francs, according to the terms of the treaty of Miramar, was thus increased by 250,000,000 francs, giving a total of 520,000,000 francs, which, reduced to Mexican money — and a Mexican peso at that time was at par with the American dollar — yielded the enormous figure of $253,000,000, the whole constituting a very respectable booty for Napoleon III and the speculators who formed his entourage. On the other hand, Maximilian, before leaving Europe, found it necessary to replenish his purse, and accordingly raised a loan of £8,000,000. The astute English financiers who supplied the loan took full advantage of the royal impecuniosity and *retained no less than 90 per cent. of the loan as interest and commission.* Thus in order that her *soi-disant* Emperor might enjoy the spending of £800,000, Mexico was burdened with a debt of £8,000,000, i. e., $40,000,000. This last transaction raised Mexico's foreign debt, contracted for her since the intervention, to the enormous sum of $293,000,000, bearing an annual interest of $10,000,000. And in addition to this, Maximilian from the day that he accepted the crown of Mexico at Miramar appropriated to himself a salary of $125,000 a month, and an allowance of $16,666 a month for his wife, making together a total of $1,700,000 a year; while his journey to Mexico cost $500,000, and the wages of his cooks and servants $319,000 more.

From what magic cave was this fabulous wealth to be conjured? From the wealth produced by the social labour of a Maximilian, of a Napoleon? From the coffers of the Church which had planned intervention and prayed for an emperor? No, it was to be conjured from the toil of the Mexican peons, already exhausted and famine-stricken, already in process of being robbed of their country, their lands, and their lives to pay the price of one emperor and to fill the maw of another.

But there was yet another debt the Mexican peons must pay — the debt of blood. In the years 1864 and 1865 alone they engaged the invaders in no less than four hundred and twenty-four pitched battles and skirmishes; and the years 1862 and 1863 were hardly less bloody. The conservative official estimate of the loss of life on both sides during those four years is fifty thousand, of which twenty-seven thousand were Mexican patriots and twenty-three thousand French soldiers and reactionary Mexicans. These estimates, however, are not only conservative but grossly misleading. They do not reckon the toll of maimed and wounded nor the great numbers who fell in the guerilla warfare, nor the host of non-combatants, men, women, and children, who died of starvation and misery, or at the hands of the murderous reactionary chiefs under the "Decree of October 3d."*

While the struggle between the French invaders and the Mexican patriots was at its height a papal delegate arrived at the court of Maximilian in Mexico City, bearing rigid instructions from his master, Pope Pius IX, "to insure that the government abolished the *Leyes de Reforma*, and all the laws against the sacred rights of the Church; to insure the promulgation of laws making full reparation to the Church for the injuries inflicted upon her, and abolishing religious freedom, and making full restoration of the clerical wealth and estates." These uncompromising injunctions to the papal delegate were reinforced by a mandatory letter from the Pope to Maximilian himself which we quote in full: "Your Majesty is fully aware that in order effectually to remedy the wrongs committed against the Church by the recent revolution and to restore as soon as possible her happiness and prosperity, it is absolutely necessary that the Catholic religion, to the exclusion of any other cult, continue to be the glory and support of the Mexican nation; that the bishops have complete liberty in the exercise of their pastoral ministry; that the religious orders be reorganized and reëstab-

---

*See p. 255.

lished, according to the instructions and powers that We have given; that the estates of the Church and her privileges be maintained and protected; that none have authorization for the teaching or publication of false or subversive documents; that education, public or private, be supervised and led by the ecclesiastical authorities; and, finally, that the chains be broken that until now have held the Church under the sovereignty and despotism of civil government." ("México á través de los Siglos," Vol. 5, p. 671.)

To a strong man this gigantic task of reorganizing religious orders which had already disappeared, of delivering up the democratic and enlightened educational system of Juarez to the Church, of creating an Inquisition for the abolition of religious freedom, and of restoring to the Church her vast estates, already homesteaded by the Mexican peons and colonized by the French, would have been disconcerting enough. To the frivolous, incompetent Maximilian it appeared simply preposterous. From the moment of his entry into Mexico City he had never troubled to conceal an exaggerated contempt and disdain for everything Mexican, and the thought of playing lackey to Mexican bishops filled him with exasperation. Having neither wisdom, dignity, nor self-discipline, Maximilian was not the man to negotiate a difficult situation adroitly. His refusal to comply with the papal instructions was not the refusal of a strong man to contravene his convictions, but the refusal of a pert schoolboy to perform his task; and it cost him the invaluable support of the Clerical party and the friendship of Rome. It was a tactical blunder of the worst description and one of the direct causes of his subsequent downfall.

Throughout the long struggle President Juarez with his cabinet travelled back and forth through Queretaro, Durango, Chihuahua, and the states of the west, cheering and encouraging his people, faithfully upholding the constitution and enforcing the *Leyes de Reforma*. Wherever in his travels he encountered large private estates owned by the outlawed partisans of the empire he confiscated them and reassigned them in full legal title to the peons working upon them. This policy he pursued through his three years of wandering, and in consequence vast tracts of valuable land became distributed among the people.*

Arriving at El Paso del Norte (to-day Ciudad Juarez) in November, 1864, Juarez issued the following manifesto, and caused it to be widely circulated throughout the territory under his jurisdiction: "In this city, as in any other city of the Republic in which the government may deem it convenient to reside, according to the circumstances, the Citizen President will use his utmost efforts to fulfil his duties with the same firmness and constancy as heretofore, thus performing his obligations to the Mexican people, who are yet unceasingly fighting against the invader and who must inevitably triumph in their defence of their independence and their republican institutions." A few days later the Constitutionalists recaptured Chihuahua from the imperialists, and Juarez immediately made it his seat of government.

This was the climax of the struggle. From that moment by some desperate, well-nigh inhuman effort the Constitutionalists began inch by inch the bloody reconquest of the fatherland from the invaders. Maximilian and the French commanders, alarmed at the unmistakable turning of the tide, retaliated with a campaign of the most brutal extermination, organizing to that end bodies of counter-guerillas, with orders to burn all towns, villages, and hamlets suspected of harbouring or supporting Mexican patriots. These counter-guerilla bands, recruited largely from the southern confederates and from the jails of Mexico and France, were in reality licensed gangs of murderers and marauders without military discipline or human mercy, and the outrages they wrought upon the defenceless Mexican communities can only be equalled in modern annals by the

---

*We have personally examined a number of these decrees of confiscation and reassignment in the states of Durango and Chihuahua. The original beneficiaries, of course, are dead, and their heirs, for the most part, have been ousted by Diaz and his *scientificos*.

FRENCH INTERVENTION

Turkish atrocities in Albania. Although the Mexican patriot in the field now knew that when he returned to his native town he would be likely to find his home in ashes, his wife dishonoured, and his children dead, he only turned to the fight with renewed energy. Victory after victory attended the onward march of the Constitutionalist army, and Maximilian and his "advisers" once more furiously endeavoured to strike terror into that brave host, long lost to all fear, by promulgating the notorious "Decree of October the Third." We quote it in part:

"Maximiliano Emperador de Mexico. With the counsel of our ministers we decree:

"Article I. Every one belonging to bands or armed groups not legally authorized, and proclaiming or not some political pretext, no matter how many may be the number of those who form the band, nor what may be its organization, character, or denomination, will be prosecuted by the martial courts, and if found guilty, even of being merely a member of that band, will be sentenced to capital punishment and executed within the next twenty-four hours after the sentence is given.

"Article II. Those who belong to the bands mentioned in the above article, and are arrested in armed battle, will be prosecuted by the commander of the army making the arrest, who within twenty-four hours after such arrest will make a summary investigation of the crime with a hearing of the defendant and his defence. A record will be made of this investigation, including the sentence, which will be capital punishment if the defendant is guilty even of being merely a member of the band. The commander will execute this sentence within the twenty-four hours above mentioned, giving to the culprit religious rites. After the execution the record will be sent to the War Department. . . .

"Article V. To be prosecuted and sentenced to the extreme penalty according to Article I of this law, First: Those who willingly assist the guerillas with money, or in any other way. Second: All those who give to them news, hints, or advice. Third: All those who willingly or consciously, knowing that they are guerillas, give or sell to them arms, horses, ammunition, food, or any war supplies.

"Article VI. Also will be prosecuted according to Article I: First, All those who are maintaining with the guerillas any connection that shows an understanding with them. Second: All those who willingly and knowingly secrete them in their homes or buildings. Third: All those who by word or writing produce false alarms against the public order, or start any demonstration against the public order. Fourth: All the proprietors or superintendents of country farms who do not make known the fact of such bands having passed by said farms.

"Given in the Palace of Mexico on the Third of October, 1865. Maximiliano."

Under this barbarous decree many thousands of defenceless non-combatants, aged people, women and children, were legally done to death at the whim of brutal guerila chiefs or military commanders. Maximilian committed many crimes in the course of his brief career, but none more bloody than this. Ultimately it sealed his own death-warrant.

A man utterly without principles or human feeling, frivolous, devoid even of intelligent self-interest, Maximilian, in complicity with his co-conspirators, usurped the throne of Mexico, laid waste her territories, and murdered thousands of her people, and crowned the last moment of his anti-social career by offering to betray all his supporters and friends as the price of his own wretched existence — truly a fitting agent and representative of the master class of the world, as truly as Juarez and the magnificent Constitution of 1857 were fitting representatives of the working class of the world.

CHAPTER XVII

THE WITHDRAWAL OF THE FRENCH TROOPS AND THE END OF THE EMPIRE

WE NOW come to the second and last phase of the war marked by the continual advance of the Constitutionalists, the withdrawal of the French troops, and the downfall of the empire. The causes which led to the withdrawal of the French troops from Mexico may be enumerated in the order of their importance as follows:

I. *The gross misrepresentations made to Napoleon III by the Clerical party in Mexico as to the strength of the military force required to subdue the Constitutionalists, and the subsequent disappointment and disgust of Napoleon III and the French Chamber in view of the unexpected prolongation of the war and its heavy cost in life and money.*

When Napoleon III and his coterie undertook the task of invading Mexico, and of building up a Mexican empire, they were largely influenced in their action by the idea that the entire enterprise could be accomplished with a small force of some four or five thousand troops, and in no longer time and at no greater expense than might be involved in the march from Vera Cruz to Mexico City. Colonel Valaza, chief of staff of the French invading army, suffered from the same delusion, and his letter to the French Minister of War, March 22, 1862, aptly expresses the general impression of the imperialists in regard to the easy conquest of Mexico: "These affairs at bottom are quite simple, and close as I am to them I have not the least doubt of the speedy and complete success of the establishment of that monarchical government in Mexico which is so earnestly desired by the majority of the country, and to which even the opposing minority are already resigned. . . . In spite of everything the Juarez government is becoming more disorganized every day. It is surrounded by people ready to desert it. Its military forces are disbanding. The commanders of the garrisons of Mexico are betraying the government. *I am persuaded that an armed force, no matter how small it may be, can take the capital with no more trouble than is necessary to supply it with food during the march."*

One can readily imagine, therefore, the shock with which Napoleon III and his cabal heard of the utter rout of the French at Puebla, and the impatience and disgust with which, after having increased the French army from six thousand to sixty-three thousand men, they waited year after year for news of that too readily anticipated complete conquest of Mexico. The truth is that long before the tide of war had definitely turned against the imperialists Napoleon III had become heartily tired of the whole affair, and having now well lined his pockets at Mexico's expense he was only seeking some plausible pretext to withdraw his troops and leave Maximilian to his fate.

II. *The overwhelming advance of the Constitutionalists after the fall of Chihuahua.*

Coupled with the bitter disillusionment of Napoleon III the real cause of the withdrawal of the French troops from Mexico was the overwhelming advance of the Constitutionalists subsequent to the fall of Chihuahua. Victory after victory crowned their march; each fresh achievement served only to increase their strength; and it became painfully evident to Napoleon III that if he failed to withdraw his troops there would soon be no troops to withdraw. Military authorities who have studied this campaign compute that with another twelve months of such fighting as began at Chihuahua in November, 1864, and continued throughout the year 1865, the French army would have been utterly annihilated.

CONSTITUTIONALISTS

A battery of machine guns under command of the revolutionary leader, Gen. Venustiano Carranza

Photograph by Paul Thompson, N.Y.

YAQUI REBELS IN CAMP

The commissariat of some of the bands of Constitutionalists is supplied by the women. Yet others remain behind with the old men and children to till the confiscated farms, for the support of the rebels

A REBEL BARRICADE IN JUAREZ

"They are fighting to-day as they fought in the days of Hidalgo, of Morelos, of Guerrero . . . for the land, for democracy. They will triumph"
(See page 358)

WITHDRAWAL OF FRENCH TROOPS

"He" (Napoleon III), says Bancroft, "now saw that, although defeated, the republicans were never crushed, springing up ever with renewed courage and in larger numbers, or abiding with firm and bitter purpose the moment favourable to their cause. . . . His triumphs were sterile, and the end seemed more remote the farther he advanced. He had set out primarily to recover an indebtedness; but millions had been expended and thousands of lives sacrificed without insuring even the first claim. The whole nation (France) took alarm at the gloomy prospects of an expedition which from the beginning had found many opponents, and had at last gradually encroached upon the patience of the majority." (Bancroft, "History of Mexico," Vol. 6, p. 207.)

III. *The loss of French military prestige and the consequent threatening attitude of Germany.*

Another very cogent reason for the withdrawal of the French troops from Mexico is to be found in the loss of French military prestige, and the consequent threatening attitude of Prussia toward France. Napoleon I had made France the military terror of Europe; Napoleon III made her the military laughing stock; and Germany — long held in leash by the myth of French military superiority — now threw off her fears and began vigorously to prepare for that Franco-Prussian war which later was destined to humble the bully of Mexico in the dust — an historical Nemesis usually overlooked. Too late Napoleon III recognized his monumental blunder and began the hasty withdrawal of his troops from Mexico to strengthen the home forces against the threatening invasion.

IV. *The bitter discontent of the French intellectuals and proletariat with the war.*

Almost as potent as the causes we have already cited as leading to the withdrawal of the French troops from Mexico was the bitter discontent of the French intellectuals and proletariat with the war. These men, whose fathers had produced the "Reign of Terror," and who themselves were about to exalt their names in history in the Paris Commune, were not of a spirit to remain idle before the slaughter of their Mexican brothers and the destruction of a constitution which echoed the deepest aspirations of their own hearts — much less that this slaughter and destruction were being accomplished at the hands of their own hated bourgeoisie. From the very inception of the intervention their attacks upon the government through the medium of the popular platform and press had been unceasing and bitter attacks which grew in extent and violence as the conduct of the war continued to outrage every human, and particularly every proletarian, feeling, and before this rising wrath of the commonalty Napoleon III had to bow.

V. *Maximilian's own fatuity and irresponsibility which had antagonized all his supporters, including the Pope and the Imperialist party itself.*

We have already dealt with this point in a previous chapter. There is no doubt that Maximilian's personality utterly disillusioned all the parties to intervention and hastened the withdrawal of their support. "The interested society in Mexico was unanimous in its complaint against Maximilian," says one historian, "particularly the real monarchists, who suffered to see how his Majesty had separated himself from the Conservative policy and from the men who represented it; and they were deeply offended that his Majesty saw fit to ridicule the more respectable and dignified persons in the presence of Mexicans and foreign adventurers who were known to be hostile to the empire and Catholicism." (F. Arrangoiz, "Apuntes para la historia del segundo Imperio Mexicano," p. 132.)

The exact credit due to the United States for the withdrawal of the French army from Mexico we have already discussed. Popular impressions to the contrary, we have proved as conclusively as it needs to be proved, that the United States influence was never exerted for the withdrawal of the French troops except in the mildest manner, and that it could not be rightfully regarded as even a minor factor in the final accomplishment of that withdrawal.

Accordingly, under the pressure of disillusionment, defeat, fear of foreign invasion and of domestic criticism, Napoleon III. announced on the 2d of January, 1866, to the French Chamber that orders would be given for the immediate and entire withdrawal of the French troops from Mexico. The terms of the treaty of Miramar gave him an excellent and much needed public excuse for his action. It mattered not that Maximilian, whom he had lured to his doom, was thereby left to face the avenging host of the Constitutionalists with a mere handful of Mexican reactionaries. The affair was finished, and as far as he, Napoleon, was concerned not without profit. Millions of pesos lined his coffers. As for the empire, *Eh bien!* it was a beautiful dream at least!

. . . .

The withdrawal of the French troops from Mexico was immediately followed by the overwhelming advance of the Constitutionalists. State after state and city after city fell into their hands, till Queretaro, Mexico City, and Puebla alone remained in the possession of the imperialists. Presently Puebla likewise fell into the hands of the advancing host, and Maximilian, with his two generals, Miramon and Mejia, prepared to make a last stand at Queretaro, the stronghold of the imperial forces. The Constitutionalists promptly laid siege to the city, and in two months had reduced the defenders to desperate straits. Thereupon, Maximilian, seeing that the end was near, secretly sent a message to General Escobedo, commander-in-chief of the Constitutionalist army, offering to betray the imperial forces, and deliver them up without stipulation on condition that he himself be spared and permitted to return to Europe!*

Fear that his treachery and cowardice might be discovered evidently weighed upon him, for he wrote a personal note to Colonel Lopez, his secret emissary to Escobedo, in the following

---

* A full account of this affair is given in "México á través de los Siglos," Vol. V, pp. 839-844.

terms: "My dear Colonel Lopez, we recommend to you the deepest secrecy in the matter of the commission to General Escobedo which we have entrusted to you, *because if it should become known our honour would be smirched.* Yours affectionately, Maximilian."

These two skilful commanders of the reactionary army, Miramon and Mejia, the one almost a Spaniard, and the other, strangely enough, a full-blooded native, were quite unaware of these overtures, and were full of determination to fight to the last. Undoubtedly they would have carried out their determination had the Emperor shown an equal courage. But Maximilian, having received word from Escobedo in reply to his treacherous offer that his surrender must be wholly unconditional, hoped yet to appease the wrath of the Constitutionalists by accepting their terms.

Accordingly, a few days later he surrendered, together with his generals and entire army. The three leaders, Maximilian, Miramon, and Mejia, were immediately imprisoned, court-martialed, and declared guilty — the two Mexican generals of high treason, and Maximilian of "being the main instrument for the French intervention, of being an usurper of the sovereignty of the Mexican people, of having used violence in the destruction of the life and property of Mexican citizens, of making war with the French commanders against the Mexican Republic, of being a factor in the destruction of thousands of lives of innocent people, of bringing Austrian and Belgian filibustering expeditions into Mexico, and of having given and executed the Decree of October 3, 1865, by which thousands of patriots were slain."

When an attempt was made to induce President Juarez to pardon the three convicted criminals, more especially Maximilian, he emphatically refused, supporting his refusal in the following words: "The death of Maximilian is the death of the spirit of foreign intervention, which, under leniency, will revive again and organize new armies under the pretext of moralizing the Mexican people, but in reality to bring another usurper to Mexico. It is necessary that the existence of Mexico as an independent nation be not left to the good-will of foreign potentates; it is necessary also that the reform, progress, and freedom of the Mexican people be not hampered and jeopardized by some European sovereign, who, in patronage of the so-called Emperor of Mexico, might plan to regulate the degree of slavery or liberty of the Mexican people to suit his own taste. The return of Maximilian to Europe would be used in the hands of the enemies of Mexico as a weapon for the restoration of a régime disastrous to the democratic institutions of this country. For fifty years Mexico has used a system of pardon and leniency with a resultant anarchy at home and a loss of prestige abroad. Never thus can the Republic be consolidated." Accordingly, on the 19th of May, 1867, Maximilian, Miramon, and Mejia were lined up and shot.

. . . .

European intervention was at an end. But what of that international capitalism which had invoked and sustained it for the purpose of destroying the Constitution of 1857 — that menace to the capitalist exploitation of Latin America, and unhallowed tocsin to the proletariat of Europe? International capitalism, although much incensed at first by the impudent vitality of the Mexican proletariat, nevertheless accepted the final failure of intervention philosophically. Its leaders saw with great content that the economic ruin, social disorganization, and physical exhaustion they had brought upon the Mexican people through the army of Napoleon III. would effectually delay and hamper the workings of the Constitution for many years; and their content was the greater that they recognized such a condition of society was a fertile breeding-ground for reaction and sedition. They bided their time awaiting that reaction, and in the fulness thereof, through the medium of Porfirio Diaz, their creature whom they made, supported, petted, and eulogized, they more effectually killed the Constitution of 1857, crushed the Mexican democracy, and worked their will upon Mexican labour and the vast Mexican national resources than they could have done through any successful intervention or series of interventions.

CHAPTER XVIII

REËSTABLISHMENT OF THE REPUBLIC AND THE CONSTITUTION OF 1857

ON THE 15th of July, 1867, President Juarez, with his cabinet, entered Mexico City. The French army had vanished, the Church power was crushed, the imperialist forces were vanquished, a crown and a sceptre lay shattered on the ground, and the triumphant entry of the patriot President into the capital affirmed the full reëstablishment of the social and economic system proclaimed by the Constitution of 1857. *But at what cost!* Mexico, as the price of her freedom, had been compelled to pay with the ruin of her agriculture, the destruction of her best and bravest, and the disastrous perversion of her national psychology.

The intervention, ending with the downfall of the empire, was the culminating struggle of the people against their old enemy, the economic despotism of the Church, and the opening struggle of the people with their modern enemy — the economic despotism of international capitalism. The results of one epoch are the causes of the next. It is with the results of the first struggle that we are concerned here. Only by thoroughly understanding these results can we appreciate all the factors at work in the second great struggle which began a few years later and is now culminating before our eyes. These results we may tabulate as follows:

1. The utter ruin of agriculture.

2. The heavy destruction of the more vital and valuable element of the Mexican nation.

3. The perversion of the noble spirit of the Ayutla Revolution, and the consequent development of a despotic soldiery faction.

4. The development of an unique passion in the Mexican people for the fatherland, and in consequence the development in them of a terror amounting almost to cowardice in face of threatened foreign invasion.

We shall proceed to deal with these in their order:

First: *The utter ruin of agriculture.*

The peons, who had enjoyed a brief possession of the land under the Constitution of 1857, were compelled to leave their small farms to defend the fatherland, and even those who remained on the land, to support their comrades in the fight, were subjected to wholesale murder and pillage at the hands of the revengeful reactionary forces, particularly during the operation of the iniquitous "Decree of October 3d." The beasts of burden so necessary to agriculture were not to be had; the oxen had been slaughtered for food; the horses, mules, and burros had been commandeered for the war; and the cows, pigs, and chickens had been preyed upon incessantly by famished bands of guerillas and counter-guerillas. Under such circumstances agriculture was paralyzed and the blight of famine came near annihilating the people already stricken to their knees. *Thus, when the noble work of reconstruction — begun under Juarez and continued under Lerdo de Tejada — was broken in upon by international capitalism acting through the medium of Porfirio Diaz, the people could no longer rally to the support of their government.*

Second: *The heavy destruction of the more vital and valuable element in the nation.*

The common people of any nation fall naturally into three divisions: the idealists, the small group of exalted, self-actuating souls who dream the dream of the people and vitalize the mass; the satisfying multitude of shrewd, honest, kindly folk, who, in virtue of their position as the feeders and tenders of the nation,

REËSTABLISHMENT OF THE REPUBLIC

readily participate in any social activity for the betterment of humanity, who realize on the plane of practical affairs the dream of the idealists, and who constitute the only element in society which makes for progress, liberty, and civilization: and last, the underfed, cowardly, stunted victims of class rule and economic anarchy, who, vitiated and overmastered by their environment, are destined to become the ready tools of reaction. In the progress of the mighty class war it is ever the courageous first two divisions of the proletariat who pay the heavy toll of blood for freedom and civilization at the barricades or on the battle-field, in the foetid jails, or on the reeking scaffold, leaving the piteous degenerates of the third division intact not only to propagate their kind but to become in the hands of the master class the very weapons which make the barricade, the battlefield, the jail, and the scaffold *of no avail*. Thus is humanity shorn. If this be true of the whole civilized world, and it is undeniably, tragically true, of Mexico at the period of the Restoration. The fifty-seven years of battle maintained by the Mexican people for freedom, humanity, and progress against their ruling class — Church, Army, and Aristocracy — against this ruling class allied with Spain, and then with the United States, and again with France, culminating in the Ayutla Revolution, three years of civil war, and four years more of that frightful struggle against the same ruling class, allied with the power of international capitalism, had all but annihilated that glorious element of the Mexican people to which we have referred.

Certainly the great majority of the peons were now small land-owners, and they endeavoured to the best of their ability to retain and foster the system which had made them such. But they were not the men of 1856; they lacked the vigour and the intelligence of the Avutla fighters. Thus Mexico was compelled to rebuild herself from the dregs up; thus international capitalism in the person of Diaz found ready to hand a considerable degenerate element well adapted to the purposes of reaction; and thus for forty-two years, until the blind revolt of

1910–1914, Mexico has lain prostrate — almost without a soul. And that is the great and terrible problem which the Mexican people faced in 1867 and face to-day. They have been drained of much of their best blood; the breed of Juarez is no more.

Third: *The distortion and perversion of the noble spirit of the Ayutla Revolution, and the consequent development of a despotic soldiery faction.*

Out of the travail of the Ayutla Revolution came forth a spirit of freedom, solidarity, and humanity unsurpassed in the history of the race. The fiery ordeal of the three years' civil war served but to render it more pure, powerful, and practical. But this spirit which was the redemption of Mexican society, the warranty of the constitution in the hearts of the people, was thoroughly perverted and brutalized during the long, cruel struggle against the foreign hordes of international capitalism.

Kipling in his story of the British soldier who in the fierce suffering of the Afghan campaign forgot his name, even the number of his regiment, and Zola, in his depiction of the brutalizing effects of war upon even the most noble minds, in that great psychological study of the Franco-Prussian struggle, "La Débâcle," both touch upon a profound truth: that international war not only devastates the economic resources of the nations involved but their very souls. No more terrible illustration of that truth is to be found in history than in the perversion of the sublime spirit of the Ayutla Revolution into the sordid spirit of despotic militarism which characterized the survivors of the war against French intervention.

Of the patriots who fought bitterly and tenaciously through four long years against the French and Mexican reactionary armies, however, not all succumbed to the brutalizing effects of their experience. Many, indeed the majority, returned to their lands and laboured patiently to repair the waste and loss of years. But there was also a large element of a lower type in whom the last trace of nobility had been quenched, who now regarded their services in the war as a legitimate excuse for attempting to impose themselves as a military despotic faction upon the fatherland.

From this class sprang Porfirio Diaz, the despoiler of Mexico; from this class sprang his followers; and in this class international capitalism divined the solution of its frustrated plans.

Fourth: *The development of a unique passion for the fatherland among the Mexican common people, and in consequence the development of a popular terror amounting to cowardice in the face of threatened foreign intervention.*

The common people of Mexico, as distinguished from the ruling class—and we must repeat this distinction at the risk of tediousness, for it is a genuine distinction of both class and blood — are a domestic folk, puritans in their patriarchal mode of life, great lovers of children, of the home and its simple joys. Among them, unless where they have been debauched by too close contact with the ruling class or the disintegrating life of great cities, marital infidelity, family discord, or sexual immorality is almost unknown. That this spirit of reverence for the elemental good of life still exists among them in spite of the appalling and disgusting conditions in which great numbers of them are compelled to live is a remarkable testimonial to the vitality of the Mexican character, and the most promising augury for the future of the race. Family love is the very key to Mexican psychology; out of it grows that gentle, courteous hospitality, kindly good humour and fidelity which form the chief charm of the people. To judge Mexican character from its military class on the one hand, or from the slum proletariat of Mexico City on the other, is the common error of primitive minds, of which unhappily the world is full.

What has this to do with this unique passion for the fatherland of which we propose to speak? Domestic love unmolested may well remain a sentiment bounded by the home, but domestic love violated by the oppressor, crucified by foreign legions, deepens and broadens into a profounder passion for the sanctity and inviolability of that common home, the fatherland, and becomes the strongest passion known to man. This is preëminently the case with the Mexican people. With them, under the stress of incessant foreign invasion, the hearth has widened to the national boundaries, and family love to a passion for the fatherland altogether unique in modern annals.

When Juarez began the work of reconstruction in 1867, scarcely fifty years had passed since the Independence, and in that time the Mexican common people had become stamped with the psychology of a race surrounded by enemies, and maintaining its existence at the point of the sword. For fifty years they had fought for the land without which there is no home; again and again in that time had they come almost within reach of their desire, only to see themselves hurled back by the capitalist foreign hand at the behest of their own ruling class. At every moment of triumph foreign invasion had come to tear the fruits of victory from their grasp. From Spain during the Independence, from the Southern States in the Texas war, and later from the United States, both South and North, and then from France they had seen the invader sweep down upon them to stay their hand in the struggle with the oppressor.

Finding themselves thus alone in a world apparently deprived of all sentiments of human solidarity toward them — a world powerful, subtle, murderous, a world bent upon the destruction of all they held most dear — the Mexican people inevitably conceived a hatred for the foreigner, and a passsion for the fatherland incomprehensible to more fortunate peoples. Such a passion, coupled with weakness and exhaustion, becomes a solicitude amounting to terror, and a fear of molestation amounting to cowardice. And herein lies the whole secret of Mexico's history since 1867. Rather than endure the violation of the fatherland again the people were prepared to endure all things.

None understood this better than Porfirio Diaz, and during the thirty-four years of his despotic rule over the Mexican people it was with the threat of United States intervention that he held them down in dumb submission to his will.

CHAPTER XIX

AGRARIAN AND POLITICAL DEMOCRACY

WITH the return of the constitutional government to the capital began the work of national restoration. The whole country, as we have said, lay in ruins; and upon that great promising multitude of peons who had become small farmers lay the task of rebuilding it. Scarcely was there grain enough in the land for seed. With minds dazed by long suffering, with hearts deep in mourning, the peons bowed themselves to the task of tilling the soil, rendered fertile by the patriotic blood of their fathers. The dream of the race had been realized: a plot of ground for each, a home for each, the full and free possession of the fatherland for all; and patiently they entered upon the tremendous work of reconstruction. Their humble dwellings lay in ashes; with bare hands they builded them again from the stones of the earth. Their fields were choked with the rank weeds of years; with their rusty hoes they cleared them; while from their scanty handfuls of seed, cherished as if they were ingots of gold, they began once more to raise the crops which meant life to their famishing families, and health and prosperity to the fatherland.

Cowering in the cities, scattered and shattered, were the remnants of the old ruling class, with watchful eye to the future, waiting their opportunity. Already a faction of the republican soldiery, perverted and brutalized by the war, had begun to threaten the peace of the new order. Not yet was the social body cleansed.

Under the pressure of the turmoil of the civil war and the

subsequent war of intervention President Juarez had been compelled to retain office continuously since 1858 without reëlection. Now that constitutional rule had been firmly reëstablished, he earnestly desired that it should be subjected to the proper political authorization of the people. In due time, therefore, he summoned the nation to a presidential election. In the ensuing presidential campaign three candidates appeared in the field, two of them — Benito Juarez and Lerdo de Tejada — representing the new agrarian democracy and the national aspiration for the upholding and full realization of the Constitution of 1857; the other — Porfirio Diaz — representing a small reactionary faction comprising the shattered remnants of the imperialists, together with the perverted soldiery element spawned by the recent war of intervention, and a sprinkling of astute lawyers, willing agents of Wall Street and the American railroad speculators.

Between Juarez and Lerdo de Tejada there existed no trace of political dissension or shadow of personal rivalry. They were both great-hearted patriots whose sole desire was to serve their country. Indeed Lerdo de Tejada entered the race at the express wish of Juarez as the candidate of those of the people who considered the principle of reëlection to a certain extent unfair. Both men were thoroughly identified with the principles of the constitution, were thoroughly representative of the new agrarian democracy, and accordingly enjoyed the implicit confidence of the great bulk of the nation.

Let us now glance at the third candidate. Who was this man Diaz? "Porfirio Diaz in 1876," says one of the most brilliant writers of modern Mexico, Dr. Lara Pardo, "was a military leader of medium prestige. His biographers who of late have made him a demigod, proclaiming him to be the best general Mexico has produced, have greatly exaggerated his achievements. . . . His contemporaries thoroughly agreed that General Diaz inspired them with a certain contempt by reason of his uncouthness and low intellectual calibre. The Lerdista press indeed ridiculed him and made him the mark of its biting satire on this account; and even his own partisans, the intellectual leaders of his revolt, looked upon him merely as a tool." (Dr. Luis Lara Pardo, " De Porfirio Diaz a Francisco Madero," pp. 7-19.)

In these few lines Dr. Pardo, who was closely associated with Diaz throughout his career, has well indicated the character of the future dictator of Mexico. If this was the type of man who opposed himself to the splendid constructive genius of the patriot Juarez, and the cultivated humanitarianism of Lerdo de Tejada, so intimately expressive of the new national ideals, who were his supporters? What interests and social elements did he represent? We have already briefly indicated them as the shattered remnants of the imperialists, the perverted soldiery faction spawned by the war of intervention, and a sprinkling of astute lawyers in the service of foreign capital. It is of the highest importance to the proper grasp of subsequent events that the composition of this faction be clearly understood.

The perverted soldiery were at first the only element capable of opposing the constitutional order under the guise of a political contention. They were, as we have said in the preceding chapter, the brutalized product of the long, bloody struggle with France, the disastrous aftermath of international war. Says Baz: "Those who had left whatever social position they might have had in order to adopt the profession of arms during the war of intervention now regarded themselves entitled to a recompense which the government was in no position to give. These men bitterly resented their honourable discharge at the close of the campaign . . . and accordingly formed themselves in combination with other disgruntled elements into a group of opposition, guided solely by personal interests." (Gustavo Baz, Vida de Juarez," p. 30.) The imperialists were no lovers of Diaz or of the soldiery which had helped to defeat them in the recent war. They were, however, too weak to stand alone, and consequently were glad enough to throw in their lot with any element which might promise for them opposition to the hated constitutional rule. With them also were leagued the clergy and the remnants of the landed aristocracy. In speaking of the composition of this anti-social faction, one of its most prominent leaders, and one of the most devout eulogists of Diaz, Rafael de Zayas Enriquez, says: "The opposition consisted of the soldiers who had served under Diaz, *both the professional exponents of the old régime (cuartelazo) and those who in good faith desired active progress, and even many imperialists who could not brook Juarez.* They formed a heterogeneous party as far as the number of its groups was concerned, but a homogeneous one in the common aspirations which it saw personified in its leader." (Rafael de Zayas Enriquez, "Porfirio Diaz," p. 100.) The distinction between the social *quality* of these two opposing elements, the new agrarian democracy and this small faction of reactionaries, is masterfully drawn by Dr. Lara Pardo in the following words: "Juarez was in reality *the first instance in Mexico of a civil power*, a civil power which effectually checked the *military despotism* — that degenerate product of the war — instead of submitting to it. But this military despotism would not tolerate relegation to second place. The soldiery, covered in martial glories, real or spurious, and spurred by dishonest ambitions, deemed it necessary to assail the presidency of the restored Republic as a coveted booty of war." (Dr. Luis Lara Pardo, "De Porfirio Diaz a Francisco Madero," p. 8.)

Thus in this Diaz faction we see the perverted republican soldiery, the old exponents of the cuartelazo and the disgruntled imperialists and clergy working together, apparently in a democratic political struggle for the success of Porfirio Diaz, with the secret agents and foreign ministers of international capitalism *as vastly interested spectators*.

In due time the elections were held and Juarez was reëlected to the presidency by the overwhelming vote of the new agrarian democracy, the citizens, and the intellectuals. Hardly had

AGRARIAN DEMOCRACY

Congress proclaimed Juarez chief executive by the choice of the people than cuartelazos of the disaffected soldiery broke out in the garrisons of Mexico City and Tampico. Both movements were promptly quelled, but they served effectually to indicate exactly what the civil authority must expect in the future from its opponents.

"The Porfirista party, defeated at the polls," says Baz, "gathered its forces and dashed into rebellion, resolved to gain by force of arms a victory which, according to their own pretext, had been snatched from them by governmental tactics of pressure and bribery. . . They were not the majority of the nation; *the majority was anxious for peace.* The people saw themselves protected in their dearest interests by a government undeniably Liberal, and they firmly supported that government against the cuartelazos." (Gustavo Baz, "Vida de Juarez," p. 301.)

Undoubtedly it was only the exhausted condition of the people which emboldened this disaffected element to rear its head, and only that same exhausted condition of the people which saved that element from immediate extermination.

Following the disturbances in Mexico City and Tampico, cuartelazos broke out in Guaymas and Durango, while in the states of Sonora and Yucatan the feudal aristocracy endeavoured to inflame the unsophisticated Mayas into rebellion against the very system which alone could protect them in the possession of their lands. Meanwhile the bulk of the people went forward with the task of cultivating their farms, confident of the ability of the government to deal with the disturbers. It was under these circumstances that the President's term of office again expired and the new elections were held. As in the first election after the Restoration the candidates were, for the people and the constitution, Benito Juarez and Lerdo de Tejada; for the perverted soldiery, clergy, imperialists, and American railroad speculators, Porfirio Diaz. Again Juarez was reëlected by an overwhelming majority, with Lerdo de Tejada as President of the Supreme Court. Diaz received a ludicrous minority, and the reactionaries, beaten at the polls, immediately prepared to place their tool in power by those methods of brute force with which alone they were really conversant.

The impudence of this reactionary faction reached its logical climax on the 7th of November, 1871, in the promulgation of a manifesto known as the Plan de la Noria, followed by a widespread cuartelazo in its support. The manifesto, although signed by Diaz, in reality was drawn up by Justo Benitez, one of those astute lawyers with Wall Street affiliations who constituted the brains of the revolt. Indeed, Diaz in all his eighty-odd years was never more than the tool of superior minds, and never attained even the ability to express himself intelligibly in writing.

The Plan de la Noria was exactly similar in every respect to the militarist manifestos of Iturbide, Bustamante, and Santa Ana, to whom in truth Porfirio Diaz bears a strict analogy. It proclaimed that the government was unlawfully established, and consequently was not to be regarded as a constituted authority; that the most *noted men* of the country would convene, at a date and place to be decided later, for the purpose of establishing a *real national government;* that Porfirio Diaz, as leader of the revolt, would become President of the Republic. This crude attempt to replace the enlightened modern democratic system of Mexico with the brutal brigandage of the old military dictatorships brought such a storm of indignation from the nation that the revolt suffered the most complete collapse. The real cause of its failure, however, lay in the fact that it was essentially *domestic and inadequately supported from without.*

International capitalism at this time, although it was watching Mexican affairs with keen interest, and although its agents formed the brains of the disaffection, had not yet definitely decided upon the expensive policy of financing another revolution. It had nothing to hope from Juarez, it is true, but Juarez was now an old man worn out by his tremendous labours on

AGRARIAN DEMOCRACY

behalf of the new democracy; in the logic of events he could live but a few years longer, and those exponents of international capitalism who were chiefly interested in Mexico — the American railroad and mining speculators — were willing to trust to finesse in the hope that his successor would prove more amenable to their control. As we shall see, it was not until the accession of the patriotic Lerdo de Tejada to the presidency of the Republic had blighted the hopes of the American railroad speculators in this respect that Diaz was summoned to his famous three months' conference with them at Brownsville, Texas, whence he returned to Mexico fully financed and equipped for his first successful, and hence final, assault upon the constitutional government.

Throughout all these disturbances the power of the common people remained firmly established as the ruling power of the nation. In spite of the efforts of the reactionaries to abort the national rebirth, and in spite of a series of severe droughts, which seriously afflicted agriculture at this time, the work of reconstruction went steadily forward. It is true that the period was one of transition, and that the people were in process of accommodating themselves to a system of landed property entirely new and strange to them, but such was the general goodwill that this vast homesteading of a nation was effected almost without friction.

In this connection we take the opportunity of noting a fact later to become fraught with tragic import. The peons, unused to legalities, and possessing implicit confidence in the permanence of the constitutional government, considered the record of their land made by the municipal authorities for the purposes of taxation sufficient documentary evidence to their proprietorship, and accordingly made no further effort to establish and confirm their titles. Had they not indeed in the Leyes de Reforma itself the supreme title to that land? What need had they of another? But a few years later when Diaz gave authority to the Mexican and American land speculators to expropriate all the *unrecorded land*, this naïve failure of the peons to record their holdings was made the pretext for dispossessing and evicting two millions of them from their lands and homes.

The constitutional government by no means confined its attention to the rational solution of the land question. It considered the establishment of a prosperous agrarian democracy as only the first if the most fundamental step in the national development. Industries were stimulated by the new freedom. Mining and weaving began again to assume importance, and Juarez, seeing the day when the private and unregulated exploitation of the means of wealth production, known as the capitalist system, would enmesh the nation in a new servitude as narrow as the old, vigorously pushed forward the policy laid down in the constitution and reënunciated in his own manifesto of July, 1859, which aimed at the national construction, ownership, and operation of all the means of transportation and communication within the country. He recognized that the railroad and telegraph completely control industry, and that *if the people control the government*, and the government own the railroad and telegraph, the people are in a position to impose their own terms upon industrial corporations, pending the ultimate expropriation of all the means of wealth production by the collectivity.

This was the very essence of the magnificently sane and human constructive programme which Juarez contemplated — *and the prime cause of the new intervention.* This policy which guaranteed the economic freedom of the Mexican people *shut out the foreign speculator*. When the American railroad corporations, which regarded Mexico as their private booty, saw themselves balked by this national railroad policy, initiated under Juarez, and faithfully maintained by his successor, Lerdo de Tejada, they decided the time for action had come, and gave to Diaz and his perverted soldiery their financial and moral support.

The United States capitalist press at that period never tired of ridiculing the great national railroad policy of Juarez, just as their successors to-day never weary of lauding Diaz as the

"Maker of Mexico," and the author of her wonderful railroad system! The truth is that in President Juarez, Vice-President (afterward President) Lerdo de Tejada, and Minister of Mexico in the United States Matias Romero, Mexico possessed the three greatest practical economists of modern times. Forty years ago they foresaw the octopus which is strangling the United States to-day, and just as they had saved Mexico from the clutches of the Church, the military despot, and the feudal aristocrat, so they now strove in the light of their keen scientific vision, and in the passion of their patriot hearts, to save her from a worse fate at the hands of the land speculator, the railroad monopolist, and the industrial magnate. They were well aware of the real history of American railroads. They knew that these roads, built by the labour of the common people, financed by the wealth of the common people, were the private property of speculators who spent neither money nor labour in their construction; they saw before their eyes the heavy tribute these roads levied upon the nation, and they were fully conversant also with that adroit system of mergers, pools, agreements, and interlocking directorates by which these railroad owners unified and consolidated their despotic power over the people. Juarez and his associates saw these things clearly and in their real light long before the modern "muck-raker" came to elucidate them to the common mind, and they would have none of them. If the American nation in its strength could endure the capitalist ordeal and survive, not so the infant Mexican democracy.

Juarez, as we have said, was cruelly ridiculed in the American press as an ignorant barbarian, suspicious of civilization, and endeavouring timorously to withhold Mexico from legitimate development. These writers were undoubtedly sincere. They took it for granted, as the great majority of their kin to-day take it for granted, that *development* and *capitalistic exploitation* are synonymous. There is even a theory current in the rank and file of the Socialist party itself to the effect that all societies in the course of their economic evolution must pass through the successive stages of communism, chattel slavery, feudalism, and, finally, capitalism as the last step to collectivism. The answer to that is, looking backward, *all societies have so evolved*, but, looking forward, *no society need now so evolve*. Society has been compelled to pass through the brutal capitalist stage *because it knew no better way*. And a society, like Mexico, bursting its pupa shell of feudalism at a time when world-capitalism had already evolved the science of economics, modern industrial machinery, and the full knowledge of the laws which governed human production, needed only to take advantage of that knowledge to pass from feudalism directly into collectivism. There was no reason in heaven or earth why it should toil through the byway of capitalism to arrive at a knowledge already to hand. Having once proved that two times two are four, we do not have to verify our formula every time we use it. Indeed there is neither economic, sociological, or psychological reason why Mexico or any nation to-day in feudalism shall not effect the gradual but direct transition to collectivism — i. e., the collective ownership and the administration of the means of wealth production.

Juarez understood this. His railroad policy was not meant merely to save Mexico from the ordeal of foreign railroad speculation, but to save her from the whole needless ordeal of capitalism, and lead her in the light of the knowledge won under capitalism by the other nations of the earth into the promised land of collectivism by a direct if gradual transition. That this glorious consummation was never fulfilled is due absolutely and entirely to the American railroad and industrial corporations of 1867 and to Porfirio Diaz, their tool.

Not only did Juarez, as the expression of the will of the people, carry into effect the great fundamental principle of that people's constitution — namely, free and universal access to the land — not only did he carry out the second great principle, the national construction, ownership, and operation of the means of transportation and communication, but he carried out the third great principle, that education shall be free, adequate, universal, and non-sectarian, by establishing throughout the land in every city, town, and village, and even hamlet, a chain of free public schools, staffed by the most cultivated and devoted men and women of the day. The fact that Juarez himself was a full-blooded Zapoteca, an offshoot of the Aztec race, and the majority of his advisers were of the same stock is profoundly significant in view of this educational policy. None knew better than they the vigour and brilliancy of the native mind; none understood better than they the thirst of the people for knowledge. Within a few years of the establishment of these schools the intellectual ardour of the ancient Mexican races, repressed and choked for four hundred years, had burst forth in a veritable national renaissance. Indeed, all Mexico's modern achievements in the fields of philosophy, science, art, and technology spring from this period — a period in which she gave to her children even in the remotest villages the free services of her brightest spirits as educators, and ranked those educators in emoluments and prestige with the highest officers of the public service. That these public educators were influenced by the sheer love of their labour, and the desire to aid in the unfolding of the spirit of the race, to the utter disregard of the financial reward, is vividly shown in the fact that when Diaz deliberately ruined this school system of Juarez, 80 per cent. of these educators continued their labour without pay for two years, and, indeed, would have continued indefinitely had not Diaz discharged them and ordered the schools to be closed. No more striking contrast between the spirit that is democracy, and love, and enlightenment, and the spirit which is autocracy, brutality, and ignorance could be drawn than this incident affords. To the American railroad speculators and the American industrial corporations, interested in exploiting Mexican labour and resources, an educated Mexico was an intolerable menace, and through the medium of their personal representative, Porfirio

Diaz, they plunged the people into the depths of ignorance and slavery and held them there. To Diaz himself the annihilation of education was a jest. "Compadre Porfirio," said his crony, the notorious Gonzalez, "if the time comes that I want to put you out of the way I will make you a school teacher and let you die of starvation." And both laughed at the joke!

In spite of the severe droughts of those years, and the consequent widespread destruction of crops, such was the economic and honest handling of the national finances by the Juarez administration, that not only were all the necessary expenses of the government duly covered, but a considerable surplus was put to reserve for the construction of the national railways.

"During the period of the constitutional rule from 1867 to 1871," says one historian, "in spite of the difficulties which sprang up at every step, and the military mutinies and cuartelazos which embarrassed the work of social reconstruction, a number of material improvements of far-reaching importance were accomplished, and a still larger number were inaugurated. The system of legislation was reformed; new civil and penal codes were established; the national treasury system was improved and treaties were made with the United States, Germany, and Italy; while, notwithstanding the unusual drain upon the exchequer involved in the suppression of the military revolts, all the state administration expenditures were covered without recourse to extraordinary taxation, and a great part of the new Mexican National railroad was built. . . ." (Gustavo Baz, "Vida de Juarez," p. 230.)

The great burden of the fraudulent foreign debts still weighed heavily on the country. At the time of the intervention of the allies these debts, it will be remembered, had been prudently recognized by Juarez on behalf of Mexico as national obligations to the English, French, and Spanish governments. But the action of these governments in subsequently recognizing Maximilian was a breach of neutrality according to international law, and constituted good grounds for Mexico's repudiation of their claims. Juarez, however, with characteristic wisdom, preserved the dignity of the nation, and at the same time avoided a clash with the allies by refusing to recognize these debts as obligations to the English, French, and Spanish governments as such, but only as obligations due to the individual creditors of those countries. Under this arrangement he called the creditors together for an agreement of settlement at the discretion of the Mexican Government.

During the few brief years of the Restoration period vast strides were made toward the realization of the Constitution of 1857 on the plane of practical affairs. Juarez and his cabinet, supported by the agrarian democracy, by the citizens and intellectuals, toiled at their task of national reconstruction with an ardour, faith, and wisdom unsurpassed in history.

The renaissance which followed the economic and intellectual emancipation of the people found the fullest expression under a régime of complete freedom of speech and press. Never has the intellectual heritage of Mexico given such proof of its vitality and power as during these years. Then there sprang from the genius of the race, as it were, in a night all those splendid creations in the fields of science, art, and literature which have won for Mexico her rightful place among the intellectual nations of the earth. All that Mexico has produced of worth was produced at this time or later as a result of the intellectual impetus imparted to society at this time. If then the social genius of the Mexican people had awaked, if it had thus begun to expand with a vigour fraught with all promise, whence came the sordid shambles, unillumined, ungraced, except by the reckless valour of the peons which we know as Mexico to-day?

Let Zayas Enriquez, the friend and eulogist of Diaz, reply to that question. "This profound desire for peace began in the time of Juarez when the empire had been destroyed, and with it the reactionary party. Juarez himself would have accorded peace if *we Porfiristas had not hindered him with our systematic and unbridled opposition* and our disorderly outbreaks." (Zayas

Enriquez, "Porfirio Diaz," p. 120.) And these "disorderly outbreaks" were destined later to become, under the providence of international capitalism, the darkest despotism the world has known. That is the reason of the "Barbarous Mexico" we know to-day.

Toward the year 1872 the health of Juarez began to fail. Heart weakness, coupled with the shock caused by the death of his wife, to whom he was the most devoted husband, hastened the end. "It seems that Juarez," says Bancroft, "had a presentiment that his own end was near; for in conversing with his friends he expressed regret that it would be out of his power to reconstruct the affairs of his country, wherein he said almost every effort hitherto had been directed to destroy. Nevertheless amidst all the turmoil he was beginning to see the realization of his heartfelt wish for peace when death overtook him." (Bancroft, "History of Mexico," Vol. 6, p. 385.) On the 18th of July, 1872, he died. Juarez was a fully developed man; in other words, a genius; but it must never be forgotten that true genius is collective in impulse if individual in expression. Wherever it be found it is invariably the focus of the high energies of the great multitude of common people. The products of such genius may not be regarded as individual, but as the very expression of the mass in their struggle for development.

Juarez was mourned by the nation with a profound sorrow, darkened and embittered by presentiments of evil days to come. Lerdo de Tejada, as president of the Supreme Court, and thus interim President of the Republic, summoned the people, according to the law, for presidential elections to be held on the 13th and 27th of October, 1872, at the same time proclaiming a general amnesty to all rebels and political offenders in order that no unfairness to his opponents might taint the elections.

Porfirio Diaz, who since the collapse of the Plan de la Noria had remained hiding in the mountains of Tepic, consorting with a band of desperadoes under Manuel Lozada, refused the magnanimous offer of Tejada, in the hope of casting a stain upon the legality of the elections and of exalting himself in the eyes of the nation. Later, however, when he found that society had forgotten him, he yielded, and Tejada was so chivalrous as to restore him to full military rank as a general of the regular army. In due time the elections were held and Lerdo de Tejada was placed in office by an almost unanimous vote of the people. Bancroft, in spite of his glorification of Diaz and hence depreciation of the great Constitutionalists, Juarez and Tejada, honestly describes the reason for the people's choice of president in this election when he says: "The people were inclined to associate him (Lerdo de Tejada) in great part with the beneficent policy of the recent administration. . . . the country had suffered so severely under the bad management of military chieftains that the majority regarded these candidates as unfitted for the presidential office, and as inclined to give a dangerous preference to the army." (Bancroft, "Porfirio Diaz, Su Biografia," p. 89.)

A few days after the presidential inauguration construction began on the railroad between Mexico City and Vera Cruz, the first step toward the materialization of the constitutional principle which established the democratic construction, ownership, and operation of the national railroads.

With the submission of Diaz and his subsequent restoration to military rank, peace was restored throughout the country. In Lerdo de Tejada and his cabinet the people had executives devoted to the constitution and unwearying in their efforts to realize its principles in the economic and social life of the country. Under their administration the agrarian democracy continued to flourish and expand, and the last traces of peonage, which had still lingered in some parts of the country owing to the dense ignorance of the people, were thoroughly destroyed; the national construction of railroads was vigorously promoted, and the educational system founded by Juarez was fostered and developed. In coöperation with the national Congress, the state legislatures and executives, and even with the city and rural councils, the administration continued to enforce the independence of Church and State, the freedom of religious creed, the full establishment of marriage as a civil contract, the suppression of religious oath and the clerical disabilities in respect to the acquisition of land. In spite of the peace and prosperity of the country, however, the government recognized that the reactionary faction still constituted a serious menace to the established order. They considered indeed that no social stability would be possible until the complete suppression of the soldiery had become an accomplished fact. Meanwhile they resolutely denied the soldiery and their reactionary allies any share in the government affairs. The attitude of the administration is aptly summed up by the Porfirista, Zayas Enriquez, when he says: "Lerdo was like Juarez in that he was the most vigorous advocate of civil administration as opposed to militarism." (Zayas Enriquez, "Porfirio Diaz," p. 110.)

But the unprecedented liberty which characterized the new democratic system only served to embolden the reactionaries in their attacks upon the government, and in their intrigues for its overthrow. As we have said, imperialists, big land-owners, clergy, lawyer agents of the American railroad speculators, outlaws, and professional bandits clustered around the main phalanx — the perverted soldiery, forming a faction diverse enough in its composition but a unit in its desire to overthrow the hated reign of economic freedom, prosperity, and peace established under the constitution, and to substitute therefor an era of brigandage, presided over by Diaz and protected by the power of international finance.

Yet another element was destined to add strength to this disaffected element. Mexico was now experiencing a bountiful prosperity. The productive power of the people had increased tenfold under the new economic freedom, while to the years of drought and the painful restoration of the devastated farms had succeeded years of plentiful rain and rich harvests. This accumulating wealth of the people was regarded with covetous eyes by the speculators and rising industrial capitalists of the time. Under the stern hand of the constitutional government their desire to appropriate this wealth and exploit the workers remained unsatisfied, and they accordingly threw their whole weight into the support of the reactionary faction, thereby adding very materially to its strength.

Since the restoration of Diaz to his military rank the soldiers had been disciplining and organizing their forces, while the clergy as perniciously active as ever had been preaching sedition from every pulpit, inflaming the natives of the remoter districts with the old cry of "holy war." The nuns had endeavoured to organize their monastic and conventual orders again, and the government had been compelled to suppress them with severity. This, of course, gave an additional strength to the reactionary faction, while every criminal and outlaw in the country continued to flock to its standard.

Porfirio Diaz meanwhile drew his salary as a general in the government army, held aloof from politics, and perfected his plans for the future. While outwardly taking no part in the reactionary agitation, in secret he harassed the government continually by instigating mutinies and religious riots. His main business at this time, however, was the debauching of the army, with the view of leading it into a powerful cuartelazo against the government when the opportune moment for a *coup d'état* should arrive.

.   .   .   .

Juarez and the members of the constitutional government had fully recognized that the real menace to the civil authority lay in the soldiery. The Church and Aristocracy had been crushed under the rule of the empire never again to raise their heads as the controlling force in the nation. But in a new form militarism still remained, and it was against this surviving evil that they directed their efforts, while coöperating with the people in the work of economic and social reconstruction. It was necessary, of course, that an adequate standing army should be maintained for the nonce, if only to oppose this lawless element; but there is incontestable proof in the documents of the period that the great majority of the veteran patriots who composed this standing army were not only loyal to the constitutional government, and free from collusion with the antisocial element which made Porfirio Diaz their tool, but were so far imbued with the spirit of democracy and reverence for the civil authority as to endorse the government proposals for their own suppression whenever their services should no longer be required for the maintenance of order. They themselves were at one with the constitutional government in upholding the principle that a standing army, no matter how loyal, is by its very existence a menace to a free society; and they regarded with full approval the administrative policy which aimed at the ultimate suppression of the army, and the restoration of the old bodies of civicos or national guard for the purposes of maintaining domestic order or resisting foreign invasion.*

To aid in this patriotic undertaking, and to offset the intrigues of the reactionaries, a special Masonic order, called the Mexican National Rite, was created, and provision made for its establishment throughout the country. To international capitalism in the person of American, British, and French railroad and industrial speculators, acting through their tools, the soldiery under Porfirio Diaz, is directly due the failure of these great plans. Neither the suppression of the army, the restoration of the civicos, nor the establishment of the Mexican National Rite was destined to be materialized. Before the constitutional government could thus strengthen itself the foreign hand had struck, not openly as in former invasions and interventions, but in shelter, silence, and stealth, as is the modern way.

---

*Our researches in this matter brought to light a surprisingly complete correspondence between President Juarez and the officers of the republican army, particularly with Generals Ignacio Pesqueira and José Maria Morales, in which the government's plans for the suppression of the army and the restoration of the civicos were freely and fully discussed.

CHAPTER XX

THE DIAZ CUARTELAZO

DURING President Lerdo de Tejada's first term of office the Diaz faction had thoroughly organized and disciplined their forces. Recognizing that the people would have none of them, that their cause, as a political movement, was dead, they abandoned all attempts at constitutional action and concentrated their attention upon preparations for a *coup d'état*. President Lerdo de Tejada's unblemished record in office had marked him out for certain reëlection, and the Diaz faction, foreseeing in that event a reaffirmation of the popular will, and the strengthening of the hands of the government most dangerous to the success of their conspiracy, decided to strike while there was yet time. Accordingly, early in the new year, 1876, the signal was given and cuartelazos burst forth in all parts of the country. In Lower California the soldiery overthrew the constitutional governor and installed their leader, Colonel Emiliano Ibarra, in his place; the garrisons at Tepic and a number of other cities mutinied, while in Mexico City several generals of the regular army were arrested for endeavouring to excite the garrison to revolt. The movement culminated on the 15th of January, 1876, when General Fidencio Hernandez headed a powerful uprising at Oaxaca, proclaimed General Porfirio Diaz as commander-in-chief of the revolution, and promulgated the programme of the revolution in the Plan de Tuxtepec, so called from the name of the city in which it was signed. The principles of this programme, henceforth the accepted standard of the Porfiristas, were as follows:

I. The amendment of the constitution to prohibit the re-election of the President of the Republic and the governors of the states.

II. The discharge of Lerdo de Tejada from the presidency of the Republic.

III. The appointment of the commander-in-chief of the revolutionary army to the interim presidency pending a presidential election.

IV. The discharge of the governors of the states opposed to the Plan de Tuxtepec, and the appointment of successors at the discretion of the commander-in-chief of the revolutionary army.

The enunciation of these principles was preambled by a savage attack upon the constitutional government accusing Lerdo de Tejada among many other charges — of *endeavouring to sell Mexico to the United States!*

At the beginning of the revolt Porfirio Diaz crossed the border to the safety of Brownsville, Texas, where he remained from December, 1875, to March 12, 1876, in daily conference with the agents of the American railroad speculators, the emissaries of Wall Street, and of Washington.

Meanwhile cuartelazos had broken out in favour of the Plan de Tuxtepec under Generals Donato Guerra and Galvan in the State of Jalisco, under Generals Mendez Bonilla and Carrillo in Puebla, under Colonel Garcia in Vera Cruz, under General Canto in Yucatan, under General Rocha in San Luis Potosi, and under General Couttolenne in Guerrero. The government, however, continued to hold the situation well in hand, severely defeating the rebellious soldiery in a number of engagements and driving them into the hills. In March, 1876, Generals Trevino and Naranjo headed an uprising of the garrison at Matamoros, a town immediately opposite Brownsville on the Mexican side of the line, and Porfirio Diaz, having satisfied himself it was safe to return, crossed the border. Upon hearing of the approach of the loyal troops under General Escobedo, the vanquisher of the imperialist army, he fled to New Orleans, whence, after

THE DIAZ CUARTELAZO

perfecting his arrangements for the betrayal of Mexico into the hands of the American speculators, he embarked on board the steamer *City of Havana* for Tampico. Upon his arrival at that port he was recognized by some officers of the loyal army and *only saved from arrest by claiming the United States' protection*. In speaking of this incident, Bancroft says: "Diaz, having grasped the situation, called upon the captain to afford him the protection of the American flag." (Bancroft, "Porfirio Diaz, Su Biografia," p. 502.) Thus protected, he withdrew from Tampico and sailed to Vera Cruz, whence he again disembarked under cover of the American flag, and proceeded to join the rebel forces at Oaxaca.

While the fate of the revolt was thus hanging in the balance Lerdo de Tejada's first term of office expired and new presidential elections were announced. Under the critical circumstances the President stood for reëlection unopposed and was elected to his second term by an almost unanimous vote of the people the 26th of October, 1876.

His resumption of office was immediately followed by renewed military outbreaks. Suddenly, on November 20th, scarcely a month after the government had proclaimed him its chief executive for the second time, Lerdo de Tejada resigned the presidency and left Mexico City for Acapulco, whence he embarked at once for New York.

The desertion of the President at such a crucial moment gave new life to the revolt and demoralized the Constitutionalist defence. Under the circumstances a great part of the loyal army joined the Diaz faction, and the remainder gave up the fight. In vain José Maria Iglesias, President of the Supreme Court, and hence interim President of the Republic, endeavoured to cope with the situation. In the face of a large rebel army, fully equipped and financed by foreign interests, resistance was impossible. On the 23d of November, 1876, Diaz entered Mexico City at the head of his army, and had himself proclaimed provisional President of the Republic. Two months later, January 28, 1877, a farcical congressional election was held, and the Congress thus elected under the muzzles of the rebel guns declared Porfirio Diaz President of Mexico by the unanimous vote of the people, May 2, 1877.

. . . . .

The entrance of Diaz into Mexico City brought to an end the brief glorious reign of the people and inaugurated the unbroken rule of the speculator and military despot. It annihilated "Civilized Mexico" and substituted in its place the "Barbarous Mexico" we know to-day.

The period 1867 to 1876, beginning with the Restoration and ending with the triumph of the Diaz cuartelazo, as we have seen, was one of the brightest periods in the history of modern civilization, not only in actual accomplishment but in good augury for the future. True, the turbulence of the reactionaries of the Diaz faction had obstructed the process of social reconstruction, but the power of the people was a real power; if it had been used to its fullest extent the Diaz faction would have been annihilated. This much is admitted by every writer, reactionary or radical, who has ever treated the subject; it is admitted by even the most biased of the Diaz eulogists. How, then, are we to explain the national impotence in face of the cuartelazo? Why did not the people exert their power to destroy this element which threatened their dearly bought democratic institutions? Why did they not sustain a government which they had unanimously placed in power? Why did President Lerdo de Tejada thus unreasonably forsake his trust?

The reader who has grasped the analyses set forth in the chapter on the Restoration of the Republic has already divined the answer: *The national passion for the fatherland, and the consequent terror of the people in face of a possible United States intervention.* The reactionary faction faced nothing but extinction until Diaz went to Brownsville in Texas for his famous

Copyright by Underwood & Underwood, N. Y.

PRESIDENT HUERTA AND HIS ADVISERS

Reading (from left to right): Rodolfo Reyes, Esquival Obregon, Francisco de la Barra, Gen. Manuel Mondragon, President Huerta, Vera Estañol, Garcia Granados, and Robles Gil

Enrique C. Creel　　　　José Y. Limantour

Ramón Corral

THE SCIENTIFICOS

These three men were leaders in the Diaz administration of "Scientificos." Corral was Vice-President, Limantour was Minister of Finance, and Creel, Minister of Foreign Affairs

THE DIAZ CUARTELAZO 293

conference with the American railroad speculators, and the agents of Wall Street and Washington. This movement, closely watched and widely published by the constitutional press in Mexico, struck terror into the Mexican people. They knew at once what had happened. They recognized that henceforth if they would uphold their institutions they must deal not merely with a small disaffected element headed by a military adventurer, but with the mighty foreign hand. It was a prospect fraught with all hopelessness. They bowed their heads in bitter resignation, and their President — rather than resist the power of American finance and thereby invite another devastating invasion of the fatherland — resigned and left the country. This — the fear of United States intervention — and this alone is the reason for the success of the Diaz cuartelazo and the reason for the Mexican people's dumb submission through thirty-four long years to the despotism of Diaz, the scientificos, and foreign speculators.

The Diaz victory was therefore not the result of a popular movement for change or reform, but a mere *coup d'état* supported by a handful of discontented soldiers. This is admitted by Zayas Enriquez, a Diaz eulogist: "The Porfirista revolution was not really popular, and, as I have said, Lerdo fell more on account of his own lack of faith and skepticism than because of any popular sympathy with the Revolution." ("Porfirio Diaz," p. 195.) In response to the question, "To whom was the triumph of the Revolution due?" Enriquez answers: "It is difficult to give a categorical reply to such a question; but I honestly think it was due rather to the stupidity of the government, the skepticism of Lerdo, and the lack of confidence of the army than to the political and military skill of General Diaz and the efforts of his followers." (*Ibid.*, p. 123.)

Diaz, the leader in this revolution, was not a man of large vision, anxious to safeguard the public interests while developing the resources of the country. He was not a man of education and cultivation; to him history and economics were sealed mysteries. From the beginning to the end, his vision was the vision of the barrack yard. Of the capitalist movement which filled his term of dictatorship he was the creature, not the intelligent creator. The truth of this statement is attested by Dr. Lara Pardo, a man closely associated with Diaz and possessing an intimate knowledge of his character: "For myself, knowing how little the Dictator understood the benefits the railroads might bring, and seeing him constantly favour the most inane schemes and oppose the most beneficial plans for the nation, when unsupported by foreign pressure or the supplications of his friends, his glorification becomes a myth. In my regard these exploits (the introduction of American railroads) which have been so greatly exaggerated, simply show that when his triumph was consummated the American interests were prompt to compel the new ruler to fulfil his promises of generous concessions." ("Dr. Luis Lara Pardo, De Porfirio Diaz a Francisco Madero.")

Such a revolution, carried out by such a man would never have succeeded if it had not been for the aid which he received from capitalistic interests in the United States. On this point Dr. Pardo who was, as we have said, intimately associated with Diaz, writes: "It is beyond doubt that in the United States General Diaz received the military supplies for the troops with which he opposed the government in the struggle. It is certain that he obtained moral support there; it is also incontestable that he obtained the direct support of the American interests offering in exchange free-hand concessions. . . . The history of his government is the most complete confirmation of this statement. In an interview published by the newspaper *El Imparcial* it is seen that Diaz's first action after his occupation of the capital was to sign the contract for the construction of the Central Railroad. ("Porfirio Diaz a Francisco Madero," p. 17.)

Finally the revolution, brought about by such a leader, supported by such sinister interests, was maintained by the constant threats of Diaz that any disturbance of his rule would bring intervention from the United States. This is no figment of the imagination. It is admitted by Enriquez, in his panegyric on Diaz: "This served also as a powerful check upon the turbulent elements of the interior, to make them understand that any one who conspires against the government [the Diaz government] might thereby precipitate American intervention, thus endangering the nationality of Mexico itself. This has been in reality one of the principal factors in the pacification of the country and the maintenance of permanent peace."

To sum up, we have established:

1. That from 1867 to 1876 the Mexican people were in the full enjoyment of constitutional rule: that in spite of the turbulence of a small disaffected faction there was peace, in spite of drought, prosperity, and that society had firmly established itself upon the basis of a developing agrarian democracy.

2. That the people having achieved this democracy only after fifty-seven years of the most bloody struggle against the Church, the Army, and Aristocracy, and against the foreign hand, were now deeply anxious for peace, and that they enforced that peace.

3. That the people's government not only upheld and enforced the constitution, but devoted itself unremittingly to the task of national reconstruction in the light of that constitution.

4. That in accordance with one of the fundamental principles of the constitution and of the *Leyes de Reforma*, and in full harmony with the spirit of both, the government had entered upon a policy which aimed at the national construction, ownership, and operation of the railroads, not only as a means to protect the people from the foreign speculator, but as a means to protect them from the despotism of the capitalist system, and to lay the path for their gradual transition to a purely collective administration as the normal development of an agrarian democracy.

5. That the only disorderly element in the nation was the heterogeneous party composed of the defeated imperialists, the

disgruntled clergy, the perverted soldiery, and the foreign capitalist agents, who made Diaz their figure-head.

6. That this disaffected faction, with the direct moral and financial support of the American railroad, industrial, and land speculators, and with the deliberate cognizance and connivance of the United States Government took advantage of the still unrecovered condition of the people and of their passion for peace and their terror of renewed foreign invasion to overthrow this constitutional government and destroy this enlightened democracy by the infamous method of the cuartelazo.

CHAPTER XXI

PORFIRIO DIAZ, PRESIDENT OF MEXICO

THUS we have Porfirio Diaz President of Mexico by the grace of American "Big Business" through the immediate instrumentality of an unpopular army revolt, and as a direct result of the national fear of United States intervention. Consequently, from the day of his entry into Mexico City in 1876, to the day of his flight to Paris in 1910, thirty-four years later, Diaz was supported *positively* by the psychological power of the clergy and the subsidized press, by the physical power of the Army, and by the economic power of the United States and Europe; *negatively* by the impotence of the people in face of an ever impending United States invasion. Consequently, also as *quid pro quo* of their support, these three body-guards of the new régime — the clergy, the army and the foreign speculators — enjoyed throughout this period unrestricted license in the exploitation of the national wealth and the enslavement of the people.

The first action of Diaz in power was the establishment of military rule, with the consequent forcible expulsion from Congress of every representative who insisted on expressing the will of the people, or who refused to be bought. Thus was the national council reduced as in the days of Bustamante to "an assembly of lackeys." The governors who refused to yield up the independence of their states were arrested by the soldiery and flung into jail, and their places were filled by military commanders. At first, in view of the great strength of the agrarian democratic states of the north and south, their independence was respected, but strong military contingents were dispatched to garrison their principal cities, and to watch for an opportunity to force them into line with the new régime. The situation thus produced was similar in many respects to the clerical-military despotisms of Bustamante and Santa Ana; and now, as then, men who were neither priests nor soldiers were the real brains of the government. If Santa Ana had his Lucas Alaman to instruct him in paths pleasant to the Church, Porfirio Diaz had his Justo Benitez to instruct him in the paths pleasant to the foreign speculator. In both cases was there an alliance of stupidity and ferocity with polished craft and subtilty.

The common people, although filled with solicitude for the integrity of their institutions, dumbly submitted to the new anarchy rather than face the terrible alternative, United States intervention. But it was not for several years — not, indeed, until they found themselves suddenly dispossessed of their land — that they realized the magnitude of the disaster which had befallen them.

The workers, it must be remembered, had not the opportunity of the exploiters for comprehending the march of events and cherishing their own welfare. The common people of Mexico at this time were still in possession of the land, a land that yielded them a bountiful sustenance, and they continued patiently to labour upon it, trusting that one of those swift changes of which their history was full would come to restore their Golden Age to them. In this belief they were doomed to bitter disappointment. The people's Constitution of 1857 had established as its basic principle the superiority of Man Right over Property Right. From this time Property Right began the invasion of the social field, until little by little Man Right had altogether vanished, and the complete enslavement of the masses had been accomplished.

In this gradual demolition of the magnificent democratic system of the Restoration, the Diaz cabal wisely deferred their attack upon the agrarian statutes until the right moment.

That moment naturally would be the occasion of some deliberately provoked pseudo-crisis between Mexico and the United States which would intensify the dread possibility of intervention in the minds of the people and paralyze their resistance. Pending this convenient occasion the government proceeded to entrench itself, and at the same time make of the nation a booty of war by filling all public offices with members of the new faction, and by imposing a crushing taxation upon the people to pay for the lavish upkeep of the army — in which, as of old, officers outnumbered men.

In this race for plunder, however, the United States speculators outdistanced all competitors. Scarcely had the obedient Congress proclaimed Diaz President of Mexico than the agents of the American railroad interests appeared upon the scene to demand the immediate reward of their services in placing him in power. Diaz was as prompt to comply as they to demand, and free-hand concessions to build two main lines, one from Laredo and the other from El Paso to Mexico City were immediately handed over to them.

By the terms of these concessions they were allowed to choose their own routes, and to build the lines without government supervision. Free lands were given them for the rights of way, together with a construction subsidy of eight thousand dollars per kilometer on level ground and twenty thousand dollars per kilometer in rough country! When we consider that the Mexican dollar at that time was at par with the American dollar, that the company used only the cheapest of materials in the construction of the line, and had, moreover, the advantage of forced labour at 50 cents a day; *when we consider also that they built the line in the most tortuous fashion possible in order to increase the total mileage and thus the total subsidy*, and when finally we consider that this concession was only the first of a long series of such granted by Diaz to the American railroad interests in return for their support and a personal share of the profits, we shall appreciate the anxiety of these interests to place him in power, to sustain him in power, and to hold him up before the eyes of the world as a demigod, a modern Messiah, the "Maker of Mexico!"

With the granting of these railroad concessions, however, the Diaz government had by no means satisfied its American supporters. Behind the railroad speculators now appeared large numbers of the smaller speculators eager for a share of the spoils. There were no railroad concessions for these, but not to be balked, they proceeded to revive and invent all kinds of claims for damages against Mexico, and to foist them upon the Diaz faction with the concurrence of the United States Government. Somewhat hastily assuming that their good will was of no inconsiderable importance to the maintenance of the *status quo* in Mexico, they imagined that the Diaz government would submit to be blackmailed without a protest.

"In regard," says Bancroft, "to the two thousand claims that were laid before the commission, representing the sum of $556,788,600, the great portion of them were fictitious, and the legitimate of them exorbitant. The joint commission opened up a field of peculation to every class of rascal. Every device was practised to rob one government or the other, the claimants hesitating not at all at perjury or forgery." (Bancroft, "History of Mexico," Vol. 6, p. 444.)

The outcome proved that the smaller speculators had overestimated their importance in the scale of events. A joint commission of the American and Mexican governments was formed to ajudicate upon these claims. Meanwhile Justo Benitez and his political associates, in collusion with certain interests at Washington, took advantage of the situation to work up the long desired war scare as a preliminary move to the wholesale eviction of the people from their lands. On the pretext that the enormous taxation imposed on the Mexican people was working injustice upon American citizens resident in Mexico, and other similar pretexts, Secretary Foster, with the approval of President Hayes, ordered troops to the border.

Benitez adroitly played to the United States lead by instructing Diaz also to send troops to the border. In this manner a very good semblance of an international crisis was produced, with a highly disciplinary effect upon the Mexican people. The matter of the claims, however, had become such a stench in the public nostrils that the joint commission discreetly smothered a vast number of them, allowing, indeed, only four million dollars out of the original sum of $556,788,600. The Diaz government paid this amount promptly, glad to have secured such valuable aid in terrorizing the people at such a low cost. But later, in view of the fact that no justification could be found for even this small amount, the United States Government cancelled it and restored it in part.

Subsequent to the Conquest the kings of Spain had granted to the municipalities of Mexico the right to use the belt of land immediately surrounding their townships as communal property for pasture and tilth. These communal lands, or *egidos* (shields), were of great service to the peons and poor townsfolk in eking out their miserable existence. Here they cut their fuel, pastured such few cattle as they possessed, and cultivated small patches of grain and vegetables. Even in the darkest days of the colonial régime and of the subsequent clerical and military despotisms the Church and the big land-owners had respected the *egidos*, while the Constitution of 1857 had endorsed the original grants and enforced their maintenance. It was not until the Diaz faction came into power that this elemental right of the municipalities to the communal lands was attacked. Under cover of the threatened United States invasion, to which we have referred, while the people were waiting tensely for the dread news that the American army had crossed the border, some land speculators of the Diaz faction seized the *egidos* of Juchitan, and a number of neighbouring towns of the State of Oaxaca, and proceeded to fence and occupy them. The inhabitants appealed to the authorities without response. Failing, after repeated attempts, to receive redress, they resorted to arms. Whereupon President Diaz rushed troops into the district, and a wholesale massacre ensued, in which over five hundred of the protesting villagers perished. The news of this atrocity spread in a flash to all parts of the country. *Widespread revolt seemed imminent. But at that moment President Hayes of the United States, in complicity with the Diaz faction, ordered General Ord to move his troops across the border, and the people became at once dumb and submissive.* A little later the remnants of the loyal army in the states of Guerrero, Vera Cruz, Campeche, Tamaulipas, Nuevo Leon, and Sonora rose in arms against the government, under the leadership of the veteran patriots, Generals Alvarez Pesqueira Escobedo and Amador, but again the spectre of United States invasion loomed out of the north and the movement collapsed.

It must be remembered that the American and Mexican governments then, as now, were at the back of the American and Mexican railroad, industrial, and land speculators. This coalition, having tested its solidarity and fully realized its power in the massacre of Juchitan, and the overthrow of the loyal army revolt, drew the bonds of union still closer, and proceeded to the deliberate wholesale demolition of the Mexican agrarian democracy, accompanied by the swift extermination of every trace of opposition.

The grim and bloody efficiency of this new vast Machine became speedily manifest. In 1879 a group of young men in Vera Cruz organized a political movement for the reëstablishment of the constitution. At the same time it happened that a mutiny broke out on the gunboats *Libertad* and *Independencia*, stationed in the harbour. The governor of Vera Cruz, General Luis Mier y Teran, one of the foremost adherents of the Diaz faction, deliberately charged this little group of political reformers with complicity in the mutiny. When the case was tried the federal judge, Rafael Zayas Enriquez, who sat upon the case, although a reactionary and a personal friend of Diaz, was compelled to pronounce the charge unfounded in view of complete lack of evidence to the contrary. This, however, failed to satisfy Teran, and he telegraphed his own account of the affair to Diaz, requesting instructions. Diaz, without an attempt at investigation, returned the prompt and laconic reply: "Shoot them!"

Accordingly the doomed men were dragged from their beds at midnight, torn from their wives and children, and haled to the barracks in their night clothes. Here they were turned loose in the yard and shot to death like rabbits by the soldiery. Judge Rafael Zayas Enriquez forgets for a moment his rôle of Diaz eulogist when he says in regard to this incident: "The immediate effect of this Bacchanalian orgy of blood was to strike terror to the hearts of all conspirators. That the feeling was deep and lasting is proven by the fact that it is still felt to-day, thirty years afterward." (Zayas Enriquez, "Porfirio Diaz," p. 148.)

Thus did the Machine establish its bloody peace; for the armed revolt of the people in defence of their democratic institutions, the threat of United States intervention; for the peaceful political organization of the people for the same end, wholesale murder.

In spite of the seizure of the communal lands at Juchitan, and numerous instances of individual dispossessions, the great mass of the agrarian democracy were still in possession of their farms. Their hearts were filled with forebodings for the future, but while the menace of United States invasion persisted, they knew that resistance would be useless. The impetus given to production by the individual ownership of the land established under the Restoration still continued, and agricultural prosperity abounded. Under the heavy taxation, however, the people profited little by their efforts. As in the days before the Ayutla Revolution, all their wealth above bare sustenance went to pay for the upkeep of a huge standing army, and to fill the pockets of the swarms of politicians and speculators who battened on the national treasury.

One of the outstanding characteristics of the new régime, a characteristic that has lasted to the present day, was the complete license allowed to government employees in the manipulation of the public money. From the day that Diaz came into power as the representative of American interests in 1876, to the day he fled to Paris in 1910, organized corruption reigned unchecked in the affairs of the administration, and not a single case of embezzlement, malfeasance, graft or misappropriation, in connection with the handling of the public funds, has ever been prosecuted in the courts. In this way a widely extended and infinitely ramifying collusion of interests was established between the official class and the speculators, merchants, manufacturers, and land-owners. Despotism feeds upon corruption. This system which found its master exponents in the Scientificos of recent years was no accident. It was a deliberate community of crime reaching insidiously to the most remote and unsuspected quarters, which battened as it grew and grew as it battened. In its ultimate form it became a vast, and, in a financial sense, world-wide conspiracy for the support of the Diaz faction in Mexico and the most thorough exploitation of the Mexican people.

With the expiration of Diaz's first term of office, Congress prepared to play the farce of amending the constitution according to the Plan de Tuxtepec. It will be remembered that the main principle of this plan — the standard of the Diaz cuartelazo — *was the non-reëlection of the President and the governors of the states!* Congress undoubtedly hoped that this pretence of political concession would mend its somewhat dilapidated prestige with the people and smooth the path of future fraud and exploitation.

Thus the task of appointing a successor was left to Diaz. He had proved so faithful to the interests who had placed him in power, so prompt to aid the land speculators, so energetic in nipping political opposition in the bud, that he was already regarded by his home and foreign supporters as an ideal chief executive for their purposes. A large number of them indeed were anxious to set aside the non-reëlection principle and retain him in power. Astuter counsels prevailed, however. After consultation with his political instructors and the representatives of the foreign interests, Diaz named Gen. Manuel Gonzalez as his successor. It was an excellent choice in view of the circumstances. "Then Diaz thought of Gen. Manuel Gonzalez" says Enriquez. . . ."Gonzalez was a rough man without education, without training of any kind, much less administrative knowledge. As a commander of guerillas he was brave to rashness. He had served in the ranks of the reactionaries, and afterward had gone over to the Republicans at the time of the war against the French. . . . And in addition he was one of General Diaz's most fanatical partisans." (Rafael Zayas Enriquez, "Porfirio Diaz," p. 151.)

This "rough man without education" was naturally no very acceptable candidate to the people, trained as they were in the traditions of Juarez and Tejada; consequently it was necessary to employ the same methods for his election as were used in placing Diaz in power. An election was held at the point of the bayonet, and in due time the new creature of the speculators and foreign interests was proclaimed President of Mexico.

It would be difficult to describe, with any approximation to the truth, the degradation and corruption of the new administration. That it comprised only a small number of criminals, representing the interests of the foreign speculators, and a comparatively small section of the Mexican nation, is a consoling fact; for if we were to judge the Mexican nation as a whole by the actions of this administration we should be compelled to admit that it had no further right to existence. A kind of frenzy of debauchery and an unbridled plundering of the national exchequer were the chief characteristics of the Gonzales régime. The national palace of Mexico City made sacred as a family hearth by the virtuous Guerrero, reverenced even by the military dictators in the days of the Church power, and sanctified by Juarez in the holiness of his family life, was converted by Gonzales and his politicians into a vast brothel, the scene of hideous orgies and the wholesale defamation of womanhood. Not content with such victims as Mexico offered — the demimondaines, professional prostitutes, and the ravished wives and daughters of the poor — these men even imported numbers of beautiful Circassian girls to stimulate their jaded lust. To maintain the Saturnalia the national treasury was robbed without stint or shame. "*Manuel Gonzales carried out his agreement faithfully*," says Doctor Pardo. "Very few governments, even those of Turkey and Hindoostan, and of the Spanish-American caciques, have ever offered a worse instance of prostitution and of administrative corruption. The ransacking of the public treasury was never more complete and bold; all the ordinary and extraordinary revenues went to swell the vaults of Gonzales and his favourites: new taxations were created . . . . only the army was well paid, for otherwise they knew revolt would result. . . . *That Gonzales carried on all these cynical plunderings in accord with the agreement made with Don Porfirio there is no doubt. He knew that he was to enjoy complete immunity, because General Diaz himself was the instigator and harbourer of all these crimes.*" (Dr. Lara Pardo, "De Porfirio Diaz á Francisco Madero," p. 38.)

Diaz in spite of his strict limitations was not without a certain shrewdness. He recognized clearly that "all things are lawful but all things are not expedient"; and since it was highly necessary that the predatory elements which had placed him in power should be not only appeased but glutted, he preferred that some one other than himself should bear the odium of the affair. This explains his sudden compunction in the matter of reëlection, and his adroit choice of Gonzales for the presidency. The treasury sacked, his supporters glutted, and the patience of the more respectable element exhausted, he foresaw his urgent recall to power as the saviour of society, the "Puritan Maker of Mexico." This was the "agreement" of which Dr. Lara Pardo speaks: Gonzales was to reward the Porfiristas, and reward them royally, and Diaz was to return to office in the splendour of a national saint.

During this régime the national railroad from Mexico City to Vera Cruz — that cherished project of Juarez and Tejada and the agrarian democracy — was sold for a song to the English contractors who had built it, and the proceeds went to pay for new orgies and bacchanals in the national palace. Meanwhile the American railroad speculators, taking advantage of the concessions granted them by Diaz, had already begun to build the railroads between Laredo and Mexico City, and El Paso and Mexico City.

As we have said, these roads received a construction subsidy of eight thousand dollars per kilometre on level ground, and twenty thousand dollars per kilometre in rough country. (A kilometre is 0.62137 of a mile, or 3,280 feet 10 inches.) They were built of the cheapest material, by forced labour, and in a highly circuitous fashion in order to increase the total mileage, and thus the total subsidy. At a later time, when these roads were really required for business purposes, it was found necessary to shorten them by half, and rebuild them from end to end.

Finally the corruption of the Gonzales administration reached its logical climax in two gigantic peculations: one, the debasement of the national coinage, the other, the inflation of the English credits. With the approval and authorization of Congress, debased nickel pieces of one, five, and ten cent denominations were coined and forced into circulation to the face valuation of twenty million dollars. The actual value of these coins in relation to their face value may be estimated from the fact that they were bought ready made from German manufacturers at a price equal to 15 per cent. of their face value laid down in Mexico City! The lower ranks of the government employees, including great numbers of workingmen, were forced, under threat of discharge and imprisonment, to accept their pay entirely in this spurious coinage.

The second operation — the inflation of the English credits — came near to precipitating a revolution. It will be remembered that Guadalupe Victoria, the first republican President of Mexico, contracted a government loan with English bankers for $30,000,000, of which only the sum of $20,000,000 was actually subscribed. The 5 per cent. interest on this loan had been paid more or less regularly during the Clerical régime; but thanks to the collusion of the Church with the English creditors represented by Messrs. J. de Lazardi & Co., *this original amount of twenty million dollars had increased by stealthy increments to the enormous figure of sixty-nine million dollars*. The $49,000,000 which represented the inflation had been secured by the English bankers at the comparatively trifling expenditure of a few million dollars in judicious bribes distributed amongst the various ministers and presidents of the Clerical régime. None of it ever reached the national treasury. It was the suspension of interest on this inflated credit, it will be remembered, which formed England's pretext for joining with France and Spain in the intervention of 1861. Juarez in his endeavour to avoid armed invasion had prudently recognized the debt. Subsequently, however, in reproof of the English Government's breach of neutrality in recognizing Maximilian, he refused to recognize its standing as the representative of the English creditors, consenting only to treat with these creditors as individuals, and forcing these creditors to reduce their claims. In the corruption of the Gonzales administration the English creditors now divined an excellent opportunity for further peculation; and in complicity with the President and his coterie of speculators and politicians they reintroduced this claim for recognition by Congress, *reinflated from sixty-nine million dollars to a hundred million dollars*. As in the days of Iturbide, some five or six representatives of the people had managed to effect an entrance into Congress despite the vigilance of the election officials and the soldiery. These men, refusing to be bribed, fought the recognition of this inflated credit with such vigour that the government

REBEL SCOUTS

"Badly armed, poorly organized as they were, these impetuous hosts utterly out-manœuvred and overwhelmed the 40,000 well-drilled Federal troops sent against them" (See page 345)

Photograph by Paul Thompson, N. Y.

THE PEOPLE AND WAR NEWS

"Viva la tierra! Viva la Constitución! . . . They would no longer fight for a man. Henceforth they would never lay down their arms till they themselves had consummated the economic reorganization they demanded" (See page 349)

GENERAL PASCUAL OROZCO

Leader of the revolutionist forces in the North in 1912, but later a deserter to the cause of the Federals

Copyright by The International News Service
GENERAL PANCHO VILLA

Leader of the Constitutionalist forces in the North and a strong adherent of the Agrarian Plan of seizure of estates and selling them in small parcels to native farmers

in alarm postponed debate upon it to a more convenient occasion.

While Gonzales as President was plundering the treasury and holding high bacchanal in the national palace, Porfirio Diaz, as Secretary of the Fomento department — the department of lands, mines, and industries — was quietly building up an immense political and publicity machine by the lavish distribution of land and industrial concessions to the numerous corporations, Mexican, American, and English, formed by his supporters and friends.

Herein, indeed, may be found the genesis of that monstrous "Diaz-Myth" which has held the world in the grip of a lie for thirty-four years. These concession-seeking corporations, in some instances, were joint stock concerns, composed of the most influential men in the financial and political world; in other instances they were limited liability companies comprising many thousands of shareholders in all walks of life. When we consider that many of these shareholders were professional people, lawyers, politicians, writers, preachers, editors, not only Mexican but American, English, French, and Spanish; when we consider that this policy of free-hand concessions not only in land but in railroads, industries, mines, and timber, begun by Diaz in 1876, was pursued by him until his flight to Paris in 1910, and that with each passing year thousands of new investors in all parts of the world have become interested in these concessions, we shall be able to understand a little more clearly the real nature of that vast world-conspiracy which has defamed and exploited the common people of Mexico for thirty-four years, and exalted the man who was responsible for the massacres of Juchitan, of Vera Cruz, of Papantla, of Tomochic, of Cannanea, to the position of an international hero.

It was a matter of dividends. Every investor who held stock in one of these innumerable enterprises worshipped as a god the man who made his dividends possible, *no matter how*. The great majority of the foreign investors in Mexico were, and are, Americans, hence the repeated threat of United States intervention in Mexico used by Diaz throughout his career as a bludgeon wherewith to beat the people into dumb submission while the last dividend was being ground from their quivering flesh.

Nor was Diaz blind to the possibilities of private gain in these transactions. From all concession-seeking corporations he invariably extorted 20 per cent. of the total stock as a reward for his services, a practice that, thriftily conducted, enabled him, it is charged, after thirty-four years of regal expenditure, to leave Mexico in 1910 with sixty million dollars in cash.

In regard to these land concessions it will be remembered that when the Constitution of 1857, in enunciating the principle that the sole title to personal ownership in the land rests in the personal cultivation of the land, confiscated at a blow the vast illicit holdings of the Church, and restored them to the use of the people, the peons, unused to legalities, failed to perfect their titles, justly enough regarding the constitution itself as the chief warranty of their continued possession of the land in general and the municipal tax records as sufficient evidence of their ownership in particular. This fine faith of the people now formed the pretext for their wholesale evictions from their holdings. The terms of the land concessions granted by Diaz throughout his administrative career permitted the individual or corporate concessionaire to denounce and appropriate all the *unrecorded land* within the confines of a given area.

Thus was begun the cruelest campaign of land-dispossession in history. The peon, now an independent farmer, challenged for his perfected title by the agents of the land companies, was unable to produce it. In vain he pointed to the constitution; in vain he pointed to the evidence of his proprietorship contained in the municipal tax records. Land was rising in value; the introduction of the railroads and the inrush of capital had excited the greed of the despoilers to the extreme. The peon was evicted summarily and without even the formality of investigation, and the eviction was backed by all the force of the government and army. When the peon, with that reverence for law which is his outstanding characteristic, sought the protection of the courts he found himself ruled out without a hearing, or if heard, informed that he had no case. If finally in despair he resorted to arms he was threatened with the violation of his beloved fatherland at the hands of the dreaded United States, and if still obdurate he was massacred by the government troops.

CHAPTER XXII

THE DICTATORSHIP

AT THE close of Gonzales' term of office the political agents of the foreign speculators, backed by the entire Mexican reactionary party, experienced no difficulty in setting aside the recently paraded principle of non-reëlection and in again placing Porfirio Diaz in power as President of the Republic. In this they were aided by the general reaction of honest society against the vileness of the Gonzales régime, and, of course, by the usual carefully prepared and executed "bayonet-election."

On the 1st of December, 1884, Porfirio Diaz returned to power nominally as President of Mexico, in reality as dictator, or, in other words, as the Janissary of American "Big Business." From this time until his flight to Paris in 1910, some twenty-six years later, he was maintained in office continually and without reëlection by the powers which placed him there. During this period Mexico underwent a most complete change economically and politically; the agrarian democracy gave way to a feudal and capitalist autocracy, and the constitutional government to a government which no longer depended for its sovereignty on the will of the people, but solely upon the army, the popular terror of United States invasion, and the moral support of the ever-increasing host of foreign and domestic investors in Mexican enterprises. This period, therefore, presents a continuous logical development of those forces of international capitalism which overthrew the Restoration and placed Diaz in power. Consequently it may be dealt with in its entirety as a well-marked historical epoch under the following three subdivisions:

THE DICTATORSHIP

I. The inflation of the foreign credits and their consolidation into the Mexican national debt.

II. The eviction of the people from their lands, and consequently the total destruction of the agrarian democracy, the reëstablishment of peonage, and the introduction of the most abject industrial wage slavery.

III. The establishment of a railroad and industrial policy based upon the wholesale sequestration of the national resources.

We shall proceed to deal with these in their order:

I. *The inflation of the foreign credits and their consolidation into the Mexican national debt.*

On the 22nd of June, 1885, Congress, sitting behind closed doors, unanimously passed a bill inflating the already grossly inflated foreign credits from $81,632,657.81 to $191,385,781.59, and consolidating them into a Mexican national debt. A brief review of the genesis and history of these claims will reveal the real enormity of this fraud perpetrated not only upon the Mexican people of that day but upon generations yet unborn.

In 1862, it will be remembered, the foreign credits against Mexico stood as follows:

English claims	$69,311,657.81
Spanish "	9,460,986.29
French "	2,859,917.10
Total	$81,632,561.10

With the history of the English credit we dealt in the previous chapter; its real amount was twenty million dollars. The Spanish debt, it will be remembered, began with Lucas Alaman's criminal recognition: (1) of the Spanish claim to reimbursement for the moneys expended in the Spanish campaign against the insurgents in the War of Independence; (2) of the fraudulent claims of Father Moran in regard to the confiscated estates for the support of the missions of the Holy Rosary in the Philippines. Both of these claims, it will be remembered, were repudiated by Juarez with the *sanction of the Spanish Minister, Don Miguel de los Santos Alvarez.* The French claims arose out of some trifling damages incurred by French citizens and property during the turbulent days of the Clerical military despotism. Juarez agreed to recognize these to the amount of $200,000, but, of course, repudiated them consequent upon the French invasion of Mexico. Since the Ayutla Revolution the constitutional government had endeavoured to reduce the English credit to its original proportions, and had entirely repudiated the Spanish and French credits as without foundation. Thus at the Restoration Mexico's exact legal indebtedness to Europe was only $20,000,000 due on the English credit, plus some arrears of interest. The coterie of politicians and speculators who formed the Diaz government, having optioned enormous quantities of this discredited foreign paper at ridiculously low figures, proceeded to reintroduce not only the English but the Spanish and French claims for full recognition by Congress, reinflating them in the process from $81,632,561 to approximately $144,953,785, plus arrears of interest to the amount of $46,431,996, totalling $191,385,781. Of this amount $20,000,-000 was legal indebtedness; $69,000,000 represented the result of previous peculations, and $110,000,000 represented the exact plunder of the speculators involved in the present transaction.

This colossal fraud was the foundation of many of those vast fortunes so characteristic of modern Mexico, *including those of President Diaz and his family.* Nor did the peculations of the government cease here. The same Congress which authorized the recognition of this spurious paper trebled its value by enacting a measure *which gave the bondholders of the new Mexican consolidated debt the privilege of exchanging their bonds for government (?) land at an exchange rate of* 35:100. When we consider that the owners of these bonds were members of the government, or friends and supporters of the goverment, we shall understand why this provision was made, and also why the best

THE DICTATORSHIP

irrigated lands in Mexico were sold by that government at about 7 *cents a hectare* — i. e., about 3 *cents an acre*. Thus the speculator-politician who had acquired $35,000 worth of government bonds as his share of the spoils, and at no greater cost than was involved in helping to secure the necessary legislation, could now exchange this $35,000 worth of bonds for one hundred thousand dollars' worth of irrigated lands, at the rate of 3 *cents an acre;* in other words, emerge from his strenuous labours in support of the government with approximately 3,267,000 acres of magnificent land to his credit. Thus was instituted the greatest land robbery recorded in history. *During the Diaz régime no less than* 72,000,000 *hectares* — *i. e.*, 180,000,000 *acres*, (a hectare is about $2\frac{1}{2}$ acres) — of the best lands in Mexico were acquired by land corporations and the personal friends of the administration, at a total government valuation of $5,000,000 (7 cents per hectare, or 3 cents an acre), *and at an actual payment of only* $1,750,000 *in government bonds*. The climax of this procedure was reached when these bond-holding land-speculators proceeded, with the vigorous assistance of Diaz, to evict a million independent farmers from their holdings, under the pretext that they were trespassing upon these already purchased government lands.

This plunder of an entire people and their posterity, this sequestration of an entire country, was the *pièce de resistance* of the banquet presided over by Diaz, but it was by no means the whole banquet. There were innumerable side-dishes for all those who possessed the necessary qualifications for a seat at the board.

In speaking of this period Dr. Lara Pardo says: "The Clericals — for long years excluded from the bureaucratic feasting — now received lucrative positions, fat commissions, splendid prebends; generals who fought at the side of the French against the national sovereignty were also welcome; he who had no place in the budget, nor in the secret expenditures of the State Department, got concessions, contracts, valuable land grants, similar to those of the old "Mercedes" given by the Emperor Carlos V and his descendants. . . . In the midst of this tide of generosity and liberality heads were cut off; these were the heads of the uncompromising or unsubmissive personal enemies, the obdurate rebels who were yet dreaming of disputing the supreme power of General Diaz. Murderous daggers, stray bullets, arrests, carried on with all the legal apparatus and ending in vile murder committed on the way to prison, were clearing the camp and exterminating the legitimate or the bastard opposition. This latter procedure became so common that it was baptized under the name of *ley fuga*." (Dr. Lara Pardo, "De Porfirio Diaz a Francisco Madero," p. 42.)

As Dr. Pardo indicates, the clergy had a prominent position at the banquet. Diaz and his partisans needed the moral support of the Church fully as badly as Santa Ana or Bustamante, and they were prepared to obtain it by the readiest means to hand. Indeed, never had the Church prospered as it had prospered under Diaz. Not only were the clergy given a prominent share in the Mexican national debt operations, and thus enabled again to possess themselves of vast land holdings, but immense concessions of the richest lands in Mexico were given them from time to time in such quantities, indeed, that the Church in Mexico owns more land to-day than at any time since the Conquest. Thus did the astute speculators and politicians who made Diaz their figurehead interest the whole power of the Catholic world in the support of their régime.

II. *The eviction of the people from their lands, and, consequently, the destruction of the agrarian democracy, the reëstablishment of peonage, and the introduction of the most abject wage slavery.*

Since the success of the Diaz cuartelazo, in 1877, the speculators and politicians of the new régime had not lost sight for one moment of their ultimate object — the possession of all the

THE DICTATORSHIP

valuable lands in Mexico. But it was not until 1885 that they were in a position to begin a definite and well-supported campaign of expropriation. By that time the masterly manipulation of the Mexican national debt had placed in their hands, as we have said, millions of dollars' worth of government bonds, exchangeable for land at the rate of thirty-five dollars in bonds for a hundred dollars in land; the Department of Agriculture had unblushingly fixed the price of the irrigated lands at 3 cents an acre, and the arable lands at from 1 to 2 cents an acre, and all pasture lands at 1 to ½ cent an acre; and finally President Diaz had built up a powerful engine for the suppression of revolt and the castigation of recalcitrants by the efficient organization of the army, and by the creation of a special body of fifteen thousand mounted police (rurales). These latter indeed played a highly important part in the land-evictions. Recruited from the lowest class of criminals, splendidly mounted, trained, and equipped, and wholly destitute of humanity, they were regarded by Diaz and his admirers as the chief guarantee of "peace." Conditions, therefore, were now highly favourable for a systematic attack upon the agrarian democracy.

Accordingly, in the winter of this year, 1885, the campaign was opened in the valley of Papantla in the State of Vera Cruz. This valley is one of the richest in Mexico, yielding abundant crops of coffee, cocoa, sugar-cane, pineapples, and many other tropical or sub-tropical products. At this time it supported an agrarian population of over twenty thousand honest and industrious working folk in the full enjoyment of prosperity and peace. So rich a prize as this was naturally the first to fall into the hands of the speculators.

One day a party of surveyors appeared in the valley with their transits. The people knew only too well the meaning of this invasion, and, filled with foreboding, they protested to the surveyors that they had no desire to have their lands measured even if the government had ordered it, for those lands were their own private property by the warranty of the Constitution.

The surveyors persisted and the next day reappeared with a posse of rurales. Again the people protested, but this time they were silenced by force, and in the clash that ensued several lives were lost on both sides.

Four days later a force consisting of several thousand rurales and a division of the army entered the valley and began the systematic extermination of the population. How many were killed will never be known. About ten years ago in the course of our investigations we visited this valley and endeavoured to elicit some details of the affair from the people. Neither man, woman, nor child could be induced to say a word, *because already a number of them had met death, banishment, imprisonment, and flogging for even speaking of it. In spite of this dumbness of the people, however, we obtained independent proof that for fifteen days the slaughter never ceased, that not a man escaped alive, that only a remnant of women and children were spared, and that the task of burying the dead was so great that a month later the air for miles around the valley was unbreathable owing to the stench of the thousands of putrefying corpses. To-day this whole region, where once twenty thousand peaceable, industrious folk obtained a prosperous living from the soil, belongs to a single rich family.*

In Nuevo Leon, one of those states which by reason of its great agrarian strength had managed to retain a certain independence, the local government endeavoured to protect the people in the possession of their lands. The speculators, however, were not to be balked of their prey. Accordingly Diaz, at their behest, dispatched an overwhelming force into the state, overthrew the authorities and again accomplished the wholesale eviction of the people from their lands.

The natives of Nuevo Leon, however — some of the best fighting stock in Mexico — violently resisted the government troops, and Diaz in order to quell them was compelled to resort once more to the threat of inviting United States intervention. The ruse was entirely successful. *Washington dispatched troops to the border, and the people abandoned the fight, choosing to submit*

THE DICTATORSHIP

to wholesale eviction from their farms rather than incur a new violation of the fatherland.

We have no space more than briefly to glimpse the night of horror which drew down upon the defenceless people of Mexico as happy community upon community, independent state upon state, fell victims to the greed of the speculators and the ferocity of Porfirio Diaz. Even had we the space we have not the desire. The régime of Diaz — the instrument of international capitalism in Mexico — will be placed in its true light, and thus our duty as historians will be fulfilled by the brief citation of only one or two typical episodes of the period; and even in this we confess the narration entails upon us a certain brutal effort of mind which we should be glad to relinquish. One of these is the Tomochic affair.

Following the dispossessions of Papantla and Nuevo Leon, the entire State of Chihuahua passed from the possession of hundreds of thousands of small farmers into the possession of two or three families under the leadership of one man — to-day the largest cattle owner in the world. The campaign of massacre and eviction began in the districts of Guerrero, Temosachic, and Tomochic, located on the lower range of the Sierra Madre Occidental. No worthier class of people existed on the American continent than the sturdy peasant farmers and cattle raisers of these rich districts. Puritans in their patriarchal mode of life, they added to the industry, hospitality, and courtesy of their class the mountaineer's passion for freedom.

It happened that the governor of Chihuahua, General Carrillo, an old supporter of Diaz, had his attention drawn to these lands by a lawyer named Medrano. Their richness and extent, as well as the ease with which they might be acquired, excited the cupidity of both, and they joined in a conspiracy to obtain possession of them. It was necessary, of course, to find some pretext for evicting the farmers. Such a pretext was soon to hand.

A drunken Catholic priest of Tomochic entered his pulpit

one morning to conduct mass in an unusually intoxicated condition. His abusive language and actions naturally scandalized the congregation, and the elders finally were compelled to force him out of the church. The priest thereupon went to Guerrero and complained to the authorities that the villagers of Tomochic had conspired to murder him. Acting upon the complaint, the governor dispatched a posse of rurales to arrest the elders, but Medrano, seizing the opportunity, filed charges of murder against all the farmers in the district, with the purpose of detaining them in jail indefinitely and appropriating their lands. The people, however, alive to the plot, arrested the rurales, and sent a message to the governor requesting the release of the elders and a proper examination of the facts. The governor's reply arrived fifteen days later when fifteen thousand soldiers, reinforced with a park of artillery, marched into Tomochic and began a massacre which lasted ten days and nights without ceasing.

The farmers were mountain men, hardy and capable; their women were like them. They refused to be slaughtered like sheep and sprang to arms, contesting every inch of the ground with the soldiery. Husband and wife, son and daughter fought side by side. On the tenth day every able-bodied man and woman over twelve years of age had perished, and only a handful of some two hundred old women and children remained huddled together in the church. Then the soldiers, urged on by their officers, surrounded the church with a ring of bayonets, poured oil on its doors, set fire to it, and burned it to the ground, cremating alive the throng of women and children imprisoned within.* The soldiery then ravaged the neighbouring towns of Temosachic, San Andres, and Guerrero, repeating the massacre of Tomochic again and again until the whole region was depopulated.

---

*That Diaz was directly responsible for this massacre is shown by the fact that when Heriberto Frias, an army lieutenant who witnessed this massacre, gave an exact account of it in a book called "Tomochic," he was compelled to flee Mexico for his life.

THE DICTATORSHIP

It will be remembered that during the war of intervention Juarez had made a practice of issuing decrees confiscating the immense land holdings of the imperialists and dividing them among the people. Beginning with the year 1885 a number of state legislatures, notably that of Durango, packed with the creatures of Diaz, proceeded to set aside these decrees as a preliminary step to the eviction of the farmers from their land. In every case wholesale despoliation followed. Shorn of their legal titles, harassed by rurales, threatened with United States intervention, the people yielded up their lands and sank into peonage, or, resisting, perished in entire communities.

In the State of Sonora the Yaqui Indians, a tribe of thirty thousand, had practised for centuries a system of land tenure common to all peoples in the stage of primitive communism. Under this system the land belongs to the community as a whole; one part is set aside for pasture; another for agriculture. The pasture is common to all, with certain restrictions as to the number of head of cattle permitted to any one individual; the agricultural lands are subdivided and distributed into allotments to each family. Every three years these allotments are redistributed, thus giving the due proportion of poor and rich soil to all. Brave, hardy, and industrious, and occupying a location offering excellent facilities for defence, the Yaquis from the remotest times had resisted every effort at subjugation, and had retained intact their independence and the integrity of their land system.

Owing to the general advances of society since the Ayutla Revolution, and the resulting improved methods of agriculture, this old system of redistribution of the land had dropped into desuetude among them, and by the year 1880 they had already adopted the system of private ownership in agricultural land, although the traditions of communism still swayed their actions as a collectivity. The Yaqui Valley is phenomenally rich, and the Yaquis themselves are the hardest working people in Mexico, two circumstances which excited the cupidity of the land speclators to the utmost. For if rich land is a valuable loot, not less so is the labour of an exceptionally hard-working peon. Accordingly, hardly had Diaz come into power before the land speculators invoked the combined action of the state and federal governments in an attack upon this territory.

One day, in 1880, Ramon Corral, the governor of the state, dispatched a posse of some twenty-five mescal-inflamed rurales into the Yaqui Valley to raid one of the villages while the men were absent in the fields. When the men returned home in the evening and learned that their homes had been despoiled and their women dishonoured, they went in a body to Guaymas to complain to the authorities, and, receiving no redress, proceeded to Hermosillo, the capital of the state, to lay their case before the governor. Unable to obtain aught but insult and threat from the authorities, they returned to their villages with vengeance in their hearts, and when the raids were repeated they flew to arms. This, of course, was exactly what the land speculators desired, and troops were immediately rushed into the valley to suppress the revolt and carry out the wholesale eviction of the farmers from their lands.

The task, however, proved more difficult than had been anticipated. The Yaquis are a strong race, high-hearted and of great endurance. In the Revolution of Independence, in the war with the United States, in the three years' struggle for the upholding of the constitution, and in the subsequent conflict with the French invader they had proved their patriotism and valour. To this day they venerate the names of Juarez and Lerdo de Tejada, and regard themselves as a part of the Mexican nation, sharing the responsibilities and rights of Mexican citizens. Consequently, when the government troops arrived they found themselves confronted not by a handful of terrified villagers but by an entire population, well armed, accustomed to fighting, and determined to resist eviction from their lands to the last man.

From that moment began a genuine war between the Yaqui

race and the Mexican Government which lasted for thirty years. Of course the government with its well-trained cavalry and modern artillery could have annihilated every Yaqui in Sonora at any time during the campaign. That it refrained from doing so was not due to any policy of mercy on its part, but to the fact that the land speculators needed peons. To exterminate the population was, in this instance, to destroy an invaluable labour supply. There was another cause, moreover, which saved the Yaquis from complete extermination. Ramon Corral, the governor of Sonora, and lately Vice-President of Mexico, found the maintenance of the campaign a highly profitable affair, for it provided him with good excuse for levying an enormous war tax for the upkeep of an army of ostensibly fifteen thousand soldiers. *Eight thousand of these, however, existed only on paper*, and their unclaimed pay and expenses provided a handsome perquisite for himself and his military commanders. In the course of this daily warfare the Yaquis were driven gradually from their lands into the mountains, or were forced into peonage.

In recent years President Diaz, in conjunction with his nephew, Felix Diaz, and Ramon Corral, the governor of Sonora, conducted a lucrative business in Yaqui slaves.* Their method was to round them up with posses of cavalry, ship them like cattle — men, women, and children — to Yucatan and there sell them at a price averaging sixty-five dollars apiece to the hennequin planters, admittedly the most brutal class of men in the world. Divorced from their native clime, separated from their loved ones, subjected to unnamable cruelties, the Yaquis died like flies; so fast, indeed, that the planters calculated upon buying a fresh supply every six months. Among the men, those who survived the unhealthy climate and incredible toil succumbed to the rawhide lash; among the women, those who survived the lust of the planters, and the toil of the

---

*A full and accurate account of this matter will be found in John Kenneth Turner's "Barbarous Mexico," *American Magazine*, and Kerr & Co., Chicago.

plantation, were thrown to sate the Chinamen. Thus by 1910 no more than a handful of the noble Yaqui race remained, possibly some five or six thousand, certainly not more.

These episodes are sufficient to illustrate the nature and method of the Diaz policy in regard to the agrarian democracy. Were one to make a complete compilation of all such episodes during the years 1877 to 1910, it would fill many volumes and constitute the bloodiest record since the Roman ruling class overthrew the slave revolts of Spartacus and decorated the Appian Way with living torches. Let it be sufficient for our purpose to summarize the outcome of this policy as evidenced in Mexico to-day.

As the result of these vast land despoliations the valley of Papantla, which once supported a population of twenty thousand independent farmers, to-day belongs to one rich family. The entire State of Chihuahua belongs to three families, headed by a man who is reputed the largest single cattle-owner in the world. In the State of Morelos, from which in recent times have sprung the gallant Zapata and his followers, four men, one of them the son-in-law of Diaz, own every inch of agricultural land, and two hundred thousand evicted farmers — now landless peons — till the soil for them at an average wage of $12\frac{1}{2}$ cents a day. The entire Isthmus of Tehuantepec from the Gulf of Mexico to the Pacific Ocean, formerly appropriated by Manuel Romero Rubio, Diaz's father-in-law, now belongs to a small group of interests known as the Pearson syndicate, comprising Diaz's wife, three of her sisters, José Yves Limantour, treasurer of the late Diaz government, and Lord Cowdray, formerly known as Mr. Wheetman D. Pearson.

To obtain undisputed possession of this immense region, fabulously rich in oil, as well as in first-class agricultural lands, a campaign of extermination was carried on, in the course of which whole towns, notably the town of Acayucan, and innumerable villages were completely wiped off the map. Similarly in the State of Puebla the governor, General Mucio Martinez,

THE DICTATORSHIP

in complicity with a group of land speculators and by the military assistance of Diaz, seized the entire agricultural land of the state, evicting several hundred thousand small farmers and annihilating whole towns and groups of villages in the process. By the same methods of wholesale eviction and slaughter, a single large land corporation has become possessed of all the agricultural lands of Sinaloa. In every state in Mexico the record is the same. By the year 1892 all the great bodies of agricultural land had passed from the possession of more than a million small farmers into the hands of less than fifty rich families and corporations of the Diaz clique.

In spite of these vast despoliations there yet remained, dotted here and there throughout the land, considerable numbers of scattered individual holdings which had escaped the eye of the speculator. To obtain possession of these as quickly as possible and with the least expenditure of effort, the Treasury Department on the 18th of November, 1892, issued a declaration to the effect that all owners of land formerly belonging to the Church might clear their titles and substantiate their proprietorship by registering their property and by paying a small sum into the national treasury.

The ruse worked perfectly. Terrified by the wholesale evictions they had witnessed on all sides, the remnants of the small land-owners hastened to register their property and pay the required fee. The government, having acquired a handsome sum in cash, turned over the records thus obtained to the speculators, and in the course of a few months the last of the deluded land-owners had been evicted either by some judicial trickery, or more commonly by simple force of arms.

By these methods of despoliation the agrarian democracy of Mexico was reduced to the lowest slavery. More than a million families, averaging at least five members to the family, and consequently at least a million small traders, craftsmen dependent upon the custom of these families, a total sum of six million working people, at least, were torn from independent modes of livelihood to become the peons of no more than fifty big land-owning families and corporations.

Many of these evicted farmers were possessed of so strong a passion for freedom and independent ownership of the land that they went out upon the great areas of undeveloped waterless land coveted by none, and with infinite labour wrought farms anew out of the desert. With nothing but hand-tools they dug wells, irrigated their homesteads, ploughed, harrowed, seeded them, and prepared to enjoy the fruits of their toil. Even here the pitiless eye of the despoiler was upon them. Some petty government official's cupidity would be aroused by the flourishing little farm; some day the rurales would appear — and once more the despoiled family would be turned out upon the desert to starve or sink into peonage. "Unhappy was the farmer," says Dr. Lara Pardo, "who, loving the soil inherited from his forefathers, and suddenly inspired by a spark of modernism, irrigated his heirloom, and by the use of machinery and scientific fertilizers, and by hard and patient effort, succeeded in producing unusual crops and thus attracted the attention of the neighbourhood! From that moment he had awakened the rapacity of the jefe politico, or of the military commander, or of the secretary of the governor, or of the curate, or the canon, or archbishop, and they would not rest until they had despoiled him of his property. And if he defended it with the wonderful tenacity with which the native defends his land he would be sent to the barrack, to the ignominious servitude of the prisoner-soldier, or the soldiers would take him from the jail and shoot him in the back on the highway. . . . In the court archives of Mexico there are thousands and thousands of instances of this kind; I have seen many; I know in detail histories of this kind that would fill scores of books — histories of people snatched from their farms by force with the help of the troops, in order that the governor, the military commander, or the foreigner, patronized and sustained by General Diaz, might take possession of their lands." (Dr. Lara Pardo, "De Porfirio Diaz a Francisco Madero," p. 89.)

The Church, as we have said, took a prominent share in this land despoliation as a reward for her moral support of Diaz. By the simple ruse of placing the titles of the vast estates thus acquired in the personal names of the various bishops and archbishops, the constitution was set at naught, and the Church quickly drew into her hands a vaster wealth than she had enjoyed since the Conquest. At the same time the destruction of education, and the resulting ignorance of the new generation, enabled her once more to tighten her psychological grip upon the masses. As we might be led to believe by the evidence revealed in the course of this work regarding the policy and psychology of the Roman See, this stealthy re-acquisition of wealth and power by the Church in Mexico was by no means due to the patronage of Diaz. Rather Diaz as the obedient tool of every phase of reaction enjoyed the patronage of the Church. It is rather amusing therefore to encounter the polite view of this matter taken by Zayas Enriquez in his worshipful biography of Diaz. "General Diaz," he says, "is head of the Freemasons in Mexico. He is of the thirty-third degree and Grand Commander for life. *At the same time he is the invisible head of the Catholic Church, its arch-protector and its director, influencing indirectly the appointment of bishops and archbishops, and the creation of new dioceses of archbishoprics*." (Zayas Enriquez, "Porfirio Diaz," p. 31.) The truth is the interests of the Church and the interests of International Capitalism in Mexico exactly coincided. Diaz was the serviceable, if clumsy, tool of both.

In the foregoing pages we have briefly described the manner in which Porfirio Diaz destroyed the agrarian democracy of Mexico at the behest of the land speculators and the Church and degraded the people to peonage.

We now propose to recite one or two instances illustrating the manner in which Porfirio Diaz degraded the industrial proletariat to the most abject wage slavery, and illustrating also the ferocity of the exploiters — even in fear of revolt.

In the year 1907 some forty thousand men, women, and children, employees of the Orizaba cotton mills, went on a strike for a wage of 75 cents a day for men, 40 cents for women, 30 cents for children, and a reduction of the working day from sixteen hours to fourteen hours. From the moment the strike was declared the factory superintendent, aided by the petty officials of the company, resorted to provocative tactics in the hope of creating a disturbance, and thus providing an excuse for calling in the soldiery.

Failing in this, they proceeded to cut off the strikers from the use of the wells, on the pretext that the water belonged to the company. Maddened with thirst, the people forcibly possessed themselves of the water they required. This was considered a sufficient disturbance for the purpose to hand, and the superintendent telegraphed President Diaz stating that a dangerous riot was in progress and requesting the aid of the government.

Ever prompt to comply with such requests, President Diaz sent a division of no less than fifteen thousand troops into the district. Under special instructions the troops detrained at night outside the city and secreted themselves in the factory and dominant positions of the environments.

In the morning the strikers were surprised to hear the factory bell ringing, and concluded that the company had decided to accept their terms, and was calling them back to work. Accordingly they gathered in a vast throng — men, women, and children — before the factory gates. Presently a petty company official, named Garcin, issued from the factory door and proceeded to harangue them in the most insulting fashion, calling the men hungry dogs and the women bawds. The people, all unaware of the presence of the soldiery, and enraged by these insults, endeavoured to seize Garcin. The latter immediately fled back into the factory.

This was the signal agreed upon. In a flash every window

THE DICTATORSHIP

of the factory belched fire. Volley after volley was poured into the panic-stricken mass, and the air was filled with the shrieks of women and children, and the groans of strong men piercing the continuous roar of musketry. The strikers fell in droves under the hail of lead, or trampled each other to death in maddened efforts to escape; while, urged on by the mill owners, the troops kept up an unceasing slaughter.

How many victims were left dead or struggling in their own blood in the factory yards will never be known. Some idea, however, may be gleaned from the fact that two full freight-train loads of dead and wounded were rushed to Vera Cruz under cover of night and there dumped into the bay to be eaten by the sharks which swarm in those waters. The strike was broken and the shareholders of the cotton mills filled the columns of the subsidized press, both in the United States and Mexico, with encomiums upon the efficiency of the army and the masterly discipline of Porfirio Diaz.

In 1906 ten thousand miners went out on a strike at Cannanea, demanding five pesos ($2.50 American money) a day, and an eight-hour shift. At first the superintendent of the company agreed to give the increased wage, but refused to reduce the working day. This compromise would have satisfied the strikers, but stringent orders came from President Diaz and the Secretary of the Interior, Ramon Corral, forbidding the superintendent to make the slightest concession to the miners, pointing out that to do so would be to establish a dangerous precedent and encourage industrial revolt. President Diaz backed up his orders by sending a strong division of troops into the town, and with some slight variation the massacre of Orizaba was repeated. Hundreds of miners were massacred in cold blood upon the streets, and all who were suspected of even a faint sympathy with the strike were sent to the horrors of a Mexican penitentiary. It is worthy of note that at the outbreak of the strike the mine owners sent frenzied appeals for help to the labour union officials of Arizona, *declaring that the Mexican strikers were massacring American women and children on the streets of the city!* The news sent a thrill of horror throughout the United States, and a volunteer force of three hundred American workingmen immediately crossed the border and marched on Cannanea. The report of the massacre was, of course, a pure canard. But it served its purpose — and Diaz's slaughter of the striking miners was greeted with cheers throughout the United States.

We are well aware that the policy of exterminating the more spirited section of the working class is not peculiar to Mexico, but is the policy of the capitalist class throughout the world; but Diaz's lust of blood was so wrought into the fabric of his mind that he could not conceive of the execution of the simplest project without the sacrifice of human life. An illuminating and amusing side light upon his sanguinary psychology is afforded by the following anecdote, quoted from Dr. Lara Pardo's book, "De Porfirio Diaz." For its truth we personally can vouch: "When the American Government brought pressure to bear upon President Diaz to stamp out the yellow fever then raging on the Mexican coast, protesting that it constituted a serious menace to the American cities on the Gulf and Atlantic seaboards, the President summoned Dr. Felipe Gutierrez de Lara, to whom the Superior Board of Health had given the directions of the operations against the yellow fever on the Isthmus of Tehuantepec, and ordered him to institute a well-organized campaign against the fever on the coast. "You are bearing with you," President Diaz told him, "full power: if the people resist, shoot them at once, and I assure you nobody will hold you responsible for your action; only let me know personally when you are going to do that." Dr. Gutierrez de Lara recounted the interview to me soon after it had taken place. He was greatly incensed about it. Then, when the health campaign was carried out to a happy conclusion without the necessity of shooting any one, great was the surprise of President Diaz, and he seemed quite unable to conceive that a

THE DICTATORSHIP

good work could be performed without deluging the country in blood."

. . . .

No account of this wholesale enslavement of a free people could be either convincing or complete without some reference to the spiritual blinding to which they were subjected. Diaz, it is true, placed most reliance on brute force as a method of attaining the ends desired by his masters, but these methods would have produced a violent reaction, ending in the complete destruction of his power, had he not first put out the people's eyes by way of precaution. The eyes of the people are free, adequate, and untrammelled education, free assembly, free speech, free press, and free ballot. All of these the people enjoyed to the fullest extent under Juarez and Lerdo de Tejada; all of these Diaz destroyed within a few years of his accession to power. The darkness of ignorance for nine tenths of the Mexican nation was what he planned and accomplished.

As a step toward creating this condition of affairs Diaz suppressed the teaching of the constitution in the schools. A little later he suppressed the schools themselves, except those in the larger cities. And as a result education became once more the exclusive monopoly of the wealthier classes. Juarez had established the teaching of the constitution in all the schools from the lowest to the highest, and under his régime it had been the common practice for the peasants to hire schoolboys to read its articles to them, and to repeat what they had learned about it in the schools. In that manner a pretty thorough knowledge of the constitution and all that it implied became widely disseminated among even the most illiterate. A people possessed of a full knowledge of its rights is no easy subject for enslavement. Diaz recognized this, and while hypocritically retaining the constitution on paper, even expressing a reverence for it in public, he utterly abrogated it in practice and destroyed the very knowledge of it from among the people.

Following swiftly upon the suppression of the teaching of the constitution came the destruction of the free ballot, of free assembly, of free press, and free speech. *The eyes of the people were put out.* During this régime all the hideous crimes perpetrated by the government against individuals and against whole communities of the people were wrapped in the darkest secrecy. The victims of Papantla knew only their own wrongs; they knew nothing of the wrongs of Tomochic, of Sonora, of Orizaba, of Cannanea. Thus they writhed in their bonds, dumb, impotent, blind, unable to find utterance, unable to effect concerted action, unable to see what had befallen them.

But the people of Mexico, though bound and shackled, never submitted tamely for one moment to this quenching of the light in their eyes. History bears no record of a more heroic or more useless resistance. Crimes unceasing, sinister, and bloody were committed by the Diaz government in its efforts to throttle the indignant utterances of the people; and for every martyr that fell a new hero sprang to take his place. Imprisonment or death awaited the man or woman who wrote or spoke the truth about the conditions obtaining in Mexico. Newspapers which dared to express even a mild protest against the actions of the government were raided, their printing plants wrecked, and their editors and writers were thrown into dungeons of filthy horror, there to rot, go blind, or mad. Radical writers left their homes never to return, kidnapped or stabbed to death in the dark.

In the fall of 1892, in the city of Pachuca, in the State of Hidalgo, Simon Cravioto, the governor of the state, arrested a newspaper man named Santa Maria, who had dared to attack the iniquitous policies of the government, and burned him alive at the stake. Olmos y Conteras, another Liberal publicist, while walking on the street with his wife and children was murdered in broad daylight by policemen, acting under the instructions of the governor of Puebla, Mucio Martinez. Scores of newspaper men who had gallantly protested against the wholesale butchery of people were walled up in the noisome dungeons of Belem in Mexico City, to rot in mud and excrement. That magnificent Intellectual, Jesus Carrion, a noted cartoonist of the day, and a worthy grandson of that peon hero, Pipila, who, with a flat stone on his back, set fire to the door of the castle of Granaditas in the time of Hidalgo, was one of these. When finally released he came forth blind, dying of pneumonia, and with whole portions of his body gnawed away by the rats. Thousands of brave men and women, the very flower of the nation, and the intellectual leaders of the mass, suffered unspeakable torture and death for endeavouring to save the light in the eyes of the people. Were we so minded we could fill hundreds of pages with these recitals. Let this be sufficient.

Meanwhile the subsidized press maintained a ceaseless panegyric of the Dictator. Then were uttered all those encomiums upon the character of Porfirio Diaz which the American people, and indeed the whole civilized world, have since adopted as articles of faith. Millions of dollars was expended not only to create and sustain a powerful "Diaz-Myth" and to defame the common people, but systematically to debauch every youthful Mexican Intellectual of promise.

In the University of Mexico luxurious quarters for the students were erected and supported by José Yves Limantour, the treasurer of the Diaz government, where a middle-class student could live in comparative splendour on ten dollars a month! Here he was taught to ridicule the constitution, to despise the common people, and here he was systematically trained to believe that the only path to success was to worship Diaz, to model himself on the supporters and politicians of the governing clique, forget his reason and his soul, and become an accomplished scoundrel.

This system of poisoning the spirit of the nation at its source was so far successful that there is scarcely an Intellectual in Mexico to-day whose entire theory of life is not to be as treacherous, and conscienceless, and rascally as possible. Scarcely one has even a superficial knowledge of the great social problems pressing for solution. In addition to this the subsidized press and hired publicists unceasingly represented Diaz to the Mexican people as the idol of foreign governments and nations, openly boasting that any disobedience and resistance to him on their part would be summarily dealt with by the United States army.

Not for a moment did the Mexican people peaceably submit to Diaz; but in face of the tremendous odds against them their resistance was futile. Deep in their hearts they cherished the thought of another revolution — some day perhaps when Diaz should die. Meanwhile, in spite of their hunger, misery, slavery, and ignorance, little by little they were recouping from the disastrous aftermath of the French intervention, until the day came, in 1910, when the knowledge of their power broke upon them, and they burst forth in the second Ayutla, whose end is not yet.

CHAPTER XXIII

THE RAILROADS

IF THERE is one figment of the "Diaz-Myth" more firmly implanted in the modern mind than another, it is that the introduction of railroads into Mexico was due to Diaz personally, and that this alone constitutes sufficient achievement to warrant his title as "Maker of Mexico." Exactly how much Diaz personally had to do with the introduction of the railroads and their development to their present status we propose to show by a brief examination of the facts.

In the first place, *Diaz did not introduce railroads into Mexico.* Juarez had that honour. While Diaz was hiding in the outlaw dens of the south the constitutional government in pursuance of the principles laid down in the Constitution of 1857, and reaffirmed in the *Leyes de Reforma*, had already begun the construction of the first Mexican national railroad from Mexico City to Vera Cruz. And before Diaz had betrayed his fatherland to the American railroad speculators and had been placed in power as their agent and factor, that railroad had been completed. In the second place Diaz was not personally responsible for the building of subsequent railroads. President of Mexico solely by the grace of the American railroad speculators, he had to observe his pact with them or suffer the consequences, i. e., in return for their moral and financial aid he was compelled to give them free-hand concessions to build all the roads in Mexico they desired, wherever and whenever they desired, at such terms as they desired. This lavish distribution of free-hand concessions as the price of support can scarcely be dignified with the title of a railroad policy. It was simply blackmail on the part of the speculators and common bribery on the part of Diaz.

It is also an integral part of the "Diaz-Myth," and a current article of faith, that if it was the enterprise and far-sightedness of President Diaz which inaugurated and developed a modern system of railroads in Mexico, it was American capital which built them. This is an error as radical as the other. Not a dollar of American capital has been expended anywhere or at any time in the building of the Mexican railroads. *They were built entirely by Mexican capital.* And what is more they were so immensely over-subsidized that in many cases they were built *solely for the sake of the subsidy*, and in such a fashion as to be useless for transportation; e. g., the lines from El Paso and Laredo to Mexico City. It is true that these railroad stocks were the plaything of American speculators; that such railroads as Mexico possesses have come into a bastard existence as a result of the cupidity and lawlessness of American promoters and stock gamblers, but this indicates the limit of America's service to Mexico in this respect.

Taking a broad view of the matter, the railroads entered Mexico as they entered China, Japan, and Borneo, by virtue of the necessities of that eternally expanding system of exploitation known as international capitalism. As far back as 1861 Mexico had been marked out for prey by the capitalist cabals of Europe and the United States. Mexico, however, could not be efficiently exploited without adequate means of communication and transportation — hence the railroads. That is all.

Let us now examine the next great achievement of President Diaz in the field of railroad development — the Tehuantepec railroad.

In the year 1889 Diaz signed a contract with an English financier, Edward McMurdo, for the construction of a national railroad between the ports of Coatzacoalcos on the Gulf of Mexico and Salina Cruz on the Pacific seaboard, a distance

THE RAILROADS

of one hundred and fifty miles, with the enormous subsidy of $13,500,000.* No less than ninety thousand dollars per mile! Such largess, it might be imagined, would have resulted at least in a well-built road, and in the provision of adequate rolling stock. On the contrary the road was built of the most wretched material, and by the year 1890 scarcely any of the necessary equipment had been installed. As a matter of fact McMurdo had expended no more than $2,000,000 on its construction, the remaining $11,000,000 constituting a handsome profit for himself, for Porfirio Diaz, and the small coterie of financiers and politicians immediately concerned in the transaction. More than $13,500,000 had been squandered on this project, still it was perfectly useless for commercial purposes. Diaz now gave a fresh contract for its completion to another English contractor, Wheetman D. Pearson, afterward known as Lord Cowdray. By the terms of this agreement the latter received not only a cash subsidy of $15,000,000, but a franchise to operate the road for his own benefit for fifty-one years! In due time the road was made commercially possible at an actual outlay of about $6,000,000, the remaining $9,000,000 constituting, as before, another handsome profit for all parties concerned. In addition to this, for the purpose of subsidizing a shipping line to connect with the road, Pearson obtained authorization from Porfirio Diaz to raise a loan of $17,500,000 backed by government securities, *but to be used at his own discretion*. To-day practically the entire Isthmus of Tehuantepec, with its superb agricultural lands, vast oil fields, not to speak of the railroad, is the private property of Wheetman D. Pearson in partnership with the entire Diaz family — the well-known "Pearson Syndicate."

As with the atrocities perpetrated upon the agrarian democracy and the industrial proletariat by the Diaz government, so with these colossal peculations committed upon the national treasury by this government, typical instances alone can be

*See Luis G. Labastida's "Leyes Fiscales," p. 49.

cited. The full narrative would require volumes. We have said enough, we think, to indicate the exact value of the claim that to Diaz personally was due the introduction and development of Mexico's railroad system. Not a rail was laid nor a sewer built, nor a harbour dredged in Mexico in all these years that was not a mere pretext for the unbridled plundering of the people. And it must be remembered the labour employed upon these works was in effect slave labour, lashed, starved, used up, and flung to the dogs.

These much lauded railroads and government enterprises cost the nation unnumbered millions procured only by the most extortionate taxation. Not a dollar of foreign capital was used in financing them. They were wrought out by the toil of the common people and financed by the money of the common people. Even so, for every million dollars expended in actual construction at least three million dollars was wasted in bribery and embezzlement. And as if this were not enough, the Diaz government used these enterprises as a pretext for raising foreign loans to the value of $600,000,000, not a dollar of which ever found its way to the public service.

In 1909 the colossal railroad frauds of the Diaz régime reached their climax. In that year the government effected a merger of most of the railroads in Mexico and acquired a major interest in them at the enormous figure of $230,458,000; in other words, the roads which had been built by the nation's labour, and paid for by the nation's money four times over, were now sold back to the nation at an enormous excess valuation!

It was a shrewd stroke apart from the financial aspect. The common people, imbued with the traditions of Juarez, acclaimed this nationalization of the railroads with great enthusiasm; while the whole civilized world regarded it as a vindication of the patriotic statesmanship of Porfirio Diaz! But what is still more important, it semi-officially entrenched the Mexican Government as the financial partner of the American railroad corporations, who held most of the minority stock.

THE RAILROADS

The exact strategical value of this semi-official alliance became clearly evident when President Taft rushed the American army to the border at the outbreak of the present revolution in Mexico. Fortunately the American people by 1910 had partially awaked to the real condition of affairs in Mexico, and the intended invasion on behalf of Porfirio Diaz and American "Big Business" failed to materialize, but it might easily have happened otherwise. In connection with the nationalization of the Mexican railroads the Mexican silver money was converted to the gold standard for the benefit, not of the nation, but of the speculators, an operation entailing another vast expenditure of more than $230,000,000.

. . . .

No account of the Diaz régime could be complete without some reference to the sinister group of able men who guided his policies, well known in recent times as the "Scientificos." During the early 90's the speculator-politicians who formed the real brains of the Diaz government organized themselves into a definite party, self-styled with admirable wit — the Scientificos. It was these men who ruled the country and directed the vast predatory operations upon the lands of the agrarian democracy, upon the public resources and the national treasury. To them Diaz was merely a strong-armed servitor, who in return for a share of the spoils faithfully performed the rough work of massacre, debauchery, murder, enslavement, private assassination, and imprisonment which their operations necessitated. In touch with all the great world centres of speculation, in complete control of the machinery of government, they held the nation and its wealth at their mercy, and they made the most of their opportunity. There was not a profitable enterprise in all Mexico in which they failed to take a hand.

These were the men who, with the assistance of Diaz, created "Barbarous Mexico" and the bloody revolution of 1910. Shrewd as they were, they failed to notice the coming storm.

and when it broke they failed altogether to recognize the only recourse left to them if they would save their social system from disruption. With the $80,000,000 which lay idle in the treasury at that time, they could easily have subdivided and have irrigated the government lands, and have sold them to the peons at a small profit on long instalments. Such a course as a temporary expedient would have ended the revolution in twenty-four hours. Fortunately they were not astute enough to see that half a loaf is better than no loaf — fortunately, we say, for, in spite of the fact that at the moment of writing a hundred thousand peons have lost their lives fighting for the lands which plain business common sense would have restored to them, feudalism will be overthrown, not bolstered up by a system of government land distribution on a merely "reform" basis.

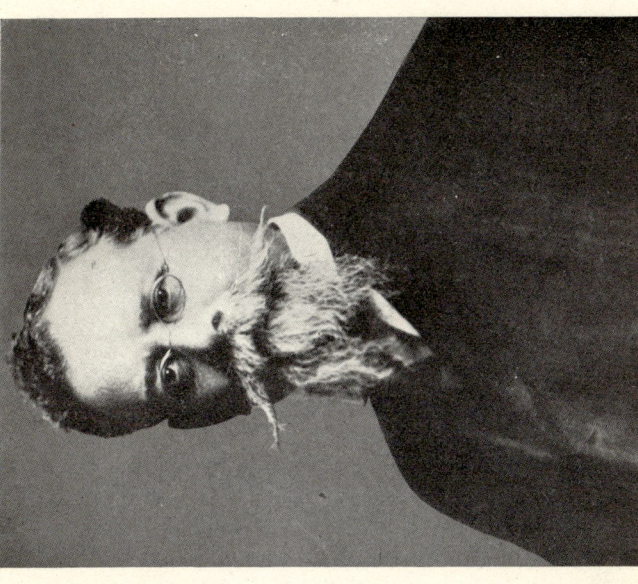

Photograph by Brown Bros.
VICTORIANO HUERTA

Copyright by Underwood & Underwood, N. Y.
VENUSTIANO CARRANZA

An interesting study in physiognomy is afforded by comparing the faces of Diaz and Huerta, the two great reactionary leaders, and Madero and Carranza, the idealistic revolutionary leaders

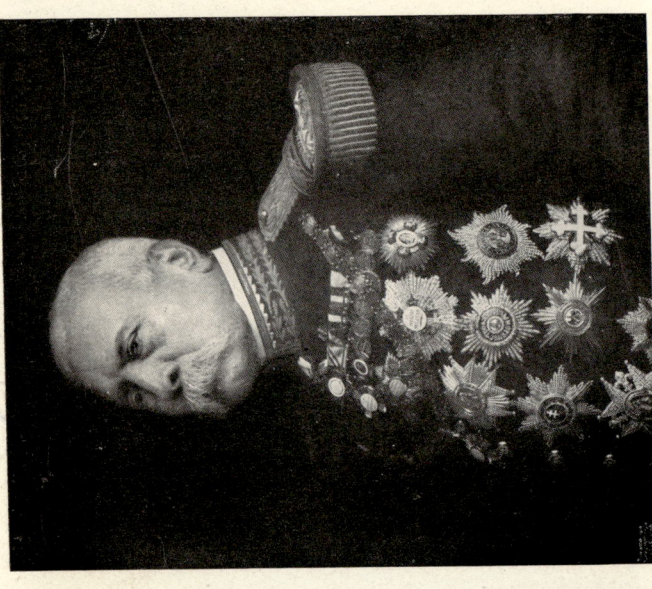

Photograph by Brown Bros.

FRANCISCO MADERO   PORFIRIO DIAZ

An interesting study in physiognomy is afforded by comparing the faces of Diaz and Huerta, the two great reactionary leaders, and Madero and Carranza, the idealistic revolutionary leaders

CHAPTER XXIV

THE REVOLUTION OF 1910-1914

NEVER for a moment since Diaz came into power in 1876 had the spirit of revolt ceased to fire the hearts of the people. Its manifestation had been repressed but the spirit lived on and grew stronger with the passing days until in the early 90's it found definite expression in the formation of the "Junta Revolucionaria del Partido Liberal Méxicano" (Revolutionary Committee of the Mexican Liberal party). Mexico under Diaz was no place for revolutionists, as the fate of Carrion, Santa Maria, and a thousand propagandists had already attested. Accordingly the group of Intellectuals who comprised the Revolutionary Committee removed from Mexico to the United States, and established their headquarters at St. Louis, Missouri. Here they proceeded to publish the official organ of the party, *Regeneracion*, circulating it widely among the Mexico peons and refugees resident in the United States, and shipping it in quantities to Mexico for secret distribution among the people.

A movement such as this, which had for its avowed object the enforcement of the Constitution of 1857 in general, and the restoration of the agrarian democracy in particular, naturally called for prompt suppression at the hands of Diaz and the Scientificos. Such a suppression, however, was not an altogether easy matter. Up to the year 1910 literally millions of dollars was expended by the Mexican Government in its efforts to stamp out this revolutionary organization, with only very partial success.

At the same time the Scientificos played into the hands of the Roman Church, with the result that Mexico was fined more than a million dollars in the matter of the restitution of the long cancelled Pious Funds formerly paid by Mexico to the Church in California for the upkeep of the missions to the Indians. The matter was arranged in this wise: Having acquainted President Roosevelt with their intention, the Scientificos proceeded to suggest to the Church in California that they enter a claim against Mexico for the restitution of the Pious Funds. It mattered not, of course, that the payment of these funds had been legally cancelled by the Constitution of 1857 and the *Leyes de Reforma*. Accordingly the Church lodged a petition with President Roosevelt to present their claims to Mexico. President Roosevelt complied and met with a polite demur from the Mexican Government. To pay the claim would be unconstitutional, said the Scientificos; they would agree, however, to arbitrate the matter before the Hague Tribunal. At The Hague the representatives of the Church in California, officially supported by the United States, argued their case for several days. The Mexican delegate spoke only a few minutes. The solemn farce ended in the sentencing of Mexico to recognize the Pious Funds, and to pay the Church of California arrears of $1,420,682 due on that fund and $43,050 annually in perpetuity!

As a flash of lightning illumines the murk of the storm, the strike of Cannanea in 1906 suddenly illumined the situation, revealing on the one hand the solidarity of the Mexican people in their sympathy for the spirit of revolt manifested in the strike, and on the other, the antagonistic attitude of certain elements of the American people toward that spirit of revolt as manifested in the applause with which they greeted the massacre of the miners. The Liberal junta thus had a double task before it, not only to educate the Mexican people in their rights and organize them into an effective weapon of revolution, but to educate the American people to the real issues involved

THE REVOLUTION OF 1910–1914 343

in that revolution, and thus to forestall the possibility of American intervention in Mexico should the revolution succeed in its objects. Against this task of the Mexican patriot, Theodore Roosevelt directed the whole weight of the federal forces.

Pursuant to orders from Washington, United States Secret Service men threw the Mexican revolutionists into jail at St. Louis, Missouri, San Antonio, and El Paso, in Texas, and upon their release pursued them across the continent to Los Angeles, where one night, without process of law or warrant of any kind, they set upon the leaders, Librado Rivera, Ricardo Flores Magon, Antonio Villareal, Manuel Sarabia, and L. Gutierrez de Lara, severely beating them and again throwing them into jail.

As fast as they were released for lack of evidence, fresh charges were preferred against them, and finally three of their number, Rivera, Magon, and Villareal were sentenced for "breach of the neutrality laws" to the Yuma penitentiary.

The Socialists of Los Angeles made the cause of these men their own and instituted a tremendous campaign of protest against this violation of law, American tradition, and humanity at the hands of the Chief Executive. The campaign spread rapidly to all parts of the United States, Canada, and Europe. Hundreds of mass meetings were held which passed unanimous resolutions expressing sympathy for the Mexican revolutionists and denunciation of the United States authorities. The American Federation of Labour, the Industrial Workers of the World, the Western Federation of Miners, the United Mine Workers of America, all officially declared themselves in sympathy with the Liberal junta and its revolutionary propaganda, and as strongly opposed to United States intervention in Mexico, backing up their declaration with substantial financial aid to the revolutionary cause.

The more Mr. Roosevelt violated the conscience of the people by this persecution of the Mexican refugees the more vigorous grew the campaign of protest. For six years the contest was waged, with what effect became apparent when, at the outbreak of the Revolution in 1910, the American people showed themselves completely opposed to a policy of intervention.

. . . .

Long immunity and an atmosphere of adulation had rendered Diaz absurdly confident in his power, and in common with the Scientificos he remained up to the last moment entirely blind to the powerful spirit of revolt among the people. On the other hand, he allowed himself to be foolishly irritated by some mild attacks made upon him by an academic politician named Francisco Madero, a member of the wealthy and influential Madero family of Jewish origin.

To draw this new enemy into the open and test his strength, Diaz cunningly announced that he would not present himself again as candidate for President. Cunningly, we say, but not wisely, for Madero immediately announced himself as candidate for President on a radical platform which insured him the support of the whole Mexican common people.

The audacity of the move caught Diaz off his guard. Unable to stem the tide of popular enthusiasm for the new candidate, he threw him into jail, and when the elections came due in July, 1910, had himself proclaimed once more President of Mexico.

Even then he failed to recognize the real seriousness of the situation, and yielding to the pressure of the wealthy and powerful Madero family he released Francisco Madero on bail, and permitted him to flee the country, confident that he had received sufficient warning to keep him from creating further disturbance. In this he was entirely mistaken. Encouraged by the tremendous success of his campaign, Francisco Madero, before leaving Mexico, drew up and signed a manifesto calling upon the people to rise in arms for the defence of the following principles:

1. Effective suffrage (free ballot).
2. Non-reëlection (single term for all executive officers throughout the country).

3. Restoration of the lands of the common people.

After he had gained the temporary safety of the United States he caused this manifesto to be widely distributed throughout Mexico. The response was tremendous. Through the activity of the Liberal junta the Mexican people were already well aware of the strong fraternal feeling of the American labour organizations toward them, and their spirit was consequently no longer crushed by fear of United States intervention.

In the month of November, 1910, Castulo Herrera, president of the Boiler Makers and Mechanics' Union, and Pascal Orozco, a small commission merchant, started the revolt with a handful of mountaineers in Chihuahua.

It was a fitting thing that the state which saw the massacre of Tomochic, Temosachic, and Guerrero should fire the first shot in the new struggle against the oppressor. Within a few weeks the entire country was ablaze. In Durango, Coahuila, in Zacatecas and Sinaloa, thousands of peons flocked to the standard of revolt. In the State of Morelos Emiliano Zapata and Eufemio Zapata, his brother, dispossessed small land-owners, gathered a strong force of peons under their leadership and entered upon an uncompromising fight for their liberties, which has endured uninterruptedly to the present day. In Guerrero, Ambrosio Figueroa headed a similar uprising, while in the old revolutionary states of Jalisco, Nuevo Leon, and Tamaulipas, where some remnants of the agrarian democracy still remained, the people rose to a man.

Badly armed, poorly organized as they were, these impetuous hosts utterly out-manœuvred and overwhelmed the forty thousand well-drilled, well-disciplined federal troops sent against them.

Meanwhile the Scientificos had awakened to the fact that Madero personally would prove as convenient a tool as Diaz, and that his installation as President would put an end at once to a condition of affairs that was beginning to prove ruinous to their financial operations. Accordingly Porfirio Diaz was dismissed from the presidency. Francisco Leon de la Barra, the recognized leader of the Catholic Church, was proclaimed provisional President in his place, and the nation was summoned to a constitutional election.

This change of tactics was entirely successful, and the peons gladly threw down their arms to engage in the political struggle. In order to keep some check upon Madero, the Scientificos then endeavoured to force the candidacy of Francisco Leon de la Barra upon the people as Vice-President; failing in this they put him forward as candidate for the presidency itself. The people, however, were fully alive to the issue and the first phase of the Revolution closed in an incredibly short space of time with the election of Madero as constitutional President of the Republic of Mexico by the largest popular vote ever cast for a President in the history of the country.

In order to render the subsequent events intelligible it will be necessary for us to glance briefly at the character of the new President. Francisco Madero was, as we have said, a member of the wealthy and influential Madero family, Mexican Jews, whose financial interests embraced every field of exploitation, including cattle ranches, cotton plantations, mines, factories, and banks. His training, association, and traditions were consequently those of a modern Mexican man of business.

For money-making, however, as a mode of life he had neither aptitude nor inclination. His aspirations were entirely literary and political. To the surprise and disgust of his hardheaded kinsmen he proved himself again and again utterly incompetent to manage the simplest business affairs placed in his charge. Indeed he preferred the pursuits of a student and the politician to the most alluring commercial enterprise. In presence he was ineffectual, in physique frail, and he was afflicted with a high falsetto voice which rendered ridiculous his attempts at public speech.

Nevertheless he was lacking neither in personal courage nor in a certain energy and shrewdness. Francisco Madero was certainly not the man to guide the mighty forces of the Revolution of 1910, but with greater maturity and experience, and under happier circumstances, he might have made a useful member of a strong Liberal government. His book, "The Presidential Succession," which first brought him into the field as a mild antagonist of Porfirio Diaz, is above the average as a political treatise, but as an expression of the needs of the Mexican people it is decidedly inadequate.

Francisco Madero, in short, was that most unhappy of all types of politicians — the bourgeois idealist; subsequent events proved him to be a political opportunist as well. Betrayed into the open by the cunning of Porfirio Diaz, he rashly embraced the cause of the people at the moment of their impassioned revolt, not from conviction, but as an alluring political expedient. Almost without effort of his own he was lifted into power by the might of the people, as a straw is lifted by a wave, only to be dashed on the rocks of a dilemma created by his own insincerity.

Exponent of the Revolution by the will of the masses he found himself in fact merely the *deus ex machina* of the Scientificos. And he had neither the knowledge, will, nor understanding to extricate himself from his false position.

Such was the man who had ridden into power on the crest of the Revolution. A constitutional President under false pretences, his whole subsequent career was a denial of the popular cause.

Scarcely had he assumed office than he ordered the national Treasury to pay his brother, Gustavo Madero, the sum of $700,000, ostensibly as indemnity for the expenses he had incurred in the support of the Revolution. There was no proof that those expenses had been incurred in total or in part, and the indecent haste with which the transaction was consummated awakened an ugly suspicion in the public mind. He then proceeded to fill his cabinet and all of the important public offices with members of his own family, who were also Scientificos.

To his uncle, Ernesto Madero, he gave the Secretaryship of the Treasury; to his cousin, Rafael Hernandez, he gave the Secretaryship of Fomento (department of mines, lands and industries); to another relative, General Gonzales Salas, he gave the Secretaryship of War; and as if this were not enough, he proceeded to thrust scores of the lesser members of the Madero clan into all the government departments. The Minister of Foreign Affairs, Manuel Calaro, was also a Scientifico.

In this way he simply built up a new Scientifico machine for the plundering of the people, differing from the old only in its personal composition. It was the Maderistas instead of the Porfiristas that revelled at the board; it was the Standard Oil Trust which dominated the foreign support of the Scientificos instead of the Southern Pacific and the Pearson Syndicate — that was all. The new administration in short, represented neither the principles of the Revolution nor even the theoretical reformism of Francisco Madero. It represented simply the private interests of the Madero clan. It is not a matter for surprise, therefore, that throughout this régime not a single measure was instituted tending toward the amelioration of the vast evils endured by the people since the Diaz cuartelazo of 1876.

Instead of disbanding the army and creating a national guard, according to the traditions of the Liberal party and the Constitution of 1857, the Madero cabal fostered and maintained it at an enormous expense as a weapon for the suppression of the people. Francisco Madero personally repudiated the *Leyes de Reforma*, and extended a cordial invitation to the Clericals to take part in the affairs of government; and at a banquet given in his honour by a group of the Scientificos he boldly denied he had ever promised to restore the lands to the people.

When the people continued persistently to demand of him the restoration of the lands for which they had fought, he endeavoured to dupe them by requesting Congress to authorize the "Caja Nacional de Ahorros" — an institution existing

THE REVOLUTION OF 1910–1914

only on paper — to raise a loan of $250,000,000 for the purpose of buying large tracts of land to be subdivided into small allotments and sold to the people on instalments! To make the mockery more complete he appointed as a committee to handle the buying and selling of these lands a group of wealthy landowners, many of them his own relatives.

The pledge of free ballot suffered the same repudiation at his hands. In the states of Puebla, Vera Cruz, Hidalgo, Tamaulipas, Sinaloa, Chiapas, and Morelos he deliberately set aside the constitutional elections and imposed governors upon the people agreeable to the schemes of his rapacious relatives. Surrounded by the old element of corrupt politicians, conscienceless peculators, brutal military and scheming prelates, Francisco Madero lost every trace of his vaunted democratic ideals and became consciously or unconsciously the mere creature of that same intolerable oppression and exploitation which had provoked the Revolution of 1910.

The people were not slow to recognize the real state of affairs. When the smoke of the Revolution cleared away they found that for all their trouble they had changed nothing but a name. The cries of "Viva Madero!" became stilled; then out of the silence of disillusionment and despair there burst forth a new cry, "Viva la Tierra! Viva la Constitucion!" as full of new hope and understanding they unstacked their rifles and prepared to continue the fight. *They would no longer fight for a man. Henceforth they would never lay down their arms till they themselves had consummated that economic reorganization they demanded.*

In this clarified attitude of the Mexican people lies the great hope of the present Revolution. No man henceforth can ride on their backs into power. They will go forward unwaveringly, irresistibly, until they have established the new social order. They have learned democracy's great lesson; *that the individual cannot assume the functions of the collectivity.*

Thus before the Madero family clique had firmly settled

themselves in power new revolts had broken out in the states of Chihuahua, Durango, Zacatecas, Puebla, Vera Cruz, Guerrero, and Morelos. In the latter state the far-sighted Zapata had never for a moment relinquished the fight, directing his forces as vigorously against Madero as against his predecessor.

Again the madness of Diaz was repeated. Millions of dollars amassed by the late administration lay idle in the national treasury. The Madero clique might easily have used this wealth in irrigating government lands, subdividing them into small allotments and selling them at the cost price, but on long instalments to the people. Such a course of action would have ended the Revolution at once, enhanced the value of all Mexican securities, restored the confidence of capital, and ushered in an era of capitalist prosperity. It is true that the restoration of the lands to the people would have ruined the slave-labour and wage-labour markets, that thereafter the industrial exploiters would have been compelled by the law of supply and demand to pay higher wages to their employees; but the Madero clique were unable to see that some alleviation of the general condition of the people was inevitable; like Diaz, they were unable to recognize that the secure possession of half a loaf is better than no loaf at all. Consequently they elected to waste the millions in the treasury in embezzlements and peculations, and in maintaining a large army in the field against the revolutionists.

Thanks to this policy of the Maderos, the policy of Diaz before them, the Mexican people are engaged to-day in a clear-cut, uncompromising *Revolution*, and are not, as they might have been, the partially contented victims of a capitalistic *reform*.

CHAPTER XXV

THE DOWNFALL OF MADERO

A SYSTEM of society based upon the disfranchisement, enslavement, and unlimited exploitation of the masses, absolutely demands a strong military dictatorship as its form of government, so the whole brunt of maintaining the Madero family in control fell upon an army, which could foresee no adequate recompense for its efforts. Day after day, week after week, month after month, the soldiery were compelled to exert inhuman efforts and to endure the cruelest privations against the indefatigable guerilla bands of the Revolution. Thousands of them perished miserably in open battle and ambuscade, and by heat, hunger, and thirst on the march. Those that survived could see no other future for themselves than eventual extermination. Always in their ears rang the high-piped, hysterical voice of Francisco Madero bidding them "Go on! Go on! and supress the Revolution;" and they knew that while they toiled across the deserts, or fell stricken in the trenches, the Madero family, whom they despised as civilians and Jews — not one of whom was a soldier, not one of whom shared their hardships — were revelling in uncontrolled possession of the national Treasury and the loot of office. It is not surprising, therefore, that the soldiery became lax, disgruntled, and demoralized, nor that, ever and anon, whole bodies of them mutinied and went over to the revolutionists.

Meanwhile the Porfirista Scientificos had equal cause for complaint. Crowded from office by the Madero parvenus, hampered in their predatory operations by the Revolution, they bitterly blamed Madero not only for disturbing the old, prosperous conditions of the Diaz régime, but for failing to reduce the country to order. Prominent among these malcontents were the members of the Diaz family, grouped, as we have said, in a gigantic financial combination under the name of the Pearson Syndicate. Owners of the vast oil fields of Tehuantepec, and consequently enjoying a complete monopoly of the oil business in Mexico, they were not slow to realize that behind Madero stood the Standard Oil Company* of the United States bent upon breaking their monopoly and capturing their immense export trade with Europe. At the same time their plantations were deserted, their oil wells idle. To them Madero's failure to suppress the Revolution meant at the best immense financial loss; at the worst complete expropriation at the hands of the triumphant people. Under the circumstances, therefore, both the higher officials of the army and the entire body of the Porfirista Scientificos headed by the Pearson Syndicate formed a solid phalanx of opposition against the Madero government; and they only awaited an opportune moment to strike a deadly blow at its power and regain control of the country.

Meanwhile in the columns of the press the great army of American investors in Mexican enterprises became daily more insistent for American intervention in Mexico. To give point to their outcries, President Taft, while carefully expressing himself as averse to intervention, kept up a significant military dumb-show on the border, mobilizing and remobilizing troops at all points of invasion, and endeavouring, it seemed, to strike terror to the hearts of the revolutionists. The American people,

---

*The Revolution of 1910 was a spontaneous uprising on the part of the evicted agrarian democracy and enslaved industrial proletariat of Mexico. It was not incited nor prompted by the Standard Oil Company, as some have averred, nor in its earlier and more precarious stages was it financially supported by that company. The Standard Oil Company only became a factor in the struggle when the success of the Revolution was all but assured; but its influence undoubtedly tended both to stay the hand of United States intervention and to hasten the inevitable triumph of the people. Its support of the Revolution was, of course, dictated by pure avarice, by a desire to break the Pearson oil monopoly in Mexico.

THE DOWNFALL OF MADERO

however, were on their guard. They not only refused to sanction hostilities against Mexico, but offered continual protests against the policy of intimidating a friendly people in the exercise of their constitutional right to revolt. At the same time the representatives of the South American republics also made it perfectly clear to President Taft that United States intervention in Mexico would be strongly resented by the South American peoples, and they did not hesitate to point out that such resentment would be likely to find expression in a retaliation decidedly injurious to United States commercial interests in South America.* Under the circumstances the cause of intervention waned to extinction.

Toward the close of 1912 the situation in Mexico became acute. The Revolution was steadily gaining ground in all parts of the country. Zapata, indeed, with a large force of veteran revolutionists hovered on the very outskirts of Mexico City; the army, wearied with the perpetual conflict, and disgusted with its position as the watch-dog of the Madero faction, was ready to mutiny at any moment. In October of that year Felix Diaz, countenanced by all the disgruntled element of the old Scientificos and financed by the Pearson Syndicate, started a cuartelazo in Vera Cruz, but the uprising proved to be ill-timed. It failed, and Felix Diaz was thrown into jail; but every one acquainted with the situation knew that violent changes were near.

---

*Our information on this matter was attained at first hand in a series of personal interviews with the ministers of the South American republics at Washington; but the antagonistic attitude of the South American republics toward United States intervention in Mexico is apparent to any one who cares to watch the editorial columns of their press. Not only does this attitude show a daily increasing strength, but we have excellent authority for stating that the obnoxious policy exercised by the United States against the South American republics generally has created such a sentiment of indignation among them that, in the event of United States hostilities with either Mexico or Japan, these countries would receive not only moral sympathy but substantial and material aid from a united Latin America. Under the Democratic administration of to-day the policy of the United States toward her sister republics will undoubtedly undergo a radical change, but it cannot be expected that even the decency and good sense of President Wilson and Secretary Bryan can immediately eradicate from the minds of the South American peoples a hatred of the United States, rooted in long years of mistreatment at her hands.

The climax came on February 9, 1913. On that date the students of the Military Academy of Tlalpan, near Mexico City, broke into the prison where General Bernardo Reyes and Felix Diaz were confined and set them free. This was the signal for a general uprising of the troops stationed in the city. At the head of several battalions Felix Diaz marched on the arsenal, where the garrison received him with enthusiasm. From that moment the cuartelazo was in full command of the situation. Mustering some five thousand men, powerfully fortified, and equipped with practically inexhaustible supplies of ammunition, the Felicistas started what was in reality a sham battle with the government troops. For days a raking fire from the opposing forces swept the city from end to end. The practised military on both sides received little hurt, but over six thousand helpless non-combatants, many of them women and children, were slaughtered in the streets.

At the critical moment General Victoriano Huerta, commander-in-chief of the government troops, having made sufficient stand to save appearances, betrayed the government and went over with all his troops to the support of General Felix Diaz, making the cuartelazo completely successful. President Francisco Madero, Vice-President José Maria Pino Suarez, and Gustavo Madero, leading politicians of the Madero faction, were arrested in the national palace. A few days later all three were murdered in cold blood under the convenient "ley fuga." Victoriano Huerta was then proclaimed provisional President, and an election was announced for October 17, 1913.

The only presidential candidates in the field at present are Victoriano Huerta, the avowed exponent of the old order of Porfiristas, and Venustiano Carranza, the chief spokesman and leader of the popular revolt. Felix Diaz, after one or two abortive attempts to oust Huerta from power, has retired to Havana, and apparently given up the contest.

THE DOWNFALL OF MADERO

The force behind Felix Diaz comprised all the worst elements of the old régime. It is these elements and these alone which are supporting the provisional President Huerta to-day. Three months before his cuartelazo in Mexico City Felix Diaz, as we have said, started a premature uprising in Vera Cruz. On that occasion the Mexican press, and various reputable organs in both England and the United States, charged Wheetman D. Pearson, better known as Lord Cowdray, with placing the sum of $15,000,000 at his disposal for this purpose, and the charge has not been refuted up to date. During the twelve days' battle in Mexico City Francisco de la Barra, Garcia Granados, Sebastian Camacho, and other prominent reactionaries and Clericals, were closeted daily with the American Minister, Henry Lane Wilson, while members of the Senate harangued the mobs in the streets, inciting them to demand the resignation of Madero.

At the firing of the first shot the American press, as if in answer to a preconcerted signal, made a tremendous final effort to stampede the American people into demanding intervention. President Taft again dispatched fresh troops to the border, and ordered American gunboats to cruise off the Mexican coast. He still professed himself averse to intervention, although proclaiming that if Congress should authorize him to intervene he would do so. But the vigorous middle-class revolt which marked the year 1912 had just culminated at that time in the election of Woodrow Wilson to power; and Congress gauged the temper of the country too well to make any such request. Again the policy of intervention fell before the awakened social sense of the people.

Henry Lane Wilson, the American Ambassador to Mexico, however, broke every tradition of diplomacy and brought disgrace upon the United States by making scarcely an effort to conceal his personal interest in the triumph of the Felicista cause; and his ill-advised message to President Taft urging the recognition of the Huerta government while the blood of the murdered

Madero was yet warm on the ground shocked American decency to the depths. In short, all the elements, both American and Mexican, which worked together with Porfirio Diaz to wreck the Mexican democracy of the Restoration and create a "Barbarous Mexico" rallied to the support of Felix Diaz.

It is not to be supposed that the late President Madero viewed with indifference the ill-concealed alliance of the United States with his enemies nor the unfriendly attitude of President Taft. Indeed, from the day of his accession to the presidency he regarded United States intervention in Mexico as a daily probability, and he shaped his foreign policy accordingly. *No more severe criticism of the short-sighted policy of the United States toward Mexico could be made than is to be found in the simple fact that Francisco Madero in order to checkmate that policy was compelled to throw himself into the arms of Japan.*

We are well aware of the importance of this statement and of its tremendous international significance, but we make it deliberately with full confidence in our authority. Not only did Madero enlist the ardent support of the South American republics in the cause of Mexico's inviolability, but he entered into negotiations with the Japanese Minister in Mexico City for a close offensive and defensive alliance with Japan to checkmate United States aggression. The consummation of these negotiations was undoubtedly only prevented by the cuartelazo of Felix Diaz. How far they had progressed may be gleaned from the following incident related to us personally by one who was the intimate friend and confidential adviser of Madero throughout his political career, and in whose veracity we have complete faith.

When during the fateful twelve days' battle in Mexico City a rumour of American intervention more alarming than usual was communicated to Madero, he replied coldly that he was thoroughly anxious for that intervention, for he was confident of the

Copyright by The International News Service

THE CLIMAX IN THE 1912–1913 REVOLT

"The climax came on February 9, 1913. On that date the students of the Military Academy of Tlalpan broke into the prison where Gen. Bernardo Reyes and Felix Diaz were confined, and set them free   (See page 354)

Copyright by The International News Service

NON-COMBATANTS IN THE BOMBARDMENT OF MEXICO CITY

"The Felicistas started what was in reality a sham battle with the government troops . . . over six thousand helpless non-conbatants were slaughtered in the streets"   (See page 354)

Copyright by Underwood & Underwood, N. Y.

NON-COMBATANTS FROM OJINAGA

Women and children refugees from the battlefield at Ojinaga, camping near Presidio, Texas, to which place they fled for safety

Copyright by Underwood & Underwood, N. Y.

FEDERAL LINES OF DEFENCE AT OJINAGA

General Salazars' men in trenches from which they were driven by the Constitutionalists after a forty-eight hour conflict, January 2 and 3, 1914

THE DOWNFALL OF MADERO

surprise the American Government would receive in discovering that they had to deal with Japan.*

Such an alliance would have been fraught, of course, with infinite disaster to the Mexican people. Japan in return for her protection must have inevitably demanded and received not only large land concessions but full economic privileges for her subjects in Mexico. Japanese immigration on a vast scale would have followed, and the Mexican people would have found themselves quietly inundated, dispossessed, and finally economically controlled by an agressive alien race, irresistibly competent in arms and commerce.

The fact that the Mexican common people to-day endorse this policy of Madero's, and prefer to encounter the manifest evils of a Japanese alliance rather than retain the integrity of their country under the sufferance of the United States, shows to what disastrous extremes the policy of the American plutocracy has driven them.

. . . .

The cuartelazo of Felix Diaz was purely a military affair. It simply changed the polite civilian dictatorship of Madero, supported by the Standard Oil interests, for the unabashed military despotism of Victoriano Huerta supported by the Pearson interests. The revolutionists watched it from afar uninterested, save in the fact that their enemies were fighting among themselves. Certain superficial modifications, it is true, appeared in the revolutionary movement as the result of the change of government. Some peon leaders like Salazar, Orozco, Chechecampos, and others, went over to the Felicistas, hoping thereby to exterminate the Madero faction as the greater evil. Some of the Maderistas frankly coöperated with the revo-

---

*To what extent Japan had compromised herself with Mexico will probably never be absolutely known. It is not without significance, however, that in the later years of the Diaz régime Japan made strenuous but unavailing efforts to obtain a naval base on the Mexican coast; and that more than four hundred Japanese veterans fought in the ranks of Madero's army, while many thousands of them who applied for enlistment were only refused by the revolutionary authorities out of deference to the prejudices of the Mexican volunteers.

lutionists, their old enemies, calling themselves constitutionalists. None of these superficial modifications, however, has altered in the least the real spirit and purpose of the great mass. *They are fighting to-day as they fought in the days of Hidalgo, of Morelos, of Guerrero, of Gomez Farias, of Juarez, for the land, for democracy. They will triumph. They must triumph. Nothing short of another criminal foreign intervention can stay their hand.*

It seems to us that the Mexico of to-day offers a significant parallel to the Mexico of the 50's immediately subsequent to the downfall of Santa Ana. The Revolution of 1910 is closely akin to the Revolution of Ayutla, which overthrew the dictatorship of Santa Ana, and embodied the ideals of the people in the Constitution of 1857. Porfirio Diaz offers a striking resemblance to Santa Ana, while Francisco Madero, the leader of the popular revolt, constitutional President by the overwhelming voice of the nation, and subsequently traitor to the cause which had placed him in power, has his prototype in Comonfort. The cuartelazo of Felix Diaz is in all respects similar to the cuartelazo which overthrew Comonfort; and Victoriano Huerta, Madero's commander-in-chief who betrayed him to the enemy, is only a twentieth century Zuloaga. To-day, as then, the people have maintained a protracted struggle for the enforcement of the constitution and the restoration of the land. To-day, as then, the people slowly, but irresistibly, are subduing their enemies.

Ultimately must come a new Restoration — a new birth of Mexican democracy — but in happier conditions than in the Restoration of Juarez. Then the world-proletariat knew little of the struggle of their Mexican brothers. Even had they known of that struggle they were impotent to support it. They themselves writhed beneath the heel of an omnipotent plutocracy. To-day how great the change! Plutocracy stands bewildered before the steady, resistless march of the world-millions of awakened workers. To-day as never before in the

THE DOWNFALL OF MADERO

history of the class-struggle, the cause of any of the most remote sections of the world's workers is the cause of all. International capitalism can no longer throttle the freedom of the Mexican people with impunity. Their first attempt to repeat the atrocities of the past will involve them in a world-wide grapple with the modern army of liberty. They are aware of it. If the workers of the world are true to their trust, the heroic struggle for democracy maintained by the Mexican people for the past one hundred years will end, and that shortly, in superb accomplishment.

A DISPATCH FROM THE FRONT

HERMOSILLO, Sonora,
December, 1913.

At this time of writing the entire states of Sonora, Chihuahua, Sinaloa, San Luis Potosi, Morelos, and Puebla, and the larger part of the states of Guerrero, Michoacan, and Durango are in complete control of the Constitutionalists. In these vast areas the federal forces are either wiped out or rendered impotent, and the peons are at last in full possession of the land.

This restoration of the land to the people has arisen irresistibly — and one might say, mechanically — out of the necessities of the case, and often against the will and interest of the more reactionary leaders who have imposed themselves upon the Revolution. As the Constitutionalist forces advanced from district to district, the landlords fled before them, leaving flourishing estates and ungarnered crops ownerless and unprotected. The revolutionary government — hard pressed for provisions and funds — was compelled to confiscate these lands and their crops for the maintenance of the campaign and the sustenance of the people. The peons — suddenly conscious of their masterless condition — willingly harvested the crops and resowed the land on behalf of their brothers in the field. And, having done so, they consider themselves to-day the owners of these lands and stand prepared to defend their proprietorship, rifle in hand.

With the progress of the Revolution and the restoration of the lands there has arisen among the peons a clear class-consciousness which daily grows more defined and aggressive; and this clarified attitude of the peons toward their own needs and their own powers is guarantee enough that, whatever may be the actions of their leaders, they themselves will never be diverted from their central purpose — the democratization of the land.

THE END

RET'D MAY 19 1986

MAY 14 1996